# REVOLT AT TAOS

## Also by James A. Crutchfield

*The Settlement of America: Encyclopedia of Westward Expansion from Jamestown to the Closing of the Frontier*, editor

*The Battle of Franklin: Twilight of the Army of Tennessee*

*Tribute to an Artist: The Jamestown Paintings of Sidney E. King*

*George Washington: First in War, First in Peace*

*The Way West: True Stories of the American Frontier*, editor

*The Grand Adventure: A Year-by-Year History of Virginia*

*Mountain Men of the American West*

*America's Yesteryears*

*Eyewitness to American History*

*Tragedy at Taos: The Revolt of 1847*

*The Santa Fe Trail*

*Tennesseans at War*

*The Natchez Trace: A Pictorial History*

*Early Times in the Cumberland Valley*

*The Harpeth River: A Biography*

JAMES A. CRUTCHFIELD

# REVOLT AT TAOS

### The NEW MEXICAN and INDIAN INSURRECTION of 1847

WESTHOLME
Yardley

First Westholme Paperback 2025
©2015 James A. Crutchfield
Maps by Tracy Dungan
Maps ©2015 Westholme Publishing

All rights reserved under International and Pan-American Copyright Conventions. No part of this book may be reproduced in any form or by any electronic or mechanical means, including information storage and retrieval systems, without permission in writing from the publisher, except by a reviewer who may quote brief passages in a review.

Westholme Publishing, LLC
904 Edgewood Road
Yardley, Pennsylvania 19067
Visit our Web site at www.westholmepublishing.com


ISBN: 978-1-59416-450-7
Also available as an eBook.

Printed in the United States of America.

*For Regena,*
*Wife, soul mate, and best friend—*
*with happy memories of our times in Taos*

"A people which takes no pride in the noble achievements of remote ancestors will never achieve anything worthy to be remembered with pride by remote descendants."
— Lord Thomas Babington Macaulay

"The New Mexican was prepared to survive in the New Mexico of the [Spanish] Conquest. He was not prepared to set forth along new cultural paths, under a new economy, and under a foreign [American] mode of administration. To the New Mexican, only the struggle for survival was real. New methods, new ideas, new horizons were incomprehensible because they were shockingly out of keeping with his experience of long standing. The rhythm of centuries had set a persistent tempo to New Mexican life. It was folly to expect that, by the magic stroke of a pen upon a treaty, the New Mexican should become an American citizen overnight."
—George I. Sánchez, *Forgotten People* (1940)

"And as for Polk himself—in the preparation of grand strategy he had a small army on Mexico's northern frontier, some maps, and an overwhelming ignorance . . . of the conditions under which armies must operate. . . . They were poor maps; if they were good ones, probably even the amateur strategists would have been deterred. If their innocence had been tarnished by knowledge of the country they proposed to campaign across they would have lost the war."
—Bernard DeVoto, *The Year of Decision: 1846* (1942)

"That men do not learn very much from the lessons of history is the most important of all the lessons that history has to teach."
—Aldous Huxley, *Case of Voluntary Ignorance* (1959)

# CONTENTS

*List of Maps* — xi
*Preface* — xiii
*Prologue* — xvii

1. Gone to Texas — 1
2. Looking West — 14
3. Without Firing a Gun or Spilling a Drop of Blood — 26
4. "Every Thing Here Is Quiet and Peaceable" — 47
5. Questions in the Nation's Capital — 56
6. "We Were Without Food and Had No Covering" — 61
7. "Dead! Dead! Dead!" — 98
8. "The New Mexicans Entertain Deadly Hatred against Americans" — 114
9. Causes and Consequences — 121

*Epilogue* — 150

*Appendix A*
*Chronology of Events Surrounding the American Occupation of New Mexico in 1846 and the Taos Revolt of 1847*    159

*Appendix B*
*General Stephen Watts Kearny's August 19, 1846, Address to the People of Santa Fe*    166

*Appendix C*
*Governor Juan Bautista Vigil y Alarid's August 19, 1846, Response to General Kearny's Address*    167

*Appendix D*
*General Stephen Watts Kearny's August 22, 1846, Proclamation to the People of Santa Fe*    169

*Appendix E*
*A Description of New Mexico in 1846*    171

*Appendix F*
*A Description of Taos and Vicinity in 1847*    172

*Appendix G*
*List of American, New Mexican, and Indian Casualties of the Taos Revolt and Its Aftermath*    174

*Appendix H*
*The Taos Revolt in the Performing Arts and Literature*    180

*Notes*    183

*Bibliography*    209

*Acknowledgments*    221

*Index*    223

## List of Maps

1. The Republic of Texas, 1836–46              7
2. Plan of Santa Fe                            51
3. A contemporary map (1847) of Taos           74
4. A map of Taos as it appeared during the revolt   76–77
5. The battle at Cañada                        86
6. The battle at Embudo                        88
7. The battle at Taos Pueblo                   94–95

# PREFACE

WITHIN THE LAST COUPLE OF YEARS OR SO, WHILE I WAS working on this book, I watched a C-Span interview featuring American historian and journalist Hampton Sides. He was talking about the thoughts and concerns he had while writing *Blood and Thunder: An Epic of the American West.* His protagonist in the book was the legendary mountain man, scout, and soldier Christopher "Kit" Carson, whose name is either revered or despised by many historians, writers, American Indians, and other aficionados of the American West. Mr. Sides revealed how he had labored over the "political correctness" issues encountered during his research and acknowledged that it would have been easy to have stepped into a literary minefield.

I think I can readily identify with Sides's concerns. The subject of my book is controversial as well and has rarely been told from a dispassionate platform. Most older studies of the Taos Revolt of 1847, when it is mentioned at all, are highly charged pro-American perspectives, tense with the drama of Manifest Destiny, while newer works, written by later generations of historians whose training was the product of America's embrace of diversity, inclusion, and multiculturalism, sympathize more heavily with the New Mexican and Indian viewpoints. The premise of my book is that surely a middle ground exists, tempered by the times in which the events occurred and the backgrounds, attitudes, and politics of the Americans, the New Mexicans, and the Indians.

It is neither my intent nor my desire to document yet another history of the Mexican-American War. I believe that a majority of present-day Americans—white and otherwise—admit that the war was at least partially provoked by US imperialism, and, if not racially motivated from the beginning, then strongly racially influenced before the end. The thoughts of white Americans of the so-called National Period between the War of 1812 and the emergence of the states' rights and slavery controversies were awash with dreams of land ownership and self-sustenance. It was the era of the common man, and if the achievement of these dreams meant that the nation must expel the Indians from their ancestral homelands, and even encroach upon foreign soil, so be it.

You will find no scathing criticisms in this book of the American invasion of Mexico, of the duplicity of Washington officialdom in dealings with the Mexican government, of the savagery and barbarism of American military forces of occupation, nor of any of the other horrific transgressions heaped upon the Mexican people that many of the more recent writers allude to in their histories of the conflict. Neither will you find page after page of anti-Mexican sentiment, with all of the responsibility for the war placed on the shoulders of our neighbors to the south, such as is found in the older books on the subject. If you are interested in these and other views of the war, you should refer to one or more of the books that profess such an objective, many of which can be found in practically any library.

You will find here what I believe to be a straightforward account of a little-known event that occurred in New Mexico shortly after Santa Fe was occupied by American military forces in August 1846. The revolt at Taos was an important incident in the conflict between Mexico and the United States, although one that has had sparse attention paid to it. In fact, scores of published works, including many recent studies, make no mention whatsoever of the episode and the events surrounding it. I must assume that their authors were either unaware of the uprising or attributed little or no importance to it. Yet to the participants on both sides of this significant issue, it was a meaningful, painful, and stressful episode that brought with it social, psychological, and political consequences that endure to this day.

No full-length book exists that documents the entire story of the rebellion, including my own *Tragedy at Taos: The Revolt of 1847*, published in 1995. The results of my present efforts follow, tempered by a desire to make readers aware of this extremely important incident in our nation's history. If this goal is successful, I shall feel that my labors were not in vain.

# PROLOGUE

During the early morning of January 19, 1847, Charles Bent, the newly appointed governor of the American-claimed territory of New Mexico, was savagely killed at his home in Don Fernando de Taos, a small, remote New Mexican town about sixty-two miles north, as the crow flies, of Santa Fe. Until the region's occupation by the US Army during the previous August, the village, often referred to simply as Taos, was the Republic of Mexico's northernmost outpost and, before that—dating back to the days of the conquistadors—part of Spain's New World empire. Those responsible for Bent's murder were Taoseños and Indians from nearby Taos Pueblo. With emotions rubbed raw by the recent American invasion, the natives continued their bloodbath until five more leading citizens, New Mexican and American, were massacred in Taos. During the ensuing months, many other American civilians and soldiers responding to the uprising, as well as scores of New Mexicans and Taos Indians, were killed and wounded.[1]

Less than a month following Bent's murder, in a battle that lasted for the better part of two days, volunteer and regular elements of an American army under the command of Colonel Sterling Price emerged victorious after bombarding the Taoseños and their Indian allies at their refuge in the church at Taos Pueblo. Many of the participants in the earlier Taos murders were arrested, tried in American-dominated courts, and, within weeks, hanged for their actions.

The murder of Bent and the others at Taos and the subsequent trials and executions brought with them misunderstanding, controversy, mistrust, and recrimination on both sides of the issue. The events also subjected President James K. Polk's administration to a great deal of embarrassment over what some critics thought was an overextension of Polk's authority in claiming New Mexico as a territory. The brief rebellion and its aftermath failed in its objective to oust the Americans from New Mexico, but not without eventually taking hundreds of lives and making political waves in both Washington, DC, and Mexico City.

*One*

# Gone to Texas

## CATALYST FOR THE MEXICAN-AMERICAN WAR

THE MEXICAN-AMERICAN WAR OF 1846–1848, OUT OF WHICH evolved the Taos Revolt of January 1847, traces its origin to the annexation of Texas by the United States on December 29, 1845, during the administration of President James K. Polk. For nearly a decade following the Texas Declaration of Independence from Mexico in March 1836, the question of whether the newly organized republic would someday attach itself to the United States had been tossed about in Washington, DC, and in Texas, as well as in Mexico City. It came as no surprise, then, that the thorny issue brought with it cries of anger and acrimony, not to mention a great deal of saber rattling from both American and Mexican authorities.

Many of the problems between the United States and Mexico began in 1821, when Moses Austin, a resident of Missouri, was granted a large expanse of land along the lower Colorado and Brazos rivers in present-day Texas, then a northern province of New Spain. Financial troubles had driven Austin to Texas, where Spanish authorities gave him permission to settle several hundred Americans on his two-hundred-thousand-acre tract. Before Austin could get under way with his colonization scheme, however, he died.[1]

In the meantime, also during 1821, a far-reaching event occurred. Mexico obtained its independence from Spain and thus became owner of the land included in Austin's grant.[2] Stephen Austin, son of Moses, pursued the matter after his father's death and persuaded the Mexican government to allow him to inherit the elder Austin's landholdings, along with his right to colonize the American families. Obtaining approval, Austin assumed command of the movement, thus heralding the first legitimate American settlement in Texas. Austin planned to work closely with Mexican authorities and visualized that the colony would operate within the government's existing framework. To Mexican officials' delight, he proved to be a patriotic citizen.

Both Austin and his followers, as well as Mexican administrators, were pleased with the arrangement. Over the next few years, more grants were issued to Americans who were eager to make new homes for themselves beyond the Mississippi River. By 1824, when the Mexican state of Texas y Coahuila was organized, several thousand Americans had already firmly established themselves in the Brazos River valley. Plenty of land existed for everyone, the Mexican government thought, and here, on the new country's remote northeastern frontier, the population was so sparse that it was better to have someone on the land, Americans or otherwise, than to leave it totally barren for the dry, summer winds to blow away. Additionally, and more importantly, the presence of these Americans, all subject to Mexican law, would serve as an excellent buffer between Mexican citizens in the south and the ever-increasing influx of even more Americans who were sure to come and perhaps not be so amenable to Mexican laws and traditions.[3]

In late 1826, a small army of about thirty American settlers, led by a disgruntled Mississippian, Benjamin Edwards, attempted to establish an independent republic of Texas. A brother of Edwards's, Haden, had acquired some three hundred thousand acres of land from the Mexican government the previous year but had disregarded the rights of earlier Americans who had already staked claims in the same area. While Haden was visiting the United States, Benjamin was confronted with the news that Mexican authorities had revoked his brother's claim and were ordering the two out of the country. Benjamin and his thirty followers occupied Nacogdoches on

December 16 and announced the Republic of Fredonia. Plans called for Texas to be divided between the Fredonians and dissatisfied Cherokee Indians, who had recently moved into the region but who could not obtain land grants on their own from the Mexican government. However, when two hundred fifty Mexican soldiers, supported by one hundred of Stephen Austin's colonists—who didn't like the Edwards brothers' tactics any more than the Mexicans did—marched on Nacogdoches in late January 1827, the revolution fizzled. Both of the Edwards brothers returned to the United States, leaving the original settlers of their massive claim breathing a sigh of relief.[4]

As more and more Americans became entrenched in their new Mexican homes, US authorities attempted to acquire Texas and Coahuila. In 1827, President John Quincy Adams—through Joel Poinsett, the US minister to Mexico—offered $1 million for the territory, only to be scorned by Mexican officials.[5]

On March 4, 1829, Andrew Jackson was inaugurated president of the United States. A product of the frontier and an acknowledged expansionist, Jackson soon made it known that Texas and Coahuila, in which so many Americans now lived, would better be a part of the United States than of a foreign power like Mexico. In a letter dated June 8, 1829, written to John Overton, his close friend and one-time law partner back in Tennessee, Jackson declared, "I have long since been aware of the importance of Texas to the United States and of the real necessity of extending our boundary west of the Sabine. . . . I shall keep my eye on this object & the first propitious moment make the attempt to regain the Territory as far south & west as the great Desert."[6] Later the same year, President Jackson attempted to purchase the Texas part of Texas and Coahuila for $5 million. Not only was his offer rejected, like President Adams's proposition a couple of years earlier, but Mexican authorities also demanded that Joel Poinsett, still the US minister, be recalled.[7]

By 1830, despite Jackson's failure to negotiate the purchase of the American-inhabited zone of Texas, thousands of Americans lived in the region. Mexico expressed second thoughts about its earlier generosity regarding colonists from the United States. The brash invaders were not so welcome anymore. A local newspaper commented about the peculiar people from the north, observing that they were "astute and agile," and "quick to seize any occurrence and turn it to . . .

advantage."[8] A contemporary Mexican observer added that in his opinion, "they are in general . . . lazy people of vicious character."[9]

After reconsidering its land-grant policies to foreigners, the Mexican government closed its frontier and made it known that no more newcomers—especially Americans—would be accepted.[10] By then, however, it was too late. The flood gates in the United States were open. All across the land back East, residents were selling their farms and stores, packing up their wagons with all of their earthly possessions, and heading for the newfound land of opportunity. "GTT" signs sprang up all over the South and East, indicating that the former property owners had "Gone to Texas." Thousands of Americans were on the move, and officials in Mexico realized more and more that they had a real problem on their hands.

In 1834, Stephen Austin presented a petition to Mexican president Antonio Lopez de Santa Anna demanding that Texas be organized into a separate state, but one still under Mexican authority. Santa Anna, who had been in and out of political power for a number of years, had Austin arrested and jailed. But while Austin brooded away in a Mexican prison, momentum rapidly snowballed for Texas independence from its mother country.

Some Texas residents were willing to use force to gain their independence. In late June 1835, William B. Travis, a former South Carolina schoolteacher and lawyer, accompanied by a few American volunteers, stormed the Mexican garrison at Anahuac on Galveston Bay, demanded its surrender, and received it. Later, during October of the same year, Travis, with a small army of Texas settlers, defeated a troop of Mexican cavalry along the Guadalupe River near San Antonio in central Texas.

On March 2, 1836, the Texas Declaration of Independence was unanimously approved by fifty-nine Texans who had gathered at Washington-on-the-Brazos, the provisional capital. Even as that historic meeting was being attended, Santa Anna was quickly tightening his grip on Texas forces gathered inside the Alamo at San Antonio. Since February 23, some four thousand Mexican soldiers had surrounded the old Spanish mission and watched as the small Texas army inside slowly ran out of food and water. During the dawn hours of March 6, the Mexican army made its final assault. All of the Anglo-Texan defenders inside the mission were killed, including Travis, Texas Ranger James "Jim" Bowie, and former Tennessee congressman David "Davy" Crockett.

Later in March, Colonel James W. Fannin—who for a brief time earlier in the year had served as commander in chief of the Texas army—and three hundred Texans were surrounded by forces of General José Urrea near Goliad. After two days of attempting to defend his position, Fannin's only choice became surrender. On March 27, 1836, counter to Urrea's promise of clemency for the Texans, all of them were massacred by order of President/General Santa Anna. Texans sprang back though. To the war cries "Remember the Alamo" and "Remember Goliad," General Sam Houston's troops defeated Santa Anna's army at San Jacinto on April 21, thus assuring, once and for all, independence for Texas.[11]

Mexican President Antonio Lopez de Santa Anna.

Texas affairs returned to near normal following the war for independence. Sam Houston, a former Tennessee congressman and governor, was elected the republic's first president, and Texas was formally recognized as a sovereign state by many countries, including the United States. But to the chagrin of Mexican officials, annexation by the United States was already being fostered by many Texans and Americans alike. It took only about ten years for the question of the permanent Texas-Mexico-United States relationship to gain a first-place spot on the agendas of many statesmen in Washington and Mexico City.

When Texas won its independence from Mexico in 1836, it finalized its southern and western border as the channel of the Rio Grande from its mouth at the Gulf of Mexico to its headwaters in present-day Colorado. From there, the boundary followed a line due north for three hundred miles to roughly the 42nd parallel, then east for about seventy miles, due south to the headwaters of the Arkansas River, east along that stream to the 100th meridian, due south to the Red River, down that river to the 94th meridian, then south to the Sabine River and down the Sabine to its mouth at the Gulf of Mexico. On a present-day map, the region includes parts of Wyoming, Colorado, Kansas, Oklahoma, and New Mexico. The real estate thus contained within the republic's borders encompassed the entire eastern half of today's state of New Mexico, including the towns of Santa Fe and Taos.12

Mirabeau B. Lamar, who succeeded Sam Houston as president of Texas, took over the reins of government in 1838. One of his first acts was to attempt to bring Texas into the modern age with improved roads and an expanded school system. The republic, however, suffered from economic bad times, and within three years from the date Lamar took office, the public debt had swelled to more than $7 million. Yet Texas officials continued to spend more than $1 million a year, while the republic's annual income was less than half a million dollars.

Lamar thought his country's economic woes could be improved if it established trade relations with the prosperous Santa Fe markets, which he believed lay within his republic's boundaries. Costly Cuban merchandise could be unloaded on the Texas gulf coast, routed through the newly organized town of Austin, then sent directly to Santa Fe, thus cutting off hundreds of miles from the traditional route between Missouri and New Mexico via the Santa Fe Trail. Lamar visualized Texas coffers filling rapidly from providing the freighting facilities for all of this rich trade.

In 1839, Lamar urged his congress to approve an expedition to Santa Fe to explore and, hopefully, confirm his trade theory. In April 1841, Lamar's operatives advertised in the *Austin City Gazette* for able-bodied "young men" to serve as escorts for a wagon train carrying "merchandise" through Comanche country to Santa Fe, promising all takers that "the expedition will furnish an ample field for adventure."13

On June 20, 1841, three hundred to four hundred men and boys, along with as many horses and a score of supply wagons, left Austin on the first leg of the so-called Texan-Santa Fe Expedition. The group traveled north out of Austin, then more or less west across the parched Llano Estacado to San Miguel in the eastern part of present-day New Mexico.

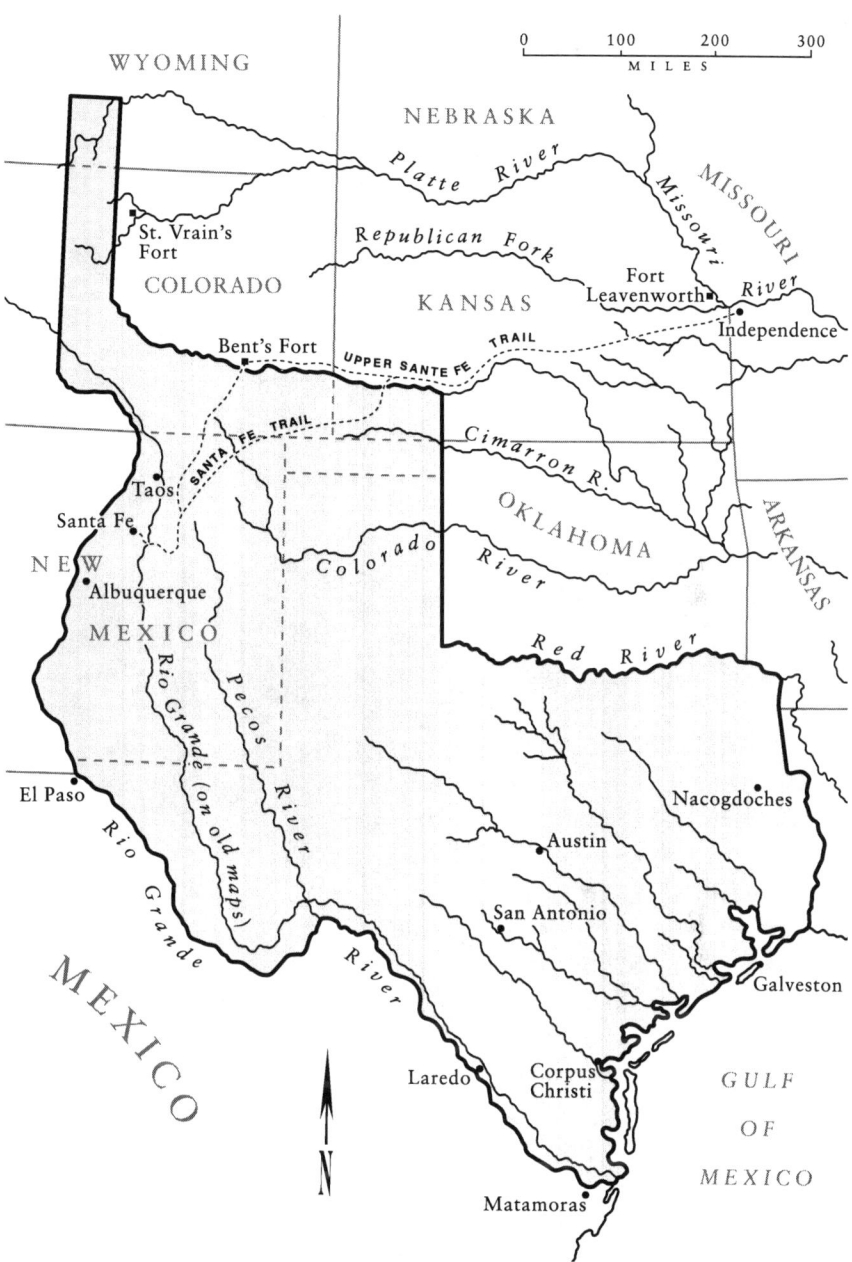

Map 1. The Republic of Texas, 1836–46

But San Miguel was as far as most of the weary travelers got. The expedition, suffering from poor planning and lack of provisions, had already divided into two groups in West Texas, both elements punished by weeks of grueling travel that quenched even the brightest fires of enthusiasm. Weary from the hunger, thirst, and threat of Indian attack, both parties straggled into San Miguel during the autumn days of 1841, only to be arrested by waiting Mexican soldiers under the command of Manuel Armijo, the governor of New Mexico.

They were then marched under armed guard to Mexico City. George Wilkins Kendall, a newspaperman and one of the captives, wrote in his book, *Narrative of the Texan Santa Fe Expedition*, published in 1844, that the prisoners were led on their forced march by an especially brutal soldier who delighted in making everyone as miserable as possible at all times. With the possibility of even worse treatment facing them when they arrived in Mexico City, Kendall reported that in the meantime, an extremely cold winter had set in, making the hundreds-of-miles journey almost impossible.[14]

President Lamar's ideas to tap the markets of New Mexico and to reap huge profits from the trade between Cuba and Santa Fe by putting Texans in a kind of middle-man position failed miserably. Instead of strengthening the claim of Texas that the Rio Grande was its western border, the ill-planned Texan-Santa Fe Expedition resulted in the deaths and incarceration of many of its participants.[15]

Few issues in American history have generated more political controversy than the annexation of Texas. The decade following its independence from Mexico was filled with debate about the wisdom of allowing the new republic to enter the Union. By 1843, however, the annexation issue had become much more heated. Former president Andrew Jackson favored adding Texas to the United States and was joined by President John Tyler and Secretary of State John C. Calhoun. Former President Martin Van Buren had publicly announced his opposition to annexation, paying for his reversal on the issue by turning Jackson against him and losing the upcoming Democratic Party nomination for the presidency to James K. Polk. Henry Clay, who would run—and lose—against Polk in the 1844

The New Mexican village of San Miguel.

election, along with most of the other Whigs, also opposed the idea.[16]

Mexico threatened war if the United States consummated its plans to annex Texas. Nevertheless, on April 12, 1844, the annexation treaty was signed between officials of the Republic of Texas and Secretary of State Calhoun for the Tyler administration. However, by the time Congress made the annexation measure official and Tyler signed it, Tyler had only three days left in his term as president. Polk was about to enter the White House, thus placing the fate of Texas in the hands of the quiet, diminutive Tennessean.

Polk was nominated by the Democrats for the presidency in 1844. Born in North Carolina in 1795, he moved to Tennessee as a young man and practiced law in Columbia, a small village about forty miles south of Nashville. He was soon elected to the Tennessee legislature and later served seven terms in the US House of Representatives, two of them as speaker. Upon his return to Tennessee, he became governor for one term before retiring to his home in Columbia. At the Democratic convention in 1844, despite his successful political career, Polk's name was still relatively unknown. Following much political infighting, he was nominated on the ninth ballot. In the election, he defeated the Whig candidate, Henry Clay, by sixty-five electoral votes but only by a little more than 38,000 popular votes out of nearly 2,640,000 cast.[17]

Polk promised voters that he would serve only one term as president but would achieve four objectives if elected: reduce the tariff, establish an independent treasury, settle the Oregon boundary question with the British, and acquire California. All four objectives were fulfilled within the single term he promised.[18]

In his inaugural speech of March 4, 1845, from the East Portico of the US Capitol, Polk left no doubt about his position on westward expansion in general, and Texas annexation in particular. He proclaimed that Texas had always desired to become a state in the American union and to "enjoy with us the blessings of liberty secured and guaranteed by our Constitution." He reminded his listeners that Texas had once been a part of the United States, referring to his firm belief that Texas was part of the original Louisiana Purchase and that the United States relinquished the territory to Spain in 1819 when Spain ceded Florida to the United States. Furthermore, he told the onlookers that Texas was an independent, sovereign nation that had the "undoubted right to dispose of a part or the whole of her territory and to merge her sovereignty as a separate and independent state in ours."[19]

Possibly to smooth the waters with an angry Mexican government, Polk added that foreign powers should consider the American annexation of Texas "not as the conquest of a nation seeking to extend her dominions by arms and violence, but as the peaceful acquisition of a territory once her own," with the full compliance of the Texas government.[20] The new president then assured his listeners that he would "endeavor by all constitutional, honorable, and appropriate means to consummate the expressed will of the people and Government of the United States by the reannexation of Texas to our Union at the earliest practicable period."[21]

Polk's political mentor and idol, Andrew Jackson, was ecstatic over the annexation news. A Washington friend wrote to him, "I congratulate you, Dear General, on the success of the great question which you put in action."[22] An elated Jackson (who was ill and had only three months to live) replied, "I not only rejoice, but congratulate my beloved country [that] Texas is re-annexed, and the safety, prosperity, and the greatest interest of the whole Union is secured by this . . . great and important national act."[23]

Mexican reaction to Polk's address was as expected. On March 6, 1845, the Mexican minister in Washington dispatched a note to Secretary of State Calhoun in which he called American plans to annex Texas a violation of Mexico's rights. Calhoun responded that as an independent republic, Texas needed no approval from the Mexican government to request admission to the United States. The minister demanded his passport, closed the diplomatic mission, and left the country. Shortly afterward, officials in Mexico City refused to meet with the American minister, who eventually departed for home.[24] On March 28, Mexico City suspended diplomatic relations with the United States, prompting the War Department to eventually dispatch General Zachary Taylor and his two-thousand-five-hundred-man army to the Corpus Christi region in anticipation of trouble. Over the next year, Taylor positioned his soldiers on the south bank of the Nueces River in the disputed zone claimed by both Mexico and the United States. During spring 1846, the army relocated to the north bank of the Rio Grande, where troops built Fort Brown across the river (and the international border) from Matamoras.[25]

President James K. Polk.

In late December 1845, less than ten months from the day he took office, President Polk oversaw the official entry of Texas into the Union. In the meantime, Mexican authorities continued to warn officials in Washington that American annexation of Texas would lead to war. On April 24, 1846, Mexican soldiers crossed the Rio Grande and killed eleven American troopers in the disputed territory claimed by both powers. With this attack, General Taylor sent a dispatch to Washington in which he proclaimed, "Hostilities may now be considered as commenced."[26] On May 3, Mexican artillery in Matamoras opened fire on Fort Brown, and on May 8 and 9, Taylor and his American troops encountered Mexican soldiers in US-claimed territory and quickly won two battles, at Palo Alto and Resaca de la Palma. "Mexico has passed the boundary of the United States, has invaded our territory and shed American blood upon the American soil. She has proclaimed that hostilities have commenced, and that the two nations are now at war," President Polk told a surprised Congress on May 11.[27] Within two hours, the House of Representatives, with a vote of 173–14, passed a declaration of war resolution.[28]

Missouri's Thomas Hart Benton, although a Democrat and the Senate's leading advocate for US westward expansion, scorned the hasty manner in which Congress approached the war. Polk recorded in his diary entry for May 11 that the senator criticized the speed with which the House passed the war resolution, adding that Benton opined that "in the nineteenth century[,] war should not be declared without full discussion, and much more consideration than had been given to it in the House of Representatives."[29] Calhoun, who had signed the original annexation treaty with Texas authorities in 1844, opposed the declaration as written and abstained from voting in the Senate, where the resolution passed 40–2, with three abstentions.[30] On May 13, Polk signed the bill declaring war with Mexico. Later in the day he placed General Winfield Scott in charge of raising an army of fifty thousand soldiers at a cost of $10 million.[31]

As expected, the moods of Americans over the war declaration were mixed. Northern Whigs, especially, adamantly opposed US involvement in Mexico and saw the entire episode as an exercise in imperialism. Philip Hone, a former mayor of New York City, expressed the attitudes of many of his Whig allies when he wrote in his diary in early May that,

> Mr. Polk and his party have accomplished their object: the war with Mexico is fairly commenced. The President (in violation of the Constitution, which gives to Congress the exclusive power to declare war) announces formally that a state of war exists, calls for volunteers and money, which Congress unhesitatingly grants; and if any old-fashioned legislator presumes to doubt the authority of Pope Polk, or questions the infallibility of his bull, he is stigmatized by some of the ruffians of the West as an enemy to his country, in league with the Mexicans.[32]

Regardless of public opinion and the criticisms of opposing party members, the war with Mexico had begun. General Taylor was already making the American military presence felt along the Texas-Mexico border, and a number of states—Alabama, Arkansas, Georgia, Illinois, Indiana, Kentucky, Mississippi, Missouri, Ohio, Tennessee, and Texas—were asked to furnish twenty thousand militia volunteers to augment the US Army, a number that grew significantly by the war's end.[33] Andrew Jackson would have been proud of the response of his home state of Tennessee to the call for volunteers (Jackson died at his estate in Nashville in June 1845). No doubt sitting president Polk, a Tennessean himself, was impressed as well. The request issued by the War Department suggested that Tennessee furnish one regiment of cavalry and two regiments of infantry, approximately two thousand eight hundred men. In response to the plea, more than thirty thousand Tennesseans joined the war effort, thus reaffirming the state's nickname—the Volunteer State—first used during the War of 1812 for a similar outpouring of patriotism.[34]

Less than a month after the declaration of war was issued, the War Department organized a military command called the Army of the West and dispatched it to New Mexico and California to occupy those two Mexican territories. The army's first major goal was the conquest of Santa Fe, a quaint little town claimed by the state of Texas and the Mexican government.[35]

*Two*

# Looking West

## THE LURE OF NEW MEXICO

WHEN TEXAS WAS ADMITTED TO THE AMERICAN UNION IN LATE 1845, the new entity claimed essentially the same boundaries as it had maintained as a republic.[1] Even with statehood, however, much of the thousands of square miles of territory lying in the northwesternmost part of the state continued to be claimed by Mexico as well, becoming a kind of no-man's-land, claimed first by both Texas and Mexico, then, after the war, by both Texas and the United States. The Compromise of 1850 finally redefined the boundaries and relinquished the disputed section previously claimed by Texas to the newly organized Territory of New Mexico.[2] Clearly, however, at the outset of the war in 1846, authorities in Washington believed that the disputed territory belonged to Mexico, since the US War Department issued explicit orders for the Army of the West to march to Santa Fe (located in Texas, according to Texas's claims) and to occupy New Mexico.[3]

Although in 1846 New Mexico was situated within the Mexican sphere of influence, a few American and European fur trappers and traders had visited the region prior to 1821, the date that signals the independence of Mexico from Spain and the first efforts of Missourians to blaze the Santa Fe Trail. Santa Fe and Taos especially became hubs for a lively trade in Rocky Mountain furs, mules, and precious metals, as well as Eastern-manufactured weapons, household goods, and hardware. Some of the Eastern newcomers even changed their citizenships and permanently relocated to New Mexico, primarily in the northern towns and villages.

One of the first white men to make the trip across the southern Great Plains was neither an American trader nor a trapper, but rather a Frenchman named Pedro Vial. At the time, New Mexico was still a possession of Spain. Vial, whose real name was Pierre Vial, made the round trip between Santa Fe and Saint Louis in record-breaking time, considering the fact that his party was captured by Indians and held for six weeks during the first stage of his journey.

Vial set out from Santa Fe in May 1792, and reached Saint Louis in early October. His return trip began in mid-June 1793, and ended in Santa Fe in mid-November. According to the commandant at Saint Louis in a letter written to the governor at New Orleans, Vial had arrived from "the town of Santa Fe, in the kingdom of New Mexico" and had been charged by Spanish authorities there to open a road between Santa Fe and Saint Louis.[4]

Prior to Vial's cross-country journey and back, other Frenchmen had already eyed the wealth of the remote villages of New Mexico. In fact, as early as 1739, the Mallet brothers, Paul and Pierre, visited Taos and Santa Fe following an overland trek that carried them through parts of present-day Missouri, Nebraska, Kansas, Colorado, and New Mexico. The Mallets lost all of their trading goods on the outward journey, and suspicious Spanish authorities detained them in Santa Fe for several months before allowing them to return to the eastern settlements. Two years later, the two attempted another passage to the region, this time via the Canadian River, but failed in their efforts.[5]

The French were not alone in casting envious eyes toward New Mexico and the riches it held. In 1804, when Meriwether Lewis and William Clark started their momentous journey to the Pacific Ocean, an American fur trader and merchant, William Morrison, of Kaskaskia, Indiana Territory, dispatched Jeanot Meteyer and Baptiste La Lande up the Missouri River with orders to cut cross-country to New Mexico.[6] They were soon followed by Lorenzo Durocher and Jacques d'Eglise. All four men made it safely to Santa Fe and traded successfully with the New Mexicans. La Lande even decided to permanently stay in the remote village, requiring the hapless Morrison to file suit against him to recover unpaid profits from the mission.[7]

In 1805, James Purcell (a.k.a., Pursley), a fur trapper from Kentucky, appeared in Santa Fe after spending close to three years in the trans-Mississippi wilderness. He liked the Spanish town and its people so well that he permanently settled there and became a carpenter.[8] He still resided there when the next American to frequent the region, Captain Zebulon Pike, arrived in March 1807.[9] Pike had been placed in command of an expedition to explore the southwestern part of the Louisiana Territory. During 1806–07, he and his companions covered many square miles of the vast wilderness and, among their other discoveries, they became the first Americans to view, but not scale, the famous mountain located in present-day Colorado later named Pike's Peak.[10]

Pike's arduous journey to New Mexico began on July 15, 1806, when he and twenty-three soldiers under the orders of Louisiana Territory's governor, General James Wilkinson, left Saint Louis, ostensibly to explore the headwaters of the Red River. Wilkinson and his close associate, former US vice president Aaron Burr, privately nurtured dreams of separating the then-southwestern part of the United States (present-day Kentucky, Tennessee, Mississippi, and Louisiana) from the rest of the country and creating a renegade Spanish-American regime in which they would be the kingpins. With this scheme in mind, Wilkinson dispatched Pike to the far West with instructions to spy out the Spanish territories and towns of northern New Spain. In late February 1807, the Americans crossed the boundary that separated Louisiana from New Spain and were confronted by Spanish soldiers near the headwaters of the Rio Grande in present-day Colorado. When questioned about his mission by the soldiers, Pike exclaimed, "What, is not this the Red River?" alluding to the generally accepted border between the United States and New Spain, but knowing full well that the stream was really the Rio Grande and that he was most likely standing on Spanish territory. Although they were not officially arrested, Pike and his companions were marched to Santa Fe for an interview with the governor.[11]

In the journal of his western travels, Pike told his readers that Santa Fe reminded him of "a fleet of the flat bottomed boats, which

A Missouri trader's caravan along the Santa Fe Trail.

are seen in the spring and fall seasons, descending the Ohio River," and that he could find but "two churches, the magnificence of whose steeples form a striking contrast to the miserable appearance of the houses."[12] Nearing the palace for an interview with the governor, Pike was confronted by a crowd of curious onlookers. He was obviously one of the few Americans that most of them had ever seen.

Governor Joachin del Real Alencaster minced no words. "Do you speak French?" he asked Pike. The American replied that he did, so the ensuing conversation was carried out in that language. It quickly became obvious to Pike that the governor was attempting to trap him into admitting that the real goal of his mission was to spy on the inhabitants and facilities of New Spain's northern frontier. In a second interview, Pike tried to assure Alencaster that he harbored "no hostile intentions toward the Spanish government." After reviewing Pike's army commission and orders, the governor "gave me his hand, for the first time, and said he was happy to be acquainted with me as a man of honor."[13]

Pike and his men were escorted by Spanish soldiers on a long journey to Chihuahua, where they were interrogated and released later in the spring. When he returned to the United States, Pike reported from memory to an anxious General Wilkinson all that he had seen and heard in New Spain. And he published the book that revealed his impressions of the wonders of the exotic territory he had visited. Pike's glowing reports of what he had seen in the vastness of New Spain served to whet the appetites of others who soon planned journeys to Santa Fe, but they also identified a downside to the region. Although later travelers and writers echoed similar attitudes, Pike's sometimes negative comments regarding the potential utility of the land through which he had passed were at least partially responsible for the creation and propagation of the "Great American Desert" myth that discouraged American emigration across the southern Great Plains for years to come.[14]

At about the same time that Captain Pike was sojourning in Santa Fe, Manuel Lisa, a well-known Missouri fur trader and organizer of the Missouri Fur Company, became interested in the fabled town. In 1807, he dispatched Jacques Clamorgan, a seventy-four-year-old employee, along with four companions and four mules loaded with trade goods, to attempt to establish a trading relationship with Santa Fe merchants, a mission that had lukewarm results. As late as September 1812, Lisa still nourished ambitions of capitalizing on the infant Santa Fe trade when he communicated to officials in the town that he desired "to engage in business and open up a new commerce," and that "as a director of the Missouri Fur Company, I propose to you gentlemen that if you wish to trade and deal with me . . . I will obligate myself to fill each year any bill of goods which shall be given me, and all shall be delivered (as stipulated) both as to quality and as to quantity, at the place nearest and most convenient for both parties, to your satisfaction."[15]

However, in time, the distant headwaters of the Missouri River captured Lisa's interest, and it was left for other men to pursue the opening of the Santa Fe trade in earnest. Over the next ten years or so, several other parties of Missouri traders made trips to Santa Fe. Because Spanish authorities there were hostile toward Americans and wary of their intense interest in the region, most of the traders were arrested and their goods confiscated.

One of the most bizarre incidents to occur during the early American attempts to open the door to the Santa Fe trade involved Missouri traders Robert McKnight, Samuel Chambers, and James

Baird. The group left Saint Louis in spring 1812, and when it arrived in Santa Fe later that year, its members were arrested by the Spanish, who seized all of their trading goods. Not only were the traders imprisoned until 1821, when the Mexicans won their independence from Spain, but the luckless Missourians were invoiced for their own upkeep while in jail at a cost of 18 3/4 cents per day, to be charged against the trade goods they had brought with them.[16]

In September 1815, two other Saint Louis fur men, Auguste P. Chouteau and Jules de Mun, with a small band of trappers, left Missouri for the headwaters of the Arkansas River, where they intended to trade with Arapaho Indians. Due to the lateness of the season, the venture was less than successful. De Mun, leaving Chouteau and a few companions behind in the wilderness, returned to Saint Louis, outfitted a new party, and headed back for the mountains in 1816. During May 1817, the trapping outfit was confronted by Spanish soldiers who arrested the entire lot and carried them to Santa Fe, where they were imprisoned for nearly fifty days. De Mun wrote a letter to William Clark, governor of Missouri Territory, in November 1817, explaining that the Spanish governor had eventually admitted the traders' innocence but nevertheless had confiscated all of their property. When the Missourians were sent home, they were ordered to leave behind more than $30,000 in earned profits. Ruefully, de Mun added, "It remains now to know whether our Government will demand satisfaction of the King of Spain for outrages committed by his ignorant Governor on American citizens."[17]

Other Americans journeyed to New Mexico during 1820, among them nineteen-year-old David Meriwether, who was accompanied by a few Pawnee Indians and a black cook named Alfred. Meriwether, born in Virginia and raised in Kentucky, was a distant kinsman of Meriwether Lewis. He had been hired by Colonel John O'Fallon of Saint Louis as a trader and sutler for Colonel Henry Atkinson's 1819–1820 Yellowstone Expedition. Following his service with Atkinson on the upper Missouri, at which time he met his companion, Alfred, Meriwether returned to Council Bluffs, in present-day Iowa, eager to make a trip to New Mexico to investigate stories of abundant gold there. While on the trip, Meriwether encountered a party of Spanish soldiers, who disarmed the Americans and stripped them of all valuables. Meriwether and Alfred were then marched west, on foot. Several days later, the entourage arrived in Santa Fe, where Meriwether was presented to the governor. Following a brief audience, since the American could speak no Spanish and the governor could speak no English, Meriwether was thrown into a dark and extremely hot prison cell.

Following a couple of days of prison life, during which time he "thought the bed bugs and fleas would eat me up," Meriwether was visited by a French-speaking priest. Since the young American also spoke French, he could now complete the interview with the governor. With the priest acting as interpreter, Meriwether attempted to explain the purpose of his visit to the disbelieving official. He was thrown back into jail but eventually was released on the promise that he would never visit New Mexico again. Vowing to follow the governor's orders, Meriwether and Alfred, with enough supplies to get them back to the United States, left Santa Fe, arriving at Council Bluffs in March 1821.[18]

David Meriwether returned to the area around Louisville, Kentucky, where he married and sired thirteen children. He pursued various business interests until June 1852, when he was appointed to fill the US Senate seat vacated by the death of Henry Clay. The following year he consented to break his thirty-year-old promise never to return to New Mexico when he was prevailed upon by President Franklin Pierce to fill the role of territorial governor.

During the years since Meriwether first traveled there in 1820, the country had won its independence from Spain, only to be occupied by the American army in the late war with Mexico. Now an American territory, it was in need of a governor who understood the land and its people and who could peacefully settle the boundary-line dispute between the two nations. Meriwether served his adopted territory well at an extremely difficult time in its existence. Animosities between the United States and Mexico remained, the border dispute was still up in the air, and Indians continued to create problems for the new American government, but Meriwether endured the storm, serving as governor until 1857, when he resigned and returned to Kentucky.[19]

In 1821, an event occurred in Spanish America that dramatically changed the attitudes that government officials and the common people of New Mexico had for Americans. In February, after years of refusal, Spain finally granted independence to Mexico, whose authorities promptly opened the doors of its northernmost region, New Mexico, to any and all Americans who wished to trade. Missourians were delighted. By the time the news reached the United States, one of them, William Becknell, a native Virginian in his early thirties, was already on his way to Santa Fe to try his hand at trading in what he thought to be a fabulously rich country.

Becknell had correctly assessed the recently received, sketchy news from Santa Fe that an overthrow of Spain was imminent. Accordingly, in June 1821, he advertised in the *Missouri Intelligencer* for men to accompany him on the journey. Instructions for would-be employees were simple: bring a good rifle, plenty of ammunition, and warm clothing to last for three months.[20] Becknell's party set out from Arrow Rock, Missouri, on September 1, 1821, only a few days before Mexico would formally declare its independence. This date marks the beginnings of serious American trade with New Mexican citizens, and because of his premier role in the historic event, William Becknell is called the father of the Santa Fe trade.

Becknell's outward journey carried him along what is now called the Mountain Route of the Santa Fe Trail. This course left Arrow Rock and traveled west past Fort Osage and the site of Kansas City, Missouri, before entering present-day Kansas. As it neared the Great Bend of the Arkansas River, it proceeded along the river's north bank to the future site of Bent's Fort near present-day La Junta, Colorado, before striking out southwest toward Raton Pass and into New Mexico. In November 1821, as Becknell and his trading party were nearing their destination, they were approached by Mexican soldiers, who warmly greeted the expedition and welcomed its members to the newly independent republic of Mexico.[21] Furthermore, Becknell was told that government officials would now not only tolerate free trade with the Americans but would actually seek and encourage it. Becknell wrote in his journal that Governor Don Facundo Melgares "expressed a desire that Americans would keep up an intercourse with that country, and said that if any of them wished to emigrate, it would give him pleasure to afford them every facility."[22]

In the meantime, two other American trading parties entered New Mexico soon after Becknell reached Santa Fe on his first trip. One group was led by trappers Hugh Glenn and Jacob Fowler, and the other included John McKnight, the brother of Robert McKnight, who years earlier had tried his hand at trading with the Mexicans, only to be imprisoned for his efforts.[23]

On May 22, 1822, Becknell, along with twenty-one men and three wagons full of top-quality trade goods, crossed the Arrow Rock ferry in Missouri, bound for his second trading mission to Santa Fe. The new expedition was a much more complex affair than Becknell's original trading party. This time, wagons, instead of mules, were used to carry the freight, and this decision brought with it logistical problems not encountered on the first trip.

After several weeks of hard travel, the party arrived in the neighborhood of present-day Dodge City, Kansas. Becknell realized that his wagons could not negotiate the steep cliffs and rocky outcroppings that were common throughout Raton Pass on the Mountain Route. Accordingly, he turned his wagons toward the southwest and drove them across the dry region lying between the Arkansas and Cimarron rivers. The new way, to be called the Cimarron Cutoff, bypassed Raton Pass and rendezvoused with the Mountain Route near present-day Watrous, New Mexico. The road traversed some extremely desolate country. Josiah Gregg, a contemporary Santa Fe trader, described this part of Becknell's journey, revealing that when the drinking water gave out, the men were reduced to killing their dogs and cutting off their mules' ears to drink the blood.[24] Despite the unfavorable traveling conditions, Becknell's second trading mission proved to be even more financially successful than the first.

It remained for Josiah Gregg to raise the American public's awareness of the opportunities afforded by the New Mexican markets and to give an in-depth look at conditions there immediately prior to the Mexican-American War. Gregg, a Tennessean who was sent west by his physician because of ill health, traveled a total of eight times across the southern plains between Missouri and New Mexico. His record, *Commerce of the Prairies, or the Journal of a Santa Fe Trader, during Eight Expeditions across the Great Western Prairies, and a*

*Residence of Nearly Nine Years in Northern Mexico*, provides a storehouse of information about the land, its people and their customs, and the natural history of New Mexico and the region along the Santa Fe Trail. Gregg saw his two-volume narrative published in 1844, but he died in an accident during the Mexican-America War, never realizing that he had produced one of the all-time classics of American historical travel literature.

Josiah Gregg.

It was a great day for Mexicans and Americans alike when a trade caravan pulled into Santa Fe. Gregg left a moving account of the arrival of one of them. He wrote that the appearance of a wagon train,

> produced a great deal of bustle and excitement among the natives. "Los Americanos!"—"Los carros!"—"La entrada de la caravana!" were to be heard in every direction; and crowds of women and boys flocked around to see the new-comers . . . [who] were prepared with clean faces, sleek combed hair, and their choicest Sunday suit, to meet the "fair eyes" of glistening black that were sure to stare at them as they passed.25

No doubt, American traders found a merchant's paradise in New Mexico. Residents of Santa Fe and numerous other villages that dotted the countryside were isolated by great distances from the large towns and markets in Mexico. Consequently, they relied on their own skills and industry to make a meager living off the dry, sparse land. Trade caravans from Mexico City and other cities to the south were few and far between, and when the first of the American traders arrived on the scene with all kinds of hard-to-find goods, the common folk embraced them enthusiastically. Over the years other Missouri traders became convinced that fortunes could be made with little effort in Santa Fe and its neighboring villages. Consequently, traffic between Missouri and New Mexico grew steadily. During the decade between 1826 and 1835, more than one thousand five hundred men, accompanied by 775 wagons and carrying nearly one and a half million dollars worth of merchandise, made the arduous journey from the United States to the rich markets at the end of the Santa Fe Trail.[26]

Prior to the war, American fur trappers also found the region around Taos and Santa Fe to be lucrative markets for selling and exchanging their furs and peltries. By the 1830s and 1840s, many of them had already discovered Taos and were dealing with its inhabitants in a rapidly developing, profitable business. The Bent brothers, Charles and William, traders from Missouri, understood the rewards to be found in the southwestern fur trade. Charles, the future governor of New Mexico and the foremost victim of the Taos Revolt, became so enamored with the region that he relinquished control of Bent's Fort—built in the early 1830s by Charles and William, along with another Missouri trader, Ceran St. Vrain—to his brother. At about the same time, he moved to Taos, married, and made the town his permanent home. Bent's Fort was situated on the Mountain Route of the Santa Fe Trail along the north side of the Arkansas River. Soon after the post's construction, it became the nerve center of a large and prosperous fur enterprise carved out of the wilderness by the Bents and St. Vrain.[27]

Although New Mexico was home to a goodly number of Americans by the 1840s, the region was still a Mexican province, inhabited primarily by Indians and Hispanos with varying degrees of loyalty to Mexico City. Americans were tolerated because they brought hard-to-find goods from the East that were not readily available in the remoteness of the New Mexican frontier, or plush furs from the Rocky Mountains that in turn could be traded to the Missouri merchants. However, the Mexican government always had claimed, and still did claim, the entire New Mexico region as its own.

In reviewing the rich and varied early history of New Mexico, it is clear that by the time the Mexican-American War began, the area had become a melting pot for several vastly different cultures. A number of Pueblo tribes and their ancestors had inhabited the land for hundreds of years before the Spanish *entrada*, and, along with the more recently arrived Apaches and Navajos, had left a rich tapestry of material culture. The appearance of the Spanish in the sixteenth century and the acculturation of the indigenous people in the area had set the stage for the development of Mexico, which, after its separation from Spain, spread its influence north. Finally, the American presence, in the guise of trappers, traders, and professional soldiers, added to the already complicated cultural milieu. It is not surprising, then, that with this montage of cultures—all with such distinctive differences in religion, mores, and lifestyles—political dissatisfaction, engendered by a questionably legal American military occupation, was soon followed by revolt.

*Three*

# Without Firing a Gun or Spilling a Drop of Blood

## The American Invasion of New Mexico

At the outset of the Mexican-American War in mid-1846, Stephen Watts Kearny, a middle-aged US Army colonel, was ordered to form a military force called the Army of the West whose mission was to occupy New Mexico and California. The assignment was a challenge that would prove to be the high point of Kearny's career.[1]

Kearny, an experienced veteran, was born in New Jersey in 1794. Barely old enough to see service in the War of 1812, he was, nevertheless, commissioned a captain in 1813, and a few years later transferred to the frontier. His association with mounted cavalry dated to the original formation of the US Regiment of Dragoons in 1833. At that time, Kearny was promoted to lieutenant colonel and second-in-command of this new mounted branch of the service.[2]

In 1836, when his commander, Colonel Henry Dodge, resigned from the army to become governor of Wisconsin Territory, Kearny assumed command of the dragoons with the rank of colonel. For several years, Kearny was the senior officer of the army's mounted troops, including a second regiment of dragoons formed in 1836.[3]

His reputation was enhanced by the army's adoption of a guide he had authored, *Carbine Manual, or Rules for the Exercise and Manoeuvers for the U.S. Dragoons*, which soon became the recognized authority on the use and care of American military shoulder arms.

Headquartered with Colonel Kearny at present-day Fort Leavenworth, Kansas, were several companies of the 1st US Dragoons. On May 13, 1846, Secretary of War William L. Marcy sent Kearny a copy of the US declaration of war with Mexico,[4] and in a separate letter, Adjutant General Roger Jones advised him that a mounted force, most likely to be commanded by Kearny himself, would soon be assembled and sent to Santa Fe in order to protect US citizens and property.[5] A dispatch, also written on May 13 and signed by the secretary of war, was sent to Missouri governor John C. Edwards, asking him to immediately raise a regiment of eight companies of mounted volunteers and two companies of volunteer artillery.[6] The following day, Adjutant General Jones again wrote to Colonel Kearny, confirming that he was to be the commander of the military force, to consist of his own 1st Dragoons along with other units.[7]

General Stephen Watts Kearny, 1st Regiment, U.S. Dragoons.

Sixteen days later in Washington, President Polk met with his cabinet to discuss the advisability of sending an army to New Mexico so late in the season.[8] Although it was only the end of May, Polk was concerned about whether the army had time to make the journey to New Mexico, conquer the region, and then march all the way to California before snow blocked the mountain passes. "In winter, all whom I had consulted agreed that it was impracticable to make the expedition,"[9] wrote the president in his diary. However, Thomas Hart Benton, the influential senior senator from Missouri who attended a number of cabinet meetings, had different ideas. Benton, who only the previous month had been so hesitant about the speedy manner in which the United States declared war on Mexico, was now one of the leading proponents for the rapid prosecution of the conflict. By the end of the cabinet meeting, Benton had convinced Polk that—given the information provided by explorer and army topographical engineer John Charles Frémont (who was Benton's son-in-law) in his book, *Report of the Exploring Expedition to the Rocky Mountains in the Year 1842, and to Oregon and North California in the Years 1843–'44*—the army could safely make its transcontinental march "provided it could move from Independence by the first of August."[10]

Satisfied that Benton knew what he was talking about and encouraged by Kearny's reputation for having recently commanded part of the 1st Dragoons on an extended journey to the Continental Divide and back, Polk continued with his plans.[11] The proposal, as submitted to his cabinet officers for discussion, was that Kearny and his soon-to-be-organized army would be dispatched to Santa Fe as early as possible. Once there, if Kearny thought he could reach California before winter threatened, he would leave that city under the command of his lieutenant colonel, "with a sufficient force to hold it," and proceed to California with the remainder of the army.[12] Kearny, in the meantime, continued to structure his regiment and asked General George M. Brooke, commander of the army's Department of the West, to immediately transfer Companies B and K of the 1st Dragoons—commanded respectively by Captains Edwin V. Sumner and Philip St. George Cooke—to Fort Leavenworth to join the rest of the unit.[13]

Without debate, Polk's proposition was approved by the cabinet, and Kearny received his orders a few days later. In a letter dated June 3, 1846, from Secretary of War Marcy, the colonel was advised that as a response to the "pending war with Mexico," an expedition was being formed to "take the earliest possession of Upper California," and that Kearny was to be its commander. In the same letter, Kearny was informed that one thousand mounted Missouri troops would follow his command and that if more soldiers were needed, he had the authority to directly contact the governor of Missouri for assistance. He was also advised that a large group of Mormons was somewhere on the plains en route to California and that they might be of service to the army in its conquest of that region. Kearny's orders, therefore, included authority to recruit a military force from these Mormons, not to exceed one-third of his entire army. The result was the famous Mormon Battalion that later followed Kearny's army to California.[14]

While Marcy's directives left no doubt that Polk fully expected Kearny to conquer New Mexico and California one way or the other, a peaceful occupation was preferred. The secretary told Kearny that if he did successfully occupy New Mexico and Upper California, he should "establish temporary civil governments therein" and that he should make every effort "to continue in their employment all such of the existing officers as are known to be friendly to the United States, and will take the oath of allegiance to them." Furthermore, according to Marcy's orders, Kearny was given authority to "assure the people of those provinces that it is the wish and design of the United States to provide for them a free government, with the least possible delay, similar to that which exists in our Territories."[15]

After Kearny received his orders, one of the first things he did was to solicit the assistance of the Mormons. On June 19, 1846, he directed Captain James Allen, one of his officers, to find the Mormon camps, meet with their leaders, and attempt to recruit four or five companies of volunteers to total 292 to 545 men.[16] Over the next several weeks, Allen visited the Mormons with a petition requesting volunteers to join his commander's unit and assist him in the occupation of California. Many of the Mormon leaders were hesitant to consider the offer and were concerned about the welfare of the women and children if the men went off to war. However, when the matter was laid before the church's highest official, President Brigham Young, he put the issue to rest, stating, "If we want the privilege of going where we can worship God according to the dictates of our consciences, we must raise the Battalion."[17]

By mid-July, Captain Allen, with the assistance of the Mormon leaders, had raised four full companies—about four hundred men—and part of a fifth. Governor Edwards of Missouri was busy raising the regiment requested by President Polk. Companies of mounted volunteers were organized and filled across the state, and by June 5, they began arriving at Fort Leavenworth, where they were soon integrated with Kearny's army. While at the fort, the new recruits underwent rigorous training in dragoon tactics.[18]

In the meantime, all the Missouri companies had arrived at Fort Leavenworth. As was the custom with volunteer forces, the men of the regiment elected their own commander. The honor fell to Alexander W. Doniphan, who was a well-known lawyer but who had volunteered in the 1st Regiment Missouri Mounted Volunteers as a private. Now, with the rank of colonel, Doniphan was second-in-command of the entire Army of the West, reporting to Colonel Kearny. C. R. Ruff was elected lieutenant colonel, and William Gilpin was commissioned major. Like Doniphan, both Ruff and Gilpin had volunteered as privates. Eight companies made up the 1st Missouri: A, B, C, D, E, F, G, and H, each company consisting of volunteers from Jackson, Lafayette, Clay, Saline, Franklin, Cole, Howard, and Calaway Counties respectively and commanded by Captains David Waldo, William P. Walton, Oliver Perry Moss, John W. Reid, John D. Stephenson, Monroe M. Parsons, Hancock Jackson, and Charles E. Rodgers. A battalion of artillery (two companies consisting of about 250 men) from Saint Louis was commanded by Captains Richard H. Weightman and Woldemar Fischer, with Major Meriwether Lewis Clark serving as field officer. Cole and Platte Counties furnished a single battalion of infantry (145 men), which was commanded by Captains William Angney and William S. Murphy. Captain Thomas B. Hudson commanded 107 members of the Laclede Rangers from Saint Louis. Monthly wages for the all volunteer force ranged from seven dollars for privates to seventy-five dollars for Colonel Doniphan.[19] By the latter part of June, the 1st Missouri Mounted Volunteers were ready to march with Kearny's 1st US Dragoons to New Mexico.

Colonel Alexander W. Doniphan, 1st Regiment, Missouri Mounted Volunteers.

The newly organized Mormon Battalion was mustered into service on July 16, 1846, at Council Bluffs, Iowa Territory.[20] From the mustering grounds, the infantrymen making up the battalion traveled to Fort Leavenworth for training. James Allen, now promoted to lieutenant colonel, commanded the unit consisting of Companies A, B, C, D, and E, which were under the orders of Captains Jefferson Hunt, Jesse Hunter, James Brown, Nelson Higgins, and Daniel Davis respectively. Soon after the battalion left Fort Leavenworth for Santa Fe, sad news arrived telling of the unexpected death of Lieutenant Colonel Allen, who had delayed his departure from the fort for a few days after the main column had left. The command of the battalion fell to 1st Lieutenant Andrew Jackson Smith of the 1st Dragoons, who marched the men to Santa Fe.[21]

In order to better feed the men and animals on the long march across the prairie and to ensure that pasturage and the water supply would not be abused by the magnitude of the troops' movement, commanders spread departure dates over several weeks. By late June 1846, several elements of the Army of the West had left Fort Leavenworth on their way to Bent's Fort, some 537 miles to the west.

The logistics of the first leg of Kearny's mission—to reach Bent's Fort—were mind-boggling. The army now numbered 1,658 men, including the combat troops, staff officers, and small contingents of sutlers, topographical engineers, medical personnel, and quartermasters.[22] Also accompanying Kearny were about fifty mounted Shawnee and Delaware Indians to serve as scouts.[23] With his command were 3,658 mules, 14,904 cattle, 459 horses, and 1,556 wagons. His artillery consisted of twelve 6-pounder cannons and four 12-pounder howitzers. The sheer magnitude of managing men and materiel of such proportions across hundreds of miles of hot, dry prairie was staggering. But the old veteran, Kearny—with the same resourcefulness and determination he had used years earlier to make the 1st Dragoons such a success—prevailed.

As the miles separating the army from Fort Leavenworth lengthened, the increasingly arid conditions of the Great Plains brought discomfort to man and animal alike. On the morning of July 12, the temperature stood at ninety-five degrees, and mirages fooled the mounted soldiers into seeing water that was not really there. Provisions ran low. Finally, however, the Arkansas River was sighted, and "Horse and man ran involuntarily into the river, and simultaneously slaked their burning thirst."[24] Herds of buffalo appeared on the endless prairies, and many were killed, cooked, and heartily devoured by the hungry soldiers. During late July, lead elements of the Army of the West approached Bent's Fort. A difficult part of the Army's journey was now over.

As the soldiers drew nearer to the fort, they were met by noted mountain man Thomas "Broken Hand" Fitzpatrick, who had guided

Colonel Kearny to the Rocky Mountains and back the previous year. Fitzpatrick, born in Ireland in 1799, began his life in America as a Rocky Mountain fur trapper, but he eventually quit the fur trade and took up scouting for emigrant parties and the military.[25] Fitzpatrick presented Kearny with intelligence he had gathered in Santa Fe that New Mexico's governor, Manuel Armijo, was preparing all parts of the region for the imminent invasion by the American army and that Kearny's "movements would be vigorously opposed."[26] Still obscure in the United States, Armijo was a legend in his native New Mexico. He had already served as New Mexico's governor from 1827 to 1829 and from 1837 to 1844. Then, in 1845, he again assumed the office, in addition to the role of commanding general of New Mexico.[27]

Mexican governor Manuel Armijo.

Kearny no doubt remembered Armijo's role in the 1841 Texan-Santa Fe Expedition, when he arrested and marched, under armed guard, several hundred Texas traders to Mexico City for detention. And he probably still recalled the 1843 attack of a group of soldiers of fortune under the command of Jacob Snively on an advance party of Armijo's army that was traveling along the Santa Fe Trail to protect a Mexican trading caravan. Snively's men killed eighteen New Mexicans, all of them Taos Indians, and captured many others. Men of Kearny's own 1st US Dragoons under the command of Captain Philip St. George Cooke were dispatched to intercept and arrest Snively's men after the incident caused a national uproar.[28]

Taking Armijo's threats into consideration, Kearny now prepared his next move, the actual occupation of New Mexico in as painless and bloodless a manner as possible.

Bent's Fort was built in 1833 by Charles Bent, his younger brother William, and Ceran St. Vrain to serve as headquarters for the far-reaching Bent, St. Vrain & Company. Originally called Fort William, it was located on the north bank of the Arkansas River along the

Mountain Route of the Santa Fe Trail in present-day southeastern Colorado near today's town of La Junta.

William Bent was born in Saint Louis in 1809. By 1824, William, deeply influenced by Charles, was trapping along the upper reaches of the Arkansas River and was well familiar with the section of the southern Great Plains through which the Santa Fe Trail ran. William Bent often chose to remain behind at the fort while Charles made the supply trips back and forth to Missouri. In time, William became the major driving force in the day-to-day management of activities at Bent's Fort, and he guided the company through its successful trading operations among the Indian tribes of the southern Great Plains. William married a Cheyenne Indian named Owl Woman and became even more Indian-like in his habits. His influence among the Indians, through his marriage to Owl Woman, did a great deal to enhance the peace between various Plains tribes and the rapidly approaching whites.[29] Ceran St. Vrain, of French descent, was born in Missouri in 1802, and as early as 1825, he was a frequent visitor to Taos in New Mexico.[30]

In the meantime, Charles Bent had established a permanent home in Taos, the small New Mexican-Indian village north of Santa Fe, and married Maria Ignacia Jaramillo, an affluent Mexican widow. Although he retained his American citizenship, he soon involved himself in the town's politics, entrenched himself in trade with the locals, and became a respected resident.

By summer 1846, when the Army of the West approached Bent's Fort, the structure was the hub for the extensive Bent, St. Vrain operations that reached into today's states of Wyoming, Utah, Colorado, New Mexico, Arizona, Texas, Oklahoma, Kansas, and Nebraska. The fort was a citadel in the wilderness and was frequented by mountain men, Missouri and Taos traders, New Mexicans, and members of several tribes of southern Plains and Southwest Indians.

Bent's Fort was a magnificent structure built of adobe bricks. Fourteen-feet-high and three-feet-thick walls surrounded the fort, which consisted of thirty-eight rooms surrounding a small courtyard. Space was provided inside the fort for corrals, wagon sheds, and a blacksmith. Although the fort was built primarily as a trading post, its strategic location hundreds of miles deep into Indian territory made it necessary that it be able to serve as a defensive structure as well. Two conical bastions perched on opposite corners protected the living quarters, storehouses, and well inside. A small cannon was placed in a watchtower above the walls, and an American flag flew proudly from a flagstaff over the gate. A visitor of the time estimated that Bent's Fort could accommodate upwards of one hundred men.[31] A welcome attraction for tired and hungry sojourners was the savory food prepared in the kitchen, supervised by Charlotte Green, the black servant of the Bent brothers who was known all over the Southwest for her pancakes and pumpkin pie.[32]

Bent's Fort reigned supreme on the Santa Fe Trail for many years. However, as more and more of the wagon traffic began to travel the shorter, smoother Cimarron Cutoff route, and as trapping activity gradually came to a close, the old fort slowly lost its importance as a dominant factor in the Santa Fe trade. Its remains finally became a stop on the Kansas City, Denver, and Santa Fe stagecoach line that was operated by the Barlow-Sanderson Overland Stage, Mail and Express Company, but not before William Bent and his family packed up their belongings and rode out of the fort, never to return. Disillusioned by the US War Department's failure to pay what he considered a fair price for the structure, Bent deliberately blew up the fort when he deserted it.[33]

Although Bent's Fort was never designed to accommodate as large a number of men as arrived there in late July, nevertheless, the owners and managers scurried about to ensure that the soldiers were as comfortable as possible. For the short time that members of the Army of the West spent at the fort, most of them bivouacked on the flatlands nine miles downstream.

Santa Fe, the target of the first phase of Colonel Kearny's operations, was only about a two weeks' journey from Bent's Fort. So while the men and animals of his mixed command rested for the upcoming march, Kearny composed a directive, which he would later distribute to the native population along the way to Santa Fe. Dated July 31, 1846, the proclamation read:

> The undersigned enters New Mexico with a large military force, for the purpose of seeking union with and ameliorating the condi-

A mid-1840s plan showing exterior and bird's eye views of Bent's Fort.

tions of its inhabitants. This he does under instructions from his government, and with the assurance that he will be amply sustained in the accomplishment of this object. It is enjoined on the citizens of New Mexico to remain quietly at their homes, and to pursue their peaceful avocations. So long as they continue in such pursuits, they will not be interfered with by the American army, but will be respected and protected in their rights, both civil and religious.

Kearny closed his speech with a not-so-subtle warning to his would-be listeners that, "All who take up arms or encourage resistance against the government of the United States will be regarded as enemies, and will be treated accordingly."[34]

On August 2, 1846, the Army of the West broke camp at Bent's Fort and began its southwestward march toward Raton Pass. Once on the other side of the Arkansas River, Kearny and his men found themselves in territory claimed by both Texas and Mexico. From there, four days of difficult travel brought the Army to Raton Pass, located along the present-day Colorado-New Mexico border. First Lieutenant William H. Emory, a topographical engineer with Colonel Kearny's command, wrote in his journal that "the view . . . is inexpressibly beautiful and reminds persons of the landscape of Palestine. . . . The general appearance is something like the pass at the summit of the Boston and Albany railroad, but the scenery bolder, and less adorned with vegetation." The following day, the crossing was made by advance elements of the army, and Emory's barometer showed the height of Raton Pass to be seven thousand five hundred feet above sea level.[35]

Another topographical engineer, 2nd Lieutenant J. W. Abert, crossed Raton Pass a few weeks following Kearny. In his diary he confirmed the difficulty that wagons had in negotiating the treacherous gap in the mountains, writing that "we commenced the passage of one of the most rocky roads I ever saw; no one who has crossed the Raton can ever forget it." The rock-strewn roadway was littered with the broken wagons of previous travelers, and "at the foot of the hill we saw many axletrees, wagon tongues, sand-boards, and ox yokes, that had been broken and cast aside."[36]

When Susan Shelby Magoffin, a nineteen-year-old newlywed and one of a handful of American women who had ever traversed the Santa Fe Trail, crossed the Raton with her trader husband one week after Kearny's main force had passed, her party was slowed to a speed of one-half mile per hour. "Worse and worse the road!" she lamented. Continuing, she explained how the going got even slower, writing that "it takes a dozen men to steady a wagon with all its wheels locked—and for one who is some distance off to hear the crash it makes over the stones, is truly alarming." On one occasion, after traveling all day, Magoffin wrote that her wagon arrived at camp after dusk and that the total progress made was only six hundred to eight hundred yards.³⁷

On the day following the Army of the West's crossing of Raton Pass, Governor Armijo issued a proclamation of his own declaring to his constituents that "the moment has arrived when our country requires of her children a decision without limit, a sacrifice without reserve, under circumstances which claim all for our salvation." The governor added that "forces of that government [the United States] are advancing in this department; they have crossed the northern frontier," and he admonished his readers to prepare for war. "Let us be comrades in arms," he declared, "and, with honest union, we shall lead to victory. . . . Rest assured that your governor is willing and ready to sacrifice his life and all his interests in the defense of his country."³⁸

Lieutenant William H. Emory photographed during the Civil War.

Once on the other side of Raton Pass, Kearny's men found travel to be easier as they continued to follow the Santa Fe Trail. The Army of the West was now eight days out of Bent's Fort, and Kearny knew that his command was traveling deep into enemy territory. Along the trail, a party of Mexicans, whose mission was to reconnoiter the American forces, was captured.³⁹ More reports of native unrest continued to make their way to the army, and on August 10, Emory wrote in his journal that an American had just arrived in camp, reporting that Armijo had raised two thousand Pueblo Indians along with three hundred Mexican dragoons and that twelve hundred more soldiers were to arrive in Santa Fe at any time.⁴⁰ On the following day, Emory wrote:

> Matters are now becoming very interesting. Six or eight Mexicans were captured last night, and on their persons was found the proclamation of the Prefect of Taos, based upon that of Armijo, calling the citizens to arms, to repel the 'Americans, who were

coming to invade their soil and destroy their property and liberties;' ordering an enrolment of all citizens over 15 and under 50.[41]

Two days later, an American named Spry entered Kearny's camp with more reports of Mexican unrest. Spry had escaped from detention in Santa Fe the night before and brought with him intelligence that a Mexican army, led by Armijo, was gathering at Apache Canyon, a few miles east of Santa Fe, and that the force intended to make a stand against Kearny's army there.[42] Undaunted, the colonel and his tired men continued their march toward Santa Fe. On August 14, extra precautions were taken among the men, and an order of march was devised so that a battle formation could be formed immediately. Later in the day, a dispatch from Armijo was delivered to Kearny. Dated two days earlier, the letter was in response to Kearny's message of July 31, sent from Bent's Fort and calling for accommodation between the two forces. A liberal translation of the message by Emory revealed that New Mexicans in large numbers had responded to Armijo's call to arms, but that Armijo still desired to avoid bloodshed.[43]

During the evening of August 14, the American army made camp on the outskirts of the small village of Vegas (present-day Las Vegas, New Mexico), about sixty miles east of Santa Fe. Around midnight, Kearny received information that six hundred battle-ready New Mexicans had assembled at a pass two miles from the American encampment. At eight o'clock on the morning of August 15, Kearny, who had just received word of his promotion to brigadier general, rode into Vegas. Amid the stares of scores of curious farmers and townspeople, the general climbed to the roof of a low building on the plaza and announced the American occupation of New Mexico. In a prepared speech to the awestruck natives, Kearny told the crowd that he, not Armijo, was now the governor of New Mexico and stated that he had come "by the orders of my government, to take possession of your country, and extend over it the laws of the United States," but "as friends—not as enemies; as protectors—not as conquerors." Kearny vowed that the US government would extend protection over his listeners, their property, and their crops but threatened to hang anyone "who promises to be quiet, and is found in arms against me." He assured them of protection from marauding Apache and Navajo

General Kearny reading his proclomation at the village of Vegas (present-day Las Vegas), New Mexico.

Indians who had raided the local villages for generations, and guaranteed that their Catholic faith would be respected and protected. Finally, as his officers prepared to administer the oath of allegiance to the United States to the town officials, he told the crowd that "resistance is useless."[44]

Kearny also promised to keep many local officials in power, and few of the Vegas villagers offered resistance to his speech. Even the town's leading citizens took the oath of allegiance, and, in a matter of hours, the Army of the West departed for its rendezvous with the six hundred Mexican soldiers who supposedly still awaited them in the pass outside the village. However, the information proved to be false, and no Mexican army was to be seen. The men of the 1st Dragoons, anxious for a fight, ended the day somewhat disappointed.

The Americans entered the village of San Miguel the next day, and Kearny made a speech similar to the one he had given at Vegas. Reports of the massive buildup of the enemy at Apache Canyon became more frequent now, and during the mid-afternoon, a friendly native rode up to Kearny and exclaimed, "They are in the Cañon, my brave; pluck up your courage and push them out."[45]

The following day, a rumor reached the American camp that the Mexican soldiers under Armijo, supposedly gathered at Apache Canyon, had fled. Indeed, they had, and for reasons known only to Kearny, Armijo, and a few of their trusted staff.

On August 1, from Bent's Fort, Kearny had dispatched James Wiley Magoffin—the brother-in-law of Susan Magoffin and one of Missouri's foremost Santa Fe traders—and Captain Philip St. George Cooke to Santa Fe for a meeting with Governor Armijo. The mission was to persuade Armijo to allow the Army of the West peaceful entry to the city and to abstain from defending New Mexico from the American occupying force. Magoffin had been summoned to Washington, DC, the previous June and had met with President Polk and Senator Benton to discuss the possibility of his participation in an effort to keep Kearny's New Mexican campaign as peaceful as possible. Polk was impressed with Magoffin and wrote in his diary that "he is a very intelligent man, and gave us much valuable information."[46] Since Magoffin knew the New Mexican people and the countryside intimately, Benton felt that his presence with the advancing American army "could be of infinite service to the invading force."[47] Magoffin had agreed to assist the occupation effort and left Washington at once. When he reached Bent's Fort on July 26, he rendezvoused with Kearny, as well as with his own brother, Samuel, and his sister-in-law, Susan. Samuel and Susan had departed Independence, Missouri, on June 11, 1846, as part of a large trading caravan on its way to Santa Fe. When the Magoffin wagons reached Bent's Fort, its members awaited the arrival of Kearny and his men.

Magoffin and Cooke arrived in Santa Fe on August 12, carrying a dispatch for Armijo written by Kearny at Bent's Fort on August 1. When the governor read the letter, he was surprised to see that, according to Kearny, the United States was only interested in the part of New Mexico that lay east of the Rio Grande. Kearny pleaded with Armijo "to submit to fate and to meet me with the same feeling of peace and friendship which I now entertain for and offer to you and to all those over whom you are governor." Kearny told Armijo that he had ample men, materiel, and supplies to overcome any size force the governor might marshal. If Armijo acted logically and accepted the American occupation, "it will be greatly to your own interest and to that of all your countrymen," but if resistance was offered, then "the blood which may follow, the suffering and the misery which may ensue, will rest on your head, and, instead of the blessing of your Countrymen, you will receive their curses."[48]

The exact details of the Magoffin-Cooke-Armijo meeting have never been revealed, and the promises, if any, that Armijo made regarding the defense of Santa Fe remain unknown. His reply of August 12 to Kearny does not mention the meeting with the American emissaries, nor does it reference a potential retreat of his armed forces or a decision to lessen the New Mexican defenses.[49] It does declare, however, that Armijo believed his troops to be sufficient in strength and arms to resist the American threat. In retrospect, it appears that by the time Santa Fe was being approached by the Army of the West, Armijo was creating a sham to protect himself from what he knew would be unrelenting criticism—not only from the central government in Mexico City but from an irate constituency as well—if it was ever discovered that he had lessened his ardor to protect New Mexico without making a pretense to fight.

Missouri trader James Magoffin.

Apparently without Armijo's knowledge, the governor's second-in-command, Colonel Diego Archuleta—who later in the year, after the American army had occupied Santa Fe, would be involved in an abortive uprising there—decided to offer no resistance to the American takeover when he was told that all of the territory west of the Rio Grande might be his for the taking, since the United States lacked interest in that part of New Mexico. Of course, the falsehood of that statement would soon become apparent to both Armijo and Archuleta when they later read Kearny's proclamation of August 22, in which it became clear that the United States intended to occupy both banks of the Rio Grande.[50]

Unaware of the real reason for the retreat of Armijo's army at Apache Canyon, Lieutenant Emory later wrote that "dissensions had arisen in Armijo's camp, which had dispersed his army, and that he had fled to the south, carrying all his artillery and 100 dragoons with him." Emory stated that all resistance had evaporated between Kearny's army and Santa Fe, adding that "the general determined to make the march in one day, and raise the United States flag over the palace before sundown."[51]

The "dissensions" in Armijo's camp were far more complex and widespread than the Americans could have imagined. In May 1910, Rafael Chácon, who had been a cadet with Armijo's artillery corps at Apache Canyon, wrote to historian Benjamin M. Read explaining what had transpired among the frenzied New Mexicans who awaited Kearny's army on August 18, 1846. Chácon disclosed that shortly before the Army of the West's final approach to Santa Fe, Armijo had ordered Chácon's father, who was a prominent judge, to "call out the militia and Indian pueblos to go out and meet the American forces that were coming to take possession of New Mexico." Chácon related that New Mexican militiamen, Pueblo Indians, and New Mexican regular army units from Santa Fe and Taos, along with a squadron of dragoons from faraway Vera Cruz—all under the command of Colonel Don Pedro Muñoz—prepared for battle. Barricades of tree trunks were quickly erected, and a near-mutiny among the militiamen was quelled. According to Chácon, as the construction of the barricades neared completion, "Armijo ordered all the men to go back to their homes, saying that he would go to the front with the regular companies and the squadron of Vera Cruz." By the time Kearny's army arrived at Apache Canyon, the region was eerily quiet, presenting little evidence that a once-powerful army had just made its exit.[52]

Chácon's description of the confusion at Apache Canyon relates closely to the recollections of 105 citizens of Santa Fe who signed a letter to the president of Mexico on September 26, 1846, only a little more than a month after Armijo's flight.[53] These leading men told the president that as early as July 1, 1846, the governor had activated all of New Mexico's militiamen and all other males ages 16 to 59, ordering most of them to report, "under arms," to Santa Fe. When a reconnaissance of the region as far east as the Vermijo River discovered only a small party of Americans who quite possibly were hunters, the governor dismissed all of the troops on July 8, telling them to stay vigilant.

A few days later, when Armijo received more reliable information that the American army was on its way, he conferred with other officials and a decision was made to resist the invaders. Armijo then exchanged letters with Colonel Kearny, who had written earlier, saying that he had been ordered by the US government to occupy New Mexico, that he came as a friend, and that he had "many more troops than sufficient to put down any opposition." Armijo responded that he had "more than enough forces to repel your aggression" and that "self-preservation is a natural thing, and whatever finds itself clearly attacked and its repose disturbed should accordingly resist."[54] Armijo again assembled his army (by this time around four thousand strong) in Santa Fe. By August 14, the governor ordered his troops to proceed to Apache Canyon.

According to the Santa Fe citizens' letter to Mexico's president, despite all of Armijo's earlier rhetoric, when Kearny's army approached Apache Canyon, Armijo declared that he "would not risk facing battle with people lacking military training, and that he would do whatever seemed fitting to him." The militiamen, Indians, and civilians were sent home, as Armijo and his regular forces resolved to do battle. However, the letter revealed that "as soon as the citizenry retired, instead of advancing he and the dragoons and artillery retreated."[55]

In a letter written a little over two weeks earlier to the Mexican minister of foreign relations, interior and police, Armijo had woven a different story. He maintained that on August 9, he learned of the American army's arrival at Bent's Fort, prompting him to activate "the auxiliary companies" and to assemble them at Santa Fe. According to the governor's figures, the total force numbered one thousand eight hundred men, as opposed to the four thousand figure referred to in the Santa Fe citizens' letter. On August 15, the army marched to Apache Canyon, where Armijo "was informed that all of the auxiliary companies were not disposed to offer resistance." Armijo then called a staff meeting and told his commanders that he thought their "advantageous position" would guarantee a "complete victory." The sense of patriotism was short-lived, however. Soldiers began a general retreat, and the governor was soon left with only two hundred fighters. By the seventeenth, only Armijo, seventy dragoons, three cannons, and one howitzer remained behind awaiting the Army of the West. The command then started its retreat toward Chihuahua, whence Armijo's letter was written.[56]

When Kearny and his army snaked through Apache Canyon on August 18, they found that Armijo had called off the defense of the

The Army of the West threading its way through Apache Canyon, where an attack by Mexican forces was anticipated, but never occurred.

canyon. According to Emory, the spot was perfect for an ambush, one that "in the hands of a skilful engineer and one hundred resolute men, would have been perfectly impregnable." Calling Armijo's defensive plans "very stupid," Emory went on to report that had Armijo defended the canyon, Kearny would have either faced a fierce resistance or been required to detour his army miles to the south.[57] When they reached Armijo's deserted position in the canyon, Kearny's soldiers were jubilant. Unaware of the secret negotiations in Santa Fe a few evenings earlier, the proud soldiers gloried in their military prowess, confident that the Mexican army had fled out of fear.

At around noon on August 18, General Kearny was approached by two New Mexicans, one of them the acting secretary of state. The men carried a letter from the lieutenant governor—now the acting governor in Armijo's absence—assuring Kearny that he would encounter no resistance and extending to him every courtesy Santa Fe could afford. Advance elements of the American army arrived in Santa Fe at around three o'clock in the afternoon, and the rear guard pulled into town three hours later. Acting governor Juan Bautista Vigil y Alarid and a score of local dignitaries met Kearny and his staff and served them refreshments consisting of wine and brandy.

While the Americans enjoyed the hospitality of the Mexican officials at the ancient Palace of the Governors on the plaza, they watched at sunset as the Mexican flag was lowered and the Stars and

General Kearny and his staff observing the American flag as it is hoisted above the Palace of the Governors in Santa Fe.

Stripes was run up the flagstaff. From the high ground behind the palace, thirteen cannons saluted the occasion. Afterward, Kearny's staff was invited to dinner, which, according to Emory,

> was served very much after the manner of a French dinner, one dish succeeding another in endless variety. A bottle of good wine from the Passo de Norte, and a loaf of bread was placed at each plate. We had been since five in the morning without eating, and inexhaustible as were the dishes was our appetite.[58]

Other than facing the usual hardships that most times accompanied the mid-nineteenth-century movement of large numbers of men, animals, and materiel in summer—hunger, extreme heat, biting insects, thirst, and the like—Kearny's mission to occupy New Mexico had proceeded remarkably well. Official reports of his army's progress were continuously relayed back to Fort Leavenworth, then forwarded to newspapers in the East for readers' eager consumption. Many of the dispatches abounded with accounts of Kearny's march across the southern Great Plains and his and his army's reception in Santa Fe. They had arrived on the frontiers of New Mexico "in fine health and spirits," reported the August 29, 1846, issue of *Niles' National Register*. The account's writer added that "far from a resistance, the

Mexicans were anxious for the arrival of the Americans" and that the "ladies of Santa Fe were making extensive preparations for a fandango dance and other sports to welcome their reception."[59]

By fall 1846, the nation's newspapers overflowed with ebullient editorials touting the Army of the West and its painless, bloodless occupation of New Mexico. The *Richmond Enquirer*, copying the *Baltimore Sun*, reported in its November 6, 1846, issue that the general was "hale and hearty at Santa Fe" and had found the local populace "in excellent spirits and delighted with the prospects of becoming citizens of the United States." The writer continued, "It is as if their property, their lives, and their prosperity had been insured to them, and they are now permitted to draw the first free breath of life." Praising the vanquished New Mexicans for their ready acceptance of the American army, the newspaper related, "Our troops throughout received nothing but the kindest treatment from the inhabitants, and were well pleased with their vocation. Their wants were liberally supplied by the hospitable people of that province, and they were treated not as enemies, but as deliverers of the country."[60]

The good news was brief, however. By the end of 1846, the honeymoon was over and both Kearny's occupying army and folks back East were rapidly learning that affairs among New Mexico's residents were not as they first appeared. Certain elements of the region's population were seething with dissatisfaction over the abrupt arrival and takeover of their homeland by the uninvited Americans and began laying the groundwork for rebellion.

*Four*

# "Every Thing Here Is Quiet and Peaceable"

### OCCUPATION

THE SANTA FE OCCUPIED BY THE ARMY OF THE WEST THAT HOT August day in 1846 was a small village that had been founded during the opening years of the seventeenth century in the northernmost reaches of New Spain.¹ By the time of General Kearny's arrival, the town numbered fewer than five thousand souls—mostly New Mexicans, but a few Americans also—living their lives as merchants, clergymen, and farmers. Lieutenant Emory recorded in his notes that "the inhabitants are, it is said, the poorest people of any town in the province." He added that most of the buildings were one story, constructed of mud bricks, with a Spanish flair. Although they were "forbidding in appearance from the outside," Emory reported that the homes were very comfortable, the thick walls allowing them to stay warm in the winter and cool in the summer. The homes of the "better" class were furnished with beds, while the "lower" class slept on animal skins pitched on the floor. Emory found that the women were more sophisticated than the men, the higher class of females dressing in similar fashion to American women. Higher class men wore attire much like their American counterparts, while the lower class, "when they dress at all, wear leather breeches, tight around the hips and open from the knee down; shirt and blanket take the place of coat and vest."[2]

When Lieutenant J. W. Abert arrived in Santa Fe in September, he recorded a vivid description of the plaza, where most of the town's business and trade were pursued. The ancient Palace of the Governors occupied the north side of the plaza, while commercial establishments and stores lined the remaining three sides. The plaza was a gathering place for farmers to sell their produce and other wares. "Trains of 'burros' are continually entering the city, laden with kegs of Taos whiskey or immense packs of fodder, melons, wood, or grapes," Abert wrote, while, "Our own soldiers, too, are constantly passing and repassing, or mingling with the motley groups of Mexicans and Pueblo Indians."[3]

Another American, John T. Hughes, a volunteer with Doniphan's Missouri regiment, reported that small as Santa Fe was, the town contained six Catholic churches. But there were "no public schools, the business of education being intrusted to ecclesiastics." Hughes wrote that "the streets are crooked and narrow," and added, "The whole presents very much the appearance of an extensive brick-yard."[4]

Frederick Adolphus Wislizenus, a German physician who had left Missouri during mid-May 1846, on a scientific journey to Mexico and California, arrived in Santa Fe on June 30. "My expectations of seeing a fine city had already been cooled down by previous accounts of travellers," he wrote, but when he observed the "irregular cluster of low, flat roofed, mud built, dirty houses, called Santa Fe, and resembling in the distance more a prairie-dog village than a capital, I had to lower them yet for some degrees." If the German doctor was unmoved by the character and looks of the town, he was at least impressed by the climate, which he found "rather pleasant." He wrote that summers were comfortably warm, but that winters were "moderately cold" and that snow was abundant.[5]

On August 17, the day prior to the American army's arrival, Acting governor Vigil y Alarid issued a proclamation to Santa Fe's residents decrying the desertion of Governor Armijo and attempting to calm their fears over the US occupation. He was concerned that many citizens were fleeing their homes in the belief that the invaders were "composed of cruel and sanguinary savages [and] that they will have no security, no protection of their lives and interests on the part of the chief who commands that army." Vigil y Alarid reminded his readers that he had posted in many public places an earlier proclamation signed by General Kearny (the document that Kearny had dispatched on July 31 from Bent's Fort ahead of his own departure), and he attached a copy of the document to his own proclamation so that all could refresh their memories.[6]

Two days later, in order to reassure Santa Fe's residents of his army's peaceful intentions, Kearny assembled them in the plaza across from the Palace of the Governors and addressed them in much the same fashion as he had the people of San Miguel and Vegas.[7] When Kearny completed his talk, Vigil y Alarid took the platform and responded to the general's entreaties. The official acknowledged that "no one in this world can successfully resist the power of him who is stronger" and offered his people's "loyalty and allegiance to the government of North America." Continuing, he admitted that while the old Mexican regime—which he compared to the mother of New Mexico—was over, it was nevertheless a sad day for the region's inhabitants. "We know that we belong to the Republic that owes its origin to the immortal Washington, whom all civilized nations admire and respect," he declared, and added, "In the name, then, of the entire Department, I swear obedience to the Northern Republic and I tender my respect to its laws and authority."[8]

The next day, August 20, several leaders of the nearby pueblos met with Kearny to "express their great satisfaction at our arrival." The chiefs gave him their promises of allegiance to the United States, and a gleeful Emory wrote, "They and the numerous half-breeds are our fast friends now and forever."[9] More delegations of local natives visited with Kearny and his staff during the remainder of the week, leaving the Americans with a feeling of security and a job well done.

On August 22, Kearny issued a second, more tersely worded proclamation to Santa Feans in which he left no doubt of his intentions and expectations. The American plan now was to occupy all of New Mexico—that is, both sides of the Rio Grande—a point quite contrary to the earlier negotiations in Santa Fe that James Magoffin had pursued with Governor Armijo and Colonel Archuleta in which Magoffin insisted that the United States was interested only in occupying the east bank of the Rio Grande.

Within the next few months, one of the promises Kearny made that day in Santa Fe would live to haunt not only him personally but the Polk administration as well. Although Kearny had been given no direct authority to bestow American citizenship on the inhabitants of occupied New Mexico, he apparently assumed he could, based on the ambiguous wording of his original orders. He declared, "It is the wish, and intention of the United States to provide for New Mexico a free government, with the least possible delay, similar to those in the United States; and the people of New Mexico will then be called on to exercise the rights of freemen in electing their own representatives to the Territorial legislature." He added, "The United States hereby absolves all persons residing within the boundaries of New Mexico from any further allegiance to the republic of Mexico, and hereby claims them as citizens of the United States. . . . Those who remain quiet and peaceable will be considered good citizens and receive protection—those who are found in arms, or instigating others against the United States, will be considered as traitors, and treated accordingly."[10]

Obviously pleased with his accomplishments so far, Kearny sent a dispatch to General Jonathan E. Wool, the American commander at Chihuahua, in which he proudly reported, "I have to inform you, that on the 18th instant, without firing a gun or spilling a drop of blood, I took possession of this city, the capital of the department of New Mexico." He expressed the prevalent mood of most Americans in Santa Fe when he wrote further, "Every thing here is quiet and peaceable. The people now understand the advantages they are to derive from a change of government, and are much gratified with it."[11]

In order to strengthen the American defense of Santa Fe, General Kearny directed that a fort be built. Placed in charge of the site selection were Lieutenant Emory of the topographical engineers and Lieutenant Jeremy F. Gilmer of the corps of engineers. An elevated site some six hundred yards northeast of the plaza, the same position

# "Every Thing Here Is Quiet and Peaceable"

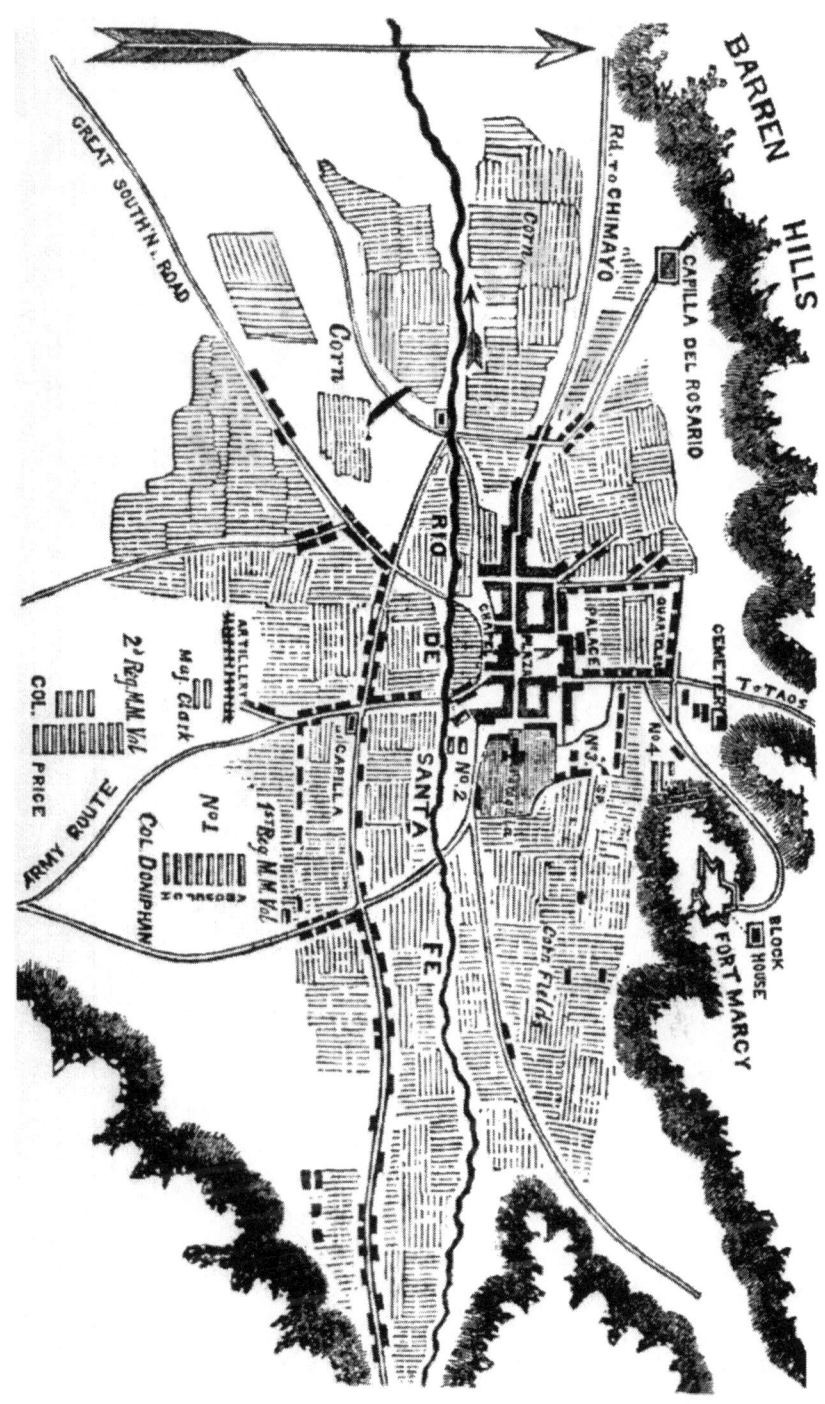

Town plan of Santa Fe from *Doniphan's Expedition* (1850).

Locals confer in front of a Santa Fe church. Note Fort Marcy in the background.

from which the cannons were fired when the American flag was raised over the Palace of the Governors on August 18, was selected, and work began on August 23. Emory thought that the site was "unfavorable for the trace of a regular work, but being the only point which commands the entire town, and which is itself commanded by no other, we did not hesitate to recommend it."[12] The construction was supervised by Gilmer and L. A. Maclean, a civilian volunteer in Colonel Doniphan's Missouri regiment. Small details of army enlisted men performed most of the work until August 27, when one hundred more soldiers were added to the crew. Four days later, twenty Mexican stonemasons were recruited. Designed to handle a garrison of 280 men, the structure was named Fort Marcy, in honor of the US secretary of war, William L. Marcy.[13]

On September 2, based on a rumor that Armijo was gathering an army to march north and attack the Americans, Kearny, several of his staff, and a number of dragoons left Santa Fe to meet him and to tour the surrounding countryside. They proceeded down the Santa Fe River, crossed over the desert to Galisteo Creek, and from there marched to the stream's confluence with the Rio Grande, near the town of Santo Domingo. Then the detail traveled the short distance to Santo Domingo Pueblo, where the men were greeted by a party of rowdy, colorfully decorated natives. From Santo Domingo, Kearny and his command descended the Rio Grande to the villages of San Felipe and Angosturas.

By September 4, in the vicinity of Bernallilo, Kearny received intelligence that Armijo's rumored buildup was most likely a ruse. Over the next few days, the soldiers marched uneventfully as far south as the village of Tome, located between the present-day cities of Belen and Albuquerque, before returning to Santa Fe on September 11. Four days later, a small detail departed for Taos, some sixty miles north of Santa Fe and the site of a large pueblo, to reconnoiter the land and determine the condition of the road connecting the two towns.[14]

Just before he departed for the conquest of California, General Kearny performed two important acts. On September 22, he made the following appointments to civil offices:

Charles Bent—governor
Donaciano Vigil—secretary
Richard Dallam, an American mining operator—marshal
Francis P. Blair, Jr., son of Francis Blair, former president Andrew Jackson's journalistic mouthpiece in Washington—US district attorney
Charles Blumner—treasurer
Eugene Seitzendorfer, a Santa Fe merchant, auditor of public accounts
Joab Houghton, a prominent American attorney, judge of the Superior Court for the First District (Santa Fe, San Miguel, and Santa Ana Counties), with court held at Santa Fe
Antonio José Otero, a native New Mexican from a distinguished Spanish family—judge of the Superior Court for the Second District (Bernalillo and Valencia Counties), with court held at Albuquerque
Charles Beaubien, a long-time French-American resident of Taos—judge of the Superior Court for the Third District (Taos and Rio Arriba Counties) with court held at Taos[15]

On the same day, Kearny sent to authorities in Washington the list of appointees as well as a copy of *Laws of the Territory of New Mexico*, which, according to the general, was "prepared for the government of the Territory of New Mexico." The document was to be officially published in Santa Fe on October 7. The laws were written by Colonel Doniphan and Private Willard P. Hall, both members of the 1st Missouri Volunteers and both renowned criminal lawyers in their native state. Translation of the code into Spanish was performed by Captain David Waldo, also of the 1st Missouri Volunteers and a prominent Santa Fe trader before the war.[16]

By late September, Kearny had completed most of his administrative chores in Santa Fe and was planning his departure. On the twenty-fifth of the month, with three hundred of his own 1st US Dragoons, he left the city for the second phase of his mission, the conquest of California. He was soon to be followed by the Mormon Battalion, now under the command of Captain Philip St. George Cooke, who had inherited the unit from Lieutenant Andrew Jackson Smith after it arrived in Santa Fe. The 1st Missouri Volunteers, commanded by Colonel Doniphan, would remain in Santa Fe until relieved by the 2nd Missouri Volunteers, led by Colonel Sterling Price and expected any day. After Price's arrival, Doniphan was to march to Chihuahua, where his regiment would become a part of General Jonathan Wool's army. Half the artillery was to accompany Doniphan when he departed for Chihuahua, and half was to remain in Santa Fe.[17]


Following the departures of Kearny (September 25) and Doniphan (October 26) and their units, Colonel Price inherited the command of all American troops and volunteer militia in New Mexico.[18] As war clouds approached in early 1846, Virginia-born Price was serving in the Congress from Missouri, but he soon resigned and petitioned President Polk to be allowed to organize the 2nd Regiment of Missouri Volunteers. The unit consisted of a full complement plus an extra battalion of mounted volunteers. The Missouri counties represented were Boone, Benton, Carroll, Chariton, Linn, Livingston, Monroe, Randolph, Sainte Genevieve, and Saint Louis, commanded by Captains S. H. McMillan (or McMillin), John Hollaway (or Holloway), R. E. Williams, William C. Holley (or Halley), Thomas Barbee, William Y. Slack, N. B. Giddings, H. Jackson, Thomas Horine, and John C. Dent, respectively. By summer, all of the troops had mustered into service, assembled at Fort Leavenworth, and begun their training. In addition to Price being elected colonel, D. D. Mitchell was selected lieutenant colonel and second-in-command, while Captain Benjamin B. Edmonson was appointed major.[19] Members of the extra battalion of cavalry, commanded by Major David Willock, hailed from Marion, Polk, Platte, and Ray Counties and were commanded by Captains Smith, Benjamin Robinson, Jesse Morin, and Israel R. Hendley. The entire regiment numbered about one thousand two hundred men, plus several artillery pieces and their crews. Elements of Price's volunteers departed Fort Leavenworth around mid-August, bound for Santa Fe, most of them arriving there between September 28 and October 12.[20]

Charles Bent, the first territorial governor of New Mexico.

The long march across the southern Great Plains on the Santa Fe Trail was a challenge to the men of the 2nd Missouri Volunteers. One of them, Sergeant William B. Drescher of the Marion County company, lost forty pounds during the journey. His reminiscences reveal that the regiment left Fort Leavenworth

> in uniform—with silk caps—(Hats was what we needed)—we suffered severely from heat and exposure under an 'August and September sun'—many failed on the way, some died—at Pawnee Fork I succumbed to heat and billious fever—brought me to death's door—but young and strong before—I rallied and arrived safely at Santa Fe.[21]

*Five*

# Questions in the Nation's Capital

### PUTTING PRESIDENT POLK ON GUARD

On December 15, 1846, General Kearny and the ragtag remnants of his Army of the West were resting and recuperating in the small Mexican town of San Diego, Upper California. They had arrived three days earlier—many of the officers and men, including Kearny, wounded, and everyone tired, hungry, and exhausted. A week had passed since the Americans and Mexicans had clashed at San Pasqual, a village on the road between Kearny's crossing of the Colorado River on November 25, and San Diego.[1] The two-day battle had left Kearny's command in shambles, prompting Lieutenant Emory, the chief topographical engineer, to write on December 7, "Day dawned on the most tattered and ill-fed detachment of men that ever the United States mustered under her colors."[2]

On the same day Kearny and his small army recovered from the fatigue and hardships of the last few weeks, a group of disenchanted New Mexicans and Indians met in Santa Fe to plan an overthrow of the recently arrived American army. Although the plot was aborted, it provided the inspiration for the highly successful revolt at Taos the following month.

A couple of thousand miles away in Washington, members of the US House of Representatives were also busy. On December 15, one week following President Polk's second annual message to Congress, the House passed a resolution that caught the president off guard. In his speech, Polk had told Congress that since

> it is the right and duty of the conqueror to secure his conquest and to provide for the maintenance of civil order and the rights of the inhabitants ... [t]his right has been exercised and this duty performed by our military and naval commanders by the establishment of temporary governments in some of the conquered Provinces of Mexico, assimilating them as far as practicable to the free institutions of our own country. In the Provinces of New Mexico and the Californias little, if any, further resistance is apprehended from the inhabitants to the temporary governments which have thus, from the necessity of the case and according to the laws of war, been established.[3]

Polk's address brought on days of spirited debate among several House members, primarily Garrett Davis, a Kentucky Whig who was anti-Polk and author of the resolution, and Hugh A. Haralson of Georgia, Stephen A. Douglas of Illinois, Robert Rhett of South Carolina, and Timothy Pillsbury of Texas, all Democrats eager to defend the president.[4] Davis's resolution called for Polk to furnish the House with copies of any and all material that had been transmitted to his military commanders in the Mexican theater that referenced "the establishment or organization of civil government in any portion of the territory of Mexico which has or might be taken possession of by the army or navy of the United States."[5]

Polk assembled his cabinet on December 19 and apprised them of the House resolution. Secretary of State James Buchanan recommended that no response be made to the request for materials. Polk disagreed and said he had resolved to cooperate and to submit to the House's appeal. As all of the pertinent documents were being read by the cabinet members, Polk singled out the recently received *Laws of the Territory of New Mexico*. One section of the document read, "The country heretofore known as New Mexico shall be known and hereafter designated as the territory of New Mexico in the United

States of America, and the temporary government of the said territory shall be organized and administered in the manner hereinafter prescribed."[6] Polk admitted that the document clearly called for "a form of Government over the conquered territory . . . which among other things declared that territory to be a part of the U.S. and provided for the election of a Delegate to the Congress of the U.S." He then opined that General Kearny "[i]n these and some other aspects . . . exceeded the power of a military commander over a conquered territory." All cabinet members agreed that when the response was written to the House, the president "must disapprove this part of the Document, though without censuring the Gen'l, who had, no doubt, acted from patriotic motives."[7] The cabinet reconvened on December 22 to consider Polk's official response, and his document was delivered to the House of Representatives later the same day.[8]

Polk told House members that although the *Laws* was intended to provide a "temporary" or provisional government, "there are portions of it which purport to 'establish and organize' a permanent territorial government of the United States over the territory, and to impart to its inhabitants political rights which, under the constitution of the United States, can be enjoyed permanently only by citizens of the United States." The president further stated that he had neither approved nor recognized these elements of Kearny's *Laws* but would sanction any "organized regulation" promulgated in "any of the conquered territories" that secured the occupation, preserved order, protected the rights of citizens, and "depriv[ed] the enemy of the advantages of these territories" as long as the military occupation continued.[9]

Turning to a defense of Kearny, Polk explained that "any excess of power" that had been demonstrated by the general or any other military officer in their duties as representatives of the American government had grown out of a "patriotic desire to give to the inhabitants the privileges, and immunities so cherished by the people of our own country." Furthermore, he added, "any such excess has resulted in no practical injury" and that it would be corrected at an early date "in a manner to alienate as little as possible the good feelings of the inhabitants of the conquered territory."[10]

On January 11, 1847, three weeks after Congress had called Polk to task, Secretary of War Marcy, following instructions from the president, dispatched a message to Kearny mildly rebuking him for overstepping his authority. Marcy explained that Kearny did not have the authority to confer citizenship on the inhabitants of New Mexico and stated this privilege could only be granted by Congress.[11] By then the general had already departed for California, but Kearny's *Laws* continued to be the only version of enforceable regulation in New Mexico.

In an interesting aside to this issue, at the very time the House called on the president for specific information that questioned the legality of declaring New Mexico a US territory, the most important document of all, *Laws of the Territory of New Mexico*, was sitting in the secretary of war's office unread. On November 23, Adjutant General Roger Jones had received the parcel containing *Laws*, as well as Kearny's list of civil appointments, both sent from Santa Fe on September 23. He promptly forwarded the package to Secretary of War Marcy for his review and disposition.[12] Marcy wrote Polk on December 21, six days after the House issued its request to the president, enclosing all of the War Department documents that were pertinent to the House resolution, including *Laws*. Marcy told Polk that since the document was "voluminous" and his time had been totally absorbed by other business, including the preparation of his report for the president's annual message, he had not "until a few days since, examine[d] it; and it was not laid before you to receive your directions in regard to it."[13] Obviously, House members had not reviewed any official documents about the matter at hand, but they most likely had read reports in local and national newspapers about the general's various proclamations declaring territorial status for New Mexico, which, added to Polk's comments in his annual message, provided more fodder for the issue.

As future events proved, Polk was premature in issuing remarks that Kearny's actions had "resulted in no practical injury." True, at

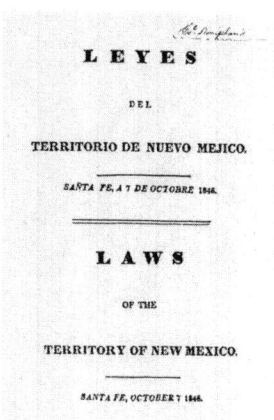

Title page of General Kearny's *Laws of the Territory of New Mexico*, also known as "Kearny's Code."

the time the president made his statement to Congress in late December 1846, his assessment of affairs in New Mexico was accurate. By spring of the following year, however, a number of the insurrectionists would be illegally tried in Taos, charged with treason against the United States based on the assumption that territorial status for New Mexico was a done deal as expressed in Kearny's *Laws*. Before clarification was forthcoming, however, one of the accused would be hanged as a traitor.

*Six*

# "We Were Without Food and Had No Covering"

## THE REVOLT

IF STEPHEN WATTS KEARNY WAS GUILTY OF MAKING ONLY ONE mistake during his brief stay in occupied Santa Fe, it was believing that the people he had just vanquished had accepted his victory in stride. Kearny naively reaffirmed his opinion of the pacifist mood of most New Mexicans on September 16, 1846, when he wrote in a dispatch to the adjutant general that the natives were "highly satisfied and contented with the change of government," adding, "There can no longer be apprehended any organized resistance in the Territory to our troops." The only concern his successor would have, declared Kearny, would be "to secure the inhabitants from further depredations from the Navajoe and Eutaw Indians."[1] As affairs turned out, however, his error in judgment proved to be costly.

Confident that matters in New Mexico were under control, Kearny and his command left Santa Fe on September 25, with hopes that the subjugation of California would be as painless as the occupation of New Mexico had proven to be. But the general could not have been more wrong in his assessment of the situation in Santa Fe and the rest of the vast region that the army now administered.

Beneath the thin veneer of joy and contentment expressed by many of the natives toward their conquerors, a powder keg of hatred and fiery rebellion was about to explode.

In defense of Kearny, however, and with the benefit of hindsight, it is apparent that he was no more ignorant of political affairs among New Mexico's inhabitants—either Indian or New Mexican—than were his superiors in Washington. Had President Polk, his cabinet, or any of the State and War Department officials involved in the execution of the war appreciated the Hispanic heritage in North America, they might have realized that rebellion among the natives had already occurred multiple times over the past three centuries. Spending a little time researching the region's complex history could have resulted in the prediction that civil unrest would most likely take place again.

Soon after Spanish conquistadors and their Catholic churchmen companions led by Hernando Cortez arrived on the shores of Mexico in 1519, they established three priorities. The first was to scour the land and native villages for gold, silver, gems, and other valuable resources that would fatten the coffers of the Spanish royalty. The second was to subjugate the native population into what, over the years, resembled a Middle Ages serfdom wherein the Spanish gentry acquired and owned the land, but the dispossessed natives performed all of the work. A system was soon established with tax structures that called for much of the Indians' hard-earned agricultural produce to be turned over to the crown. The third goal was to convert as many natives to Christianity as possible and to systematically destroy all vestiges of their ancient religions, mores, and traditions. To the Spanish invaders, it was all about glory, God, and gold—which in 1966 became the title of best-selling writer Paul Wellman's historical narrative about the period.[2]

As might be expected, New Mexico's native Americans soon became disenchanted with their Spanish overlords. In 1598, soldiers of the crown became early foreign victims of the Pueblo people's wrath when residents of the mesa-top town of Acoma, situated between present-day Albuquerque and Grants, rebelled and killed several Spanish officers and soldiers sent by Don Juan de Onate to declare Spanish sovereignty over the region. During the following year, the Spanish returned to Acoma, killed scores of the town's residents, and captured about five hundred men, women, and children. Many prisoners were punished, first by having one foot amputated, then by being placed in servitude for upward of twenty years.³

The next serious insurrection in the region was perpetrated by other normally peaceful Pueblo people who lived up and down the Rio Grande in scores of villages and spoke several different but related languages. The Pueblos were descendants of the Ancestral Puebloans, formerly called the Anasazi or Cliff Dwellers, and the collapsed Chacoan culture. They were predominantly agriculturalists who patiently coaxed corn, squash, beans, and other produce from the arid soil of their modest gardens. They lived in multistoried apartment houses, many of which are still occupied in New Mexico today. In 1630, their population was estimated by Spanish missionaries to be as high as eighty thousand.⁴

As Spanish conquistadors introduced the horse to the Southwest, several of the nomadic tribes in the region—Apache, Navajo, Comanche, Ute, and Kiowa—suddenly found extensive travel to be possible. Against such peaceful folk as the Pueblos, these tribes adopted a raider mentality, sometimes making life miserable for the passive apartment dwellers.

In 1680, residents of several of the Pueblo towns along the Rio Grande rebelled. During mid-August, a Tewa Indian named Popé who hailed from San Juan Pueblo but who had established his headquarters at Taos Pueblo, led a fifteen-hundred-man army of tribesmen from Galisteo, Pecos, Picuris, San Juan, Santa Clara, Santa Cruz, Taos, and Tesuque Pueblos against the small Spanish garrison at Santa Fe. During the nine-day siege of the town, more than four hundred residents and defenders were killed. Vastly outnumbered and cut off from their water supply, the Spanish retreated south to the present-day El Paso region.⁵

For the next twelve years, the northern New Mexico tribes lived in relative peace, at last freed from the Spanish yoke. During 1692, however, a new governor, Don Diego de Vargas, visited the pueblos, met with no resistance, and gradually supervised the reoccupation of northern New Mexico by soldiers and priests of the crown.⁶

But rebellion against authority, regardless of whether that authority was legitimate or not, was by no means limited to the Indians of the region. The descendants of the early Spanish conquerors had a flair for fomenting revolt as well. In fact, between 1821 and 1837, the government of Mexico was overturned twenty-one times, with many of its officials violently deposed.[7] During these perilous times, as historian Janet Lecompte explains, the home country was ill-equipped to be of much assistance to its distant territories.

> Governmental offices were pervaded with dissention, conspiracy, and corruption, and the public treasury was empty because of constant guerrilla warfare and huge foreign debts. With Mexico chronically on the verge of moral and financial collapse, how could she be expected to support New Mexico's commerce, church, courts, and schools, or to send soldiers and guns?[8]

In 1837, some sixteen years after Mexico had attained its independence from Spain, an armed clash erupted in northern New Mexico that ended with the murder of the incumbent governor and sixteen of his officials. Two years earlier, this governor, Albino Pérez, a polished, military-trained patrician with a background totally opposite from the poor Hispano and Indian farmers wresting a living from the unforgiving land, had come to the region from far-off Mexico City to assume his duties. Pérez brought with him a new constitution, a revised tax structure, and an attitude that won him few friends with his constituents.

During summer 1837, in response to the arrogance and excesses of Governor Pérez, villagers from across Rio Arriba, the northern half of New Mexico, organized themselves into cantóns, or independent divisions, similar to the small, autonomous provinces in Switzerland at the time. They launched a vigorous revolt, sometimes called the Chimayó Rebellion, because so many of the uprising's participants were natives of that village and the surrounding region. By August, the rebels had confronted the governor and his armed followers on several occasions, culminating with the killing spree that resulted in Pérez's death. The protesters beheaded the governor, desecrated his remains, and for a time refused to allow the body to be buried. A buffalo hunter named José Gonzales from the Taos area succeeded Pérez in the Palace of the Governors at Santa Fe, but his skills as a hunter overshadowed his abilities as an administrator, and his term as governor was short-lived. Soon former governor Manuel Armijo marched on Santa Fe, defeated the rebels, ordered them to return to their homes, and installed himself as governor.[9]

Interestingly, several players in the 1837 rebellion also would have roles in either the events surrounding the 1846 American occupation of Santa Fe or the subsequent Taos Revolt of 1847. The leader of the Taos rebels in 1837 was Pablo Montoya, who was once labeled "a brigand" and a "mischievous fool" by Pérez supporter Donaciano Vigil, Charles Bent's successor as governor after the Taos Revolt of 1847.[10] Antonio José Martínez, the curate of Taos, early on during the 1837 rebellion apparently sympathized with the rebels, although he later gave his support to Armijo, who eventually became governor. And the ever-present Armijo was involved in both the 1837 affair and the short-lived Mexican resistance to Kearny's advance on Santa Fe in August 1846.

Padre Antonio José Martínez served as priest for both the town of Taos and the Taos Pueblo for many years before, during, and after the American occupation of New Mexico.

By the time the American army arrived on the scene, New Mexicans had not only witnessed a variety of revolts and rebellions in their recent and distant pasts but were facing serious issues in the present. Arguably one of the most serious was the law that forbade the importation of weapons and ammunition into the department. As evidenced by the 1837 rebellion, Mexico City had neglected its northern-most department and had done little to endear the central government to the region's inhabitants. The rapid turnover of the last few governors, most of whom were outsiders with little or no interest in New Mexico, had left citizens unprotected from marauding Indian tribes that frequently raided the towns and villages along the upper Rio Grande.

On June 18, 1846, while Colonel Kearny was assembling the Army of the West at Fort Leavenworth, Donaciano Vigil, the former secretary to Governor Armijo and, at the time, an alternate member of New Mexico's assembly, wrote to his fellow delegates urging that the body petition the Mexican congress to legitimize the importation of arms and ammunition into New Mexico. Although, no doubt, early news of an imminent American invasion had already reached Santa Fe, Vigil's concern, as expressed in his epistle, was not the US Army but the continuing and increasingly hostile incursions from neighboring Indians. He told the assembly quite bluntly that the bows and arrows that local defenders had to use were no match for the powerful firearms that Indians had obtained through trade with the Americans. While wealthy New Mexicans might own personal firearms, the average citizen did not, wrote Vigil, adding, "Nor is it the rich who usually go in pursuit of the barbarians when they have carried out a raid."[11]

The addition of Colonel Sterling Price's 2nd Missouri Volunteers in September 1846 to the number of American troops left behind in Santa Fe when General Kearny and Colonel Doniphan departed for California and Mexico, respectively, pushed the accommodations in the small town to the breaking point. In retrospect, it would be unrealistic to believe that tensions did not reach dangerous levels between the local populace and the hundreds of occupying soldiers from the United States, consisting now of not only Price's new arrivals but a number of Kearny's infantry, the Laclede Rangers, and some artillerymen and their cannons—altogether close to two thousand men. George F. Ruxton visited Santa Fe during the early days of American occupation and found that

> Crowds of drunken [American army] volunteers filled the streets, brawling and boasting, but never fighting; Mexicans, wrapped in sarapes, scowled upon them as they passed . . . and Pueblo Indians and priests jostled the rude crowds of brawlers at every step. Under the portales [porches or arcaded buildings] were numerous montetables, surrounded by Mexicans and Americans. Every other house was a grocery, as they call a gin or whisky shop, continually disgorging reeling drunken men, and everywhere filth and dirt reigned triumphant.[12]

To ease the tension in town and to ensure the security of the surrounding region, as well as to preserve the "good order, quiet, and entire submission on the part of the malcontent New Mexicans and Pueblo Indians,"[13] Price dispatched Captain John Henry K. Burgwin[14] and the remaining two hundred 1st Dragoons to Albuquerque, some sixty miles to the south. Major Benjamin Edmonson and two hundred men of the 2nd Missouri Volunteers were sent ninety-five miles southwest to the region around the village of Cebolleta (present-day Seboyeta),[15] while Captain Israel Hendley and his company relocated to the Mora River valley about ninety miles northeast. Price's remaining officers and men were then ordered to undergo rigorous, twice-daily drills.[16]

Diego Archuleta initially resisted the American occupation, but later became a model United States citizen and served in the New Mexico territorial assembly.

During the late evening of December 15, several prominent men of the region—Tomás Ortiz, Diego Archuleta, Manuel Chávez, brothers Nicholas and Miguel Pino, and others—met at Ortiz's house to put the finishing touches on a plan that, had it been successful, could have resulted in the expulsion of the American army from Santa Fe and, ultimately, New Mexico. The scheme called for the conspirators and all of their followers to gather on the night of December 19 at a parish church, disperse from there into the streets, massacre any American they might confront, capture the army's artillery, and take Governor Bent prisoner.[17]

Fortunately for the Americans, an informer came forth and revealed the secret plot to officials. Throughout the following days, military authorities continued to gather bits and pieces of information about the failed threat to security and attempted to arrest the ringleaders. Santa Fe was in a frenzy when its residents realized that a potential revolt had been aborted. Lieutenant J. W. Abert, the topographical engineer, was out of town when the news of the uprising became public. Arriving back in Santa Fe on the morning of December 23, he wrote in his journal that all of his comrades were "in a high state of excitement from the discovery of an intended revolution," and that guards were prominently posted around town and cannons placed to commandeer the plaza. Five rebels had already been arrested and jailed, while the two ringleaders, Tomás Ortiz, half-brother of the vicar of Santa Fe Juan Felipe Ortiz, and Diego Archuleta, had escaped and were being pursued. The army's informers had discovered that the "revolutionizers had a very well-organized plot [and were] to march at dead of night and surround the houses of the Governor, Col. Price, and Maj. [Meriwether Lewis] Clark, while another party seized the guns" and "massacred" the troops.[18]

The fact that they had barely averted a catastrophe in which many American citizens might have been killed was taken rather casually by the commanders. Although extra troops were put on alert and increased precaution was taken, senior officials treated the whole affair with an almost cavalier attitude. Lieutenant Abert remarked in his diary entry of December 24 that despite the seriousness of the situation in Santa Fe, the artillery was being packed up to follow Colonel Doniphan to Mexico. He added, "I think it doubtful whether the safety of this place does not require that the artillery should remain here." On the same day, Abert heard that "San Miguel is in a state of insurrection, and the whole country seems ripe and ready for any hellish scheme to tear down the Stars and Stripes."[19]

Repeated efforts by the army to capture Archuleta failed, and on Christmas, Abert recorded that an American army officer named Walker had been sent with thirteen men to arrest the rebel at his home. Walker returned empty-handed, however, having made a quick retreat after being confronted by about one hundred angry neighbors who "seemed half inclined to attack."[20] The other primary organizer of the suppressed revolt, Tomás Ortiz, made good his escape also, fleeing first to Galisteo and then to Chihuahua. The suppression of the intended revolt and the dispersal of its would-be participants, no doubt, went a long way toward convincing American officials in Santa Fe that most, if not all, danger of a significant uprising was over.

In the meantime, a thespian society had been established by the army, and a theater, complete with sets and an orchestra, had been opened in one of the rooms in the Palace of the Governors. On Christmas night, four presentations were offered to a curious audience: a play, *Barbarossa*; a duet singing *La Polka*; a farce, *Fortune's Frolic*; and Virginia's Minstrels, featuring the popular songs of the day *You Ain't Good Looking and You Can't Come In* and *Get Along Home, You Spanish Gals*.[21]

On the following evening, a lavish party was thrown at the palace, and the young, impressionable Lieutenant Abert was there. "We had a grand feast, and all of the luxuries of an eastern table were spread before us," he declared, revealing that the menu consisted of "oysters, fresh shad, preserves, and fine champagne." With tongue in cheek, he added that "reveling in the halls of the Armijos was far above reveling in the Halls of Montezuma, for the latter was a poor uncivilized Indian, while [the former] boast[s] of being descended from the nobility of Castile."[22]

Governor Bent was concerned about affairs in the capital. While soldiers and citizens of Santa Fe were preparing to attend the dramatic event at the palace on December 26, he was writing a letter to US Secretary of State James Buchanan apprising him of recent events in the city. Bent told Buchanan about the aborted uprising and expressed hope that the two escaped leaders would soon be arrested, although he was "apprehensive that they will have made their escape from the Territory." He also expressed fears that "the occurrence of this conspiracy at this early period of the occupation of the Territory will, I think, conclusively convince our Government of the necessity of maintaining here, for several years to come, an efficient military force."[23]

Although it is highly unlikely that either Bent or the partying officers of the Army of the West grasped the degree of unrest that prevailed in the capital city and in the surrounding countryside, a real threat of rebellion still existed. If the Americans had been fooled into believing that all was well, then all the better for two other malcontents—Tomás Romero, a Taos Indian also known as Tomacito, and Pablo Montoya, a former Taos *alcalde* (mayor) and ringleader in the 1837 Rio Arriba Rebellion—who were busy secretly gathering support for a revolt of their own. Assisting Romero and Montoya were Jesus Tafoya, Pablo Chavis, and Manuel Cortez.[24] By mid-January 1847, the five revolutionaries had readied their operation for action.

On January 14, Governor Bent, still concerned about the recent state of affairs that had culminated in the quashing of the Ortiz-Archuleta plot the previous month, left Santa Fe for his home in Taos. Accompanying him were the sheriff, Stephen Lee; the circuit attorney,

James W. Leal; and a prefect, Cornelio Vigil. The ill-fated trip would prove to be all of these men's last.

Bent had frequented Taos since 1829[25] and married a well-to-do widow, Maria Ignacia Jaramillo, before settling into an adobe house north of the plaza.[26] Maria was New Mexican and related in one way or another to many of the town's most influential residents. Bent's children carried Mexican blood in their veins and were cousins to several other children in Taos. Although Bent had retained his US citizenship, as most American traders did, he quickly established himself as a man of importance and influence in Taos. He worked actively in the civic affairs of the little town and even became closely acquainted with the Mexican governor, Manuel Armijo, the man he eventually succeeded in the Palace of the Governors.

Maria Ignacia Jaramillo, Charles Bent's wife. (*Taos Historic Museums*)

Following the failed Ortiz-Archuleta uprising to overthrow the government the previous month, Bent issued a proclamation to the people of New Mexico in which he told them that they were now "governed by new statutory laws," that they had been granted "the free government promised," and that "abundant fruits . . . await you in the future." He also told his readers that "notorious" and "ambitious" men "had come forth as leaders of a revolution against the present government" but that the planned uprising had been "smothered at its birth." He pleaded with them not to foolishly throw away the benefits of their new citizenship by supporting or participating in any future overthrow effort. Finally, he revealed that reports of a Mexican army on its way north to liberate New Mexico from the Americans were untrue, and he urged his readers "to turn a deaf ear to such false doctrines and to remain quiet, attending to your domestic affairs, so that you may enjoy under the law all the blessings of peace."[27]

Regardless of Bent's popularity with the citizens of Taos, or of his perceived acceptance by them as one of their own, issues did exist that placed him in a precarious position with some of his neighbors. One item that should have concerned him was that in 1843, he raised local eyebrows when he acquired a 25 percent ownership interest in a giant real estate acquisition called the Miranda-Beaubien Land Grant, which later evolved into the Maxwell Land Grant.28 Eventually spreading across two million acres of northern New Mexico along the Cimarron, Canadian, and Vermejo rivers in present-day Colfax County, the grant had been requested by Guadalupe Miranda and Charles (Carlos) Beaubien in 1841, but was not issued by Governor Manuel Armijo until 1843, when the two requestors received a favorable hearing from Prefect Vigil, one of Bent's traveling companions to Taos. Miranda was a Mexican citizen and secretary of government at Santa Fe, and Beaubien was a native-born Canadian who had made his home in Taos since 1823, married in 1827, and become a Mexican citizen two years later.29 Complicating matters was the fact that soon after Beaubien and Miranda received their huge grant, Beaubien applied to Armijo for yet more land in the name of his young son, Narciso, and his American brother-in-law, Stephen Louis Lee, a fur trapper and Taos merchant, both of whom would also be murdered during the 1847 Taos Revolt. The two were awarded a large grant in the San Luis valley of southern Colorado, called thereafter the Sangre de Christo Grant.30

Stephen Louis Lee, the sheriff of Taos, was killed during the January 1847 uprising. (*The Mountain Men and the Fur Trade of the Far West*)

Foreign ownership of local land was much frowned upon by native New Mexicans, and although Bent thought of himself as a loyal Taoseño, some of his neighbors, especially Father Antonio José Martínez, the curate of Taos and an influential member of Taos society, believed that New Mexican land should be owned by New Mexicans and not Americans. Consequently, animosity had existed between Bent and Martínez for several years, and by the time the American occupation became fact, the two men had little regard for each other.

It is also clear from reading letters written by Bent before the American occupation that he was concerned that violence might soon erupt in Taos. He wrote to Manuel Alvarez, the American consul in Santa Fe in late February 1846, less than eleven months before he was murdered, and posed a question:

> Would it not be well to have from [Governor] Armijo . . . in wrighting, wether they will protect Americans according to the treaty ixisting. In case of warr betwean this country [Mexico] and the U States, I think it more than likely thare may be an autebreake [outbreak], sinse Parrades [President Peredes of Mexico], has come into power, he has plainly showne his views and disposition towards the U States, and thare may be verry shortely orders heare to expell uss, or doe worse, we should be prepaired and on aur gard.[31]

Many thoughts must have been running through Charles Bent's mind as he reached Taos in mid-January 1847, tired from the long, cold journey from Santa Fe. He had always loved his little hometown, which was sometimes called Don Fernando de Taos, or simply, Don Fernando.[32] Dick Wootton, a mountain man who frequented the village, recalled years later that its population was about five thousand or six thousand, but this figure, quoted by Wootton more than forty years after he was active in the region, is no doubt inflated. Other descriptions of the period picture Taos as a small village, punctuated with only a few adobe houses and one church, possibly Nuestra Señora de Guadalupe (Our Lady of Guadalupe), Father Martínez's church, located just west of the plaza. It is doubtful that more than seven hundred or eight hundred people inhabited the town in 1847. Of nearby Taos Pueblo, Wootton wrote that it was two miles from town, that its main building was six or seven stories high, that its church was built of adobe, and that perhaps as many as one thousand Indians lived there.[33]

Upon his arrival, Bent encountered a delegation of Indians from the nearby pueblo who requested that he release two of their neighbors from jail. Were the Indians testing Bent to determine if his newly assumed duties as governor would stand in the way of performing a favor for his friends? They received their answer quickly as Bent replied that he could not interfere with the processes of the law and that the matter would be handled accordingly.[34]

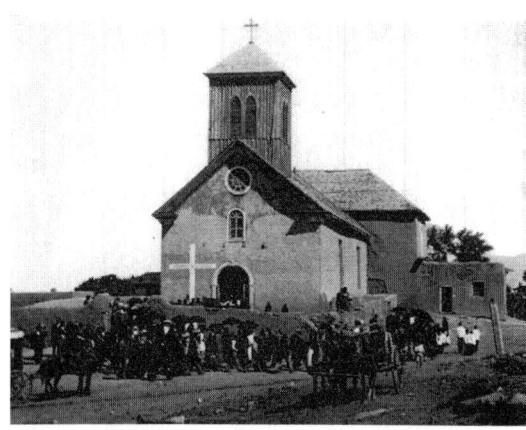

Nuestra Señora de Guadalupe (Our Lady of Guadalupe), located just west of the Taos town plaza, was headquarters for Padre Martínez's ministry. This photo dates to the late 1890s or very early 1900s, but prior to 1911 when the building was razed.

The governor had spent precious little time with his wife and children when, during the early morning hours of January 19, he was awakened and confronted in his doorway by a band of loud, angry, and armed Taoseños along with Indians from the nearby Taos Pueblo. Even in his hour of peril, Bent refused to believe that his friends and acquaintances of so many years would harm him. Making little effort to defend himself, Bent attempted to defuse the mob and to talk its participants out of doing anything foolish. Within moments he realized his mistake. While pleading with the crowd, Bent was shot in the chin and in the stomach with arrows. After gaining entry into the house, several Indians in the mob shot more arrows into Bent's body, and as he writhed in pain on the floor, he managed to free three of them from his face. Several of the angry participants slashed Bent's wrists and hands. In the meantime, Bent's wife and her sister, Josefa Jaramillo Carson, the wife of Kit Carson—along with Mrs. Bent's daughter from a former marriage, Mrs. Rumalda Luna Boggs; the Bent children; and an old Indian woman—managed to cut a hole through one of the thick adobe walls using only a fireplace poker and a spoon. In the courtyard, they found temporary respite from the violence. The governor followed them to the outside, where he was shot multiple times in the chest with firearms and scalped.[35]

The attackers soon surrounded the survivors in the courtyard, and according to later testimony from the governor's daughter, Teresina, the murderers "then left us alone with our great sorrow." The attackers issued instructions to Bent's New Mexican neighbors to offer no assistance to the terrified women and children. Teresina continued:

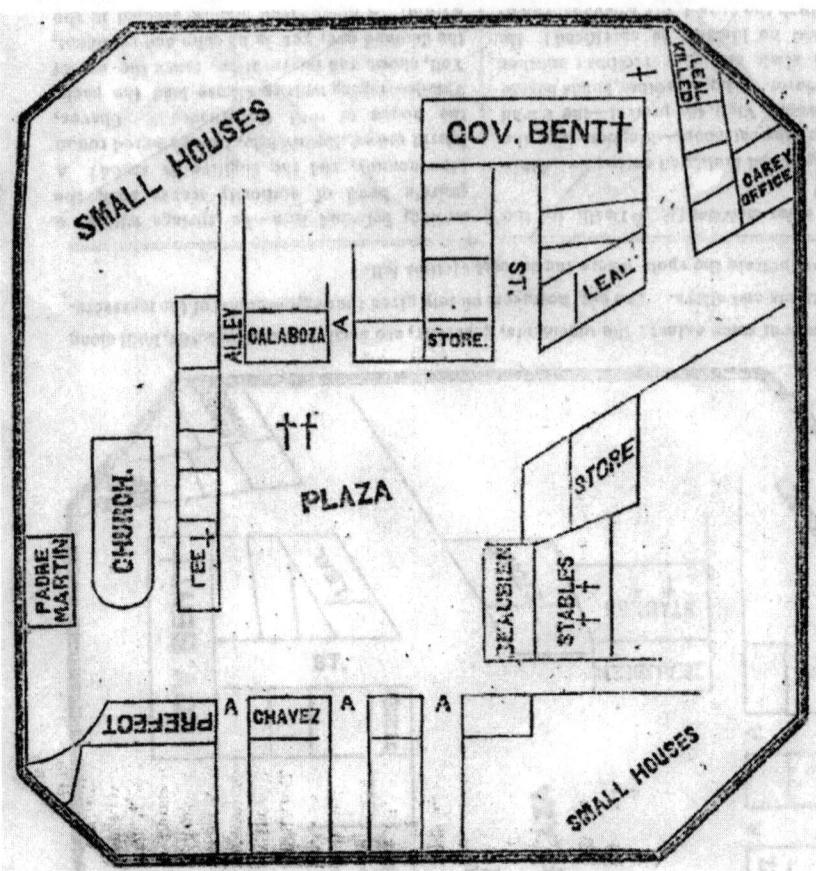

A contemporary (1847) map of Taos published within months after the revolt in the book, *Taos: A Romance of the Massacre*.

We were without food and had no covering but our night-clothing, all that day and the next night. The body of our father remained on the floor in a pool of blood. We were naturally frightened, as we did not know how soon the miscreants might return to do us violence. At about three o'clock the next morning, some of our Mexican friends stole up to the house and gave us food and clothing. That day, also, they took my father to bury him.[36]

The revolutionaries were not content with only the American governor's blood. Before the morning was over, they murdered and mutilated five more Americans and New Mexicans with American loyalties. Pablo Jaramillo, the brother of Maria Bent, and Narciso Beaubien, the circuit judge's son who had only recently returned home from attending Cape Girardeau College in Missouri, tried to hide in a nearby stable, but their refuge was revealed by a Taos woman who watched as members of the mob pierced the young boys' bodies with lances. The prefect, Cornelio Vigil; the circuit attorney, J. W. Leal; and the sheriff, Stephen Lee, were also murdered on that horrible January day.[37]

Most of the contemporary accounts of the Taos uprising vary somewhat in detail and in the victims' sequence of confrontation with their attackers. One of the more reliable witnesses appears to be Richard Smith Elliott, who accompanied the Army of the West to Santa Fe as a lieutenant in the Leclede Rangers and was also a corresponding journalist for the Saint Louis *Weekly Reveille*. Less than a month after the killings in Taos, he dispatched a report to his newspaper in which he described the incident. He related that Sheriff Stephen Lee was approached by angry Taos Indians at the "calaboose," demanding the release of three Indians being held prisoner for thievery. Since Lee had little choice except to accede to the mob's demands, he was in the process of freeing the three when Prefect Vigil appeared at the jailhouse. Vigil went into a tirade, and the insurrectionists quickly killed him, cut off his arms and legs, and dissected his corpse. Lee escaped to his home.

From the jail, according to Elliott, the culprits then visited Bent's house and, before they killed him, told him that their intent was to kill every American in Taos. Elliott's description of the governor's murder varies little from most other accounts. Meanwhile, Sheriff Lee was killed, but Elliott was not sure how. Lee's brother, General Elliott Lee, who had been visiting from Saint Louis with the sheriff, retreated to Padre Martínez's home, where the priest

> concealed him under some wheat, so that the Indians did not find him for some time; when they discovered him, they took him out to kill him, but the Priest interceded for him so strongly, that they abandoned their purpose. Gen. [ Elliott] Lee remained at the Priest's house for some time, and every few days the Indians would take him out to kill him, but would desist on the interference of the Priest.

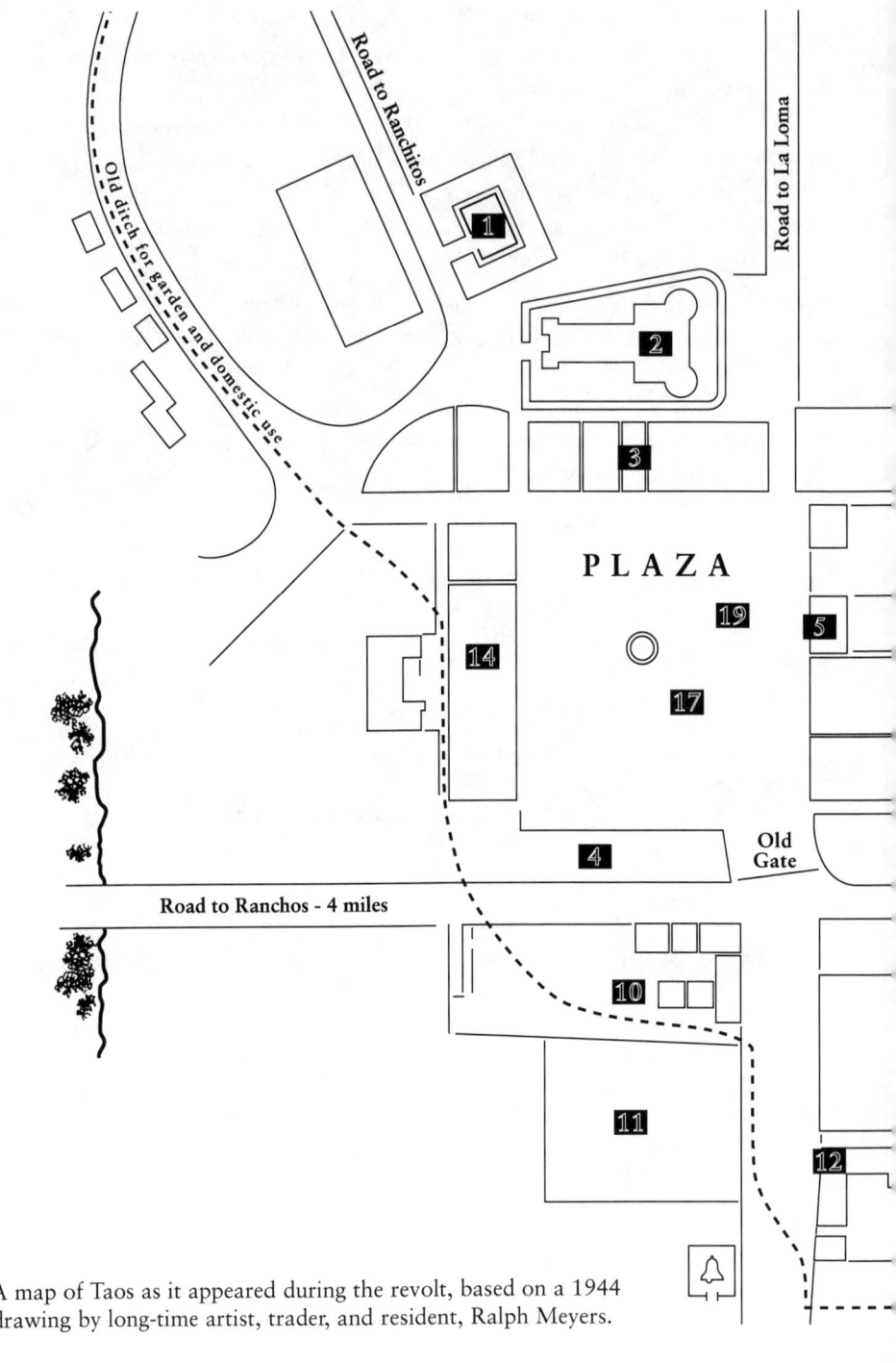

A map of Taos as it appeared during the revolt, based on a 1944 drawing by long-time artist, trader, and resident, Ralph Meyers.

## "We Were Without Food and Had No Covering"

1. Padre Martínez's residence
2. Our Lady of Guadalupe Church
3. Padre Martínez's office and printing press
4. Charles Beaubien's residence, where Narciso Beaubien and Pablo Jaramillo were killed during the revolt
5. Courthouse
6. Jail where Cornelio Vigil was killed during the revolt
7. Site of the April 9, 1847, hangings of several revolutionaries
8. Ceran St. Vrain's residence
9. Governor Charles Bent's office.
10. The Jaramillo family residence
11. Hipólito Salazar's residence
12. Kit Carson's residence and agency
13. Governor Charles Bent's residence
14. Ceran St. Vrain's merchandise store
15. Quarters for Colonel Sterling Price's troops
16. Site of the April 30, 1847 hangings of several revolutionaries
17. Site of Pablo Montoya's execution
18. Sheriff Stephen Lee's residence where he was killed.
19. Site of J. W. Leal's murder

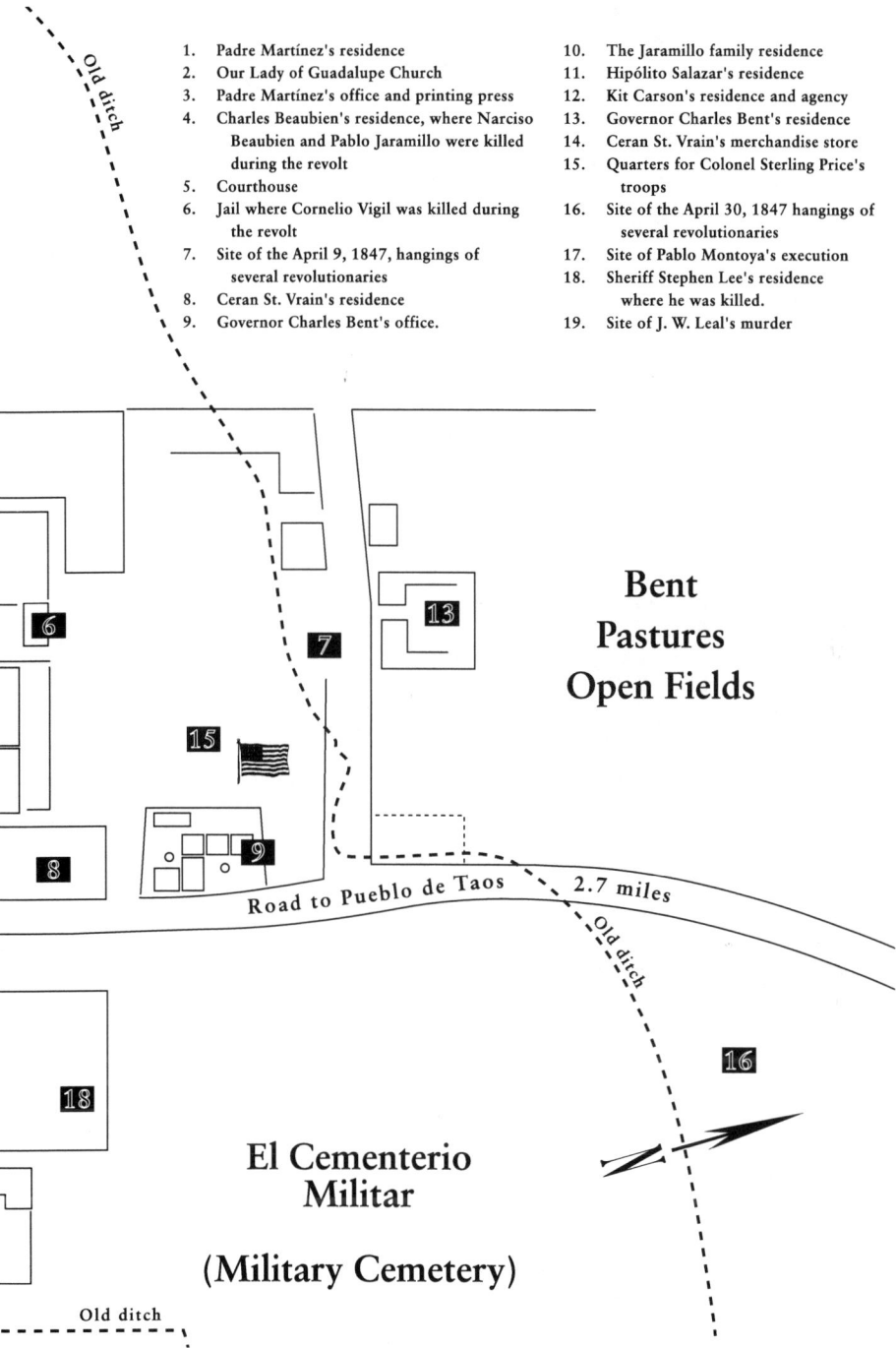

Elliott next reported that James Leal, a fellow Laclede Ranger and circuit attorney for the northern district of New Mexico at Taos, was killed. He was first captured, stripped of his clothes, and forced to march through the village, all the time being tormented and wounded with arrows. He was then returned to his home, shot multiple times with arrows, then left to die. Returning later, the mob finally killed him and threw his riddled body into the street, "where the hogs ate part of it."

Leal's murder was followed by that of Narciso Beaubien. The son of one of the three recently appointed judges for New Mexico, Narciso, "a very interesting youth of about twenty years of age," was at his father's home when the insurrectionists struck. Elliott does not mention the murder of Maria Bent's brother, Pablo Jaramillo.[38]

It is interesting that Charles Bent, Narciso Beaubien, Cornelio Vigil, and Stephen Lee—all of whom were killed in the Taos outbreak—were involved in one way or another with the disputed land grants in northern New Mexico and southern Colorado. Charles Beaubien might have been killed in the affair had he been in Taos, but he was performing his judicial duties at the time in the town of Tierra Amarilla.[39]

When they were through in Taos, the angry New Mexicans and Indians cast their eyes on other nearby American-occupied regions. At Arroyo Hondo, a few miles north of Taos, a Kentucky-born, Missouri-bred trader named Simeon Turley lived with his wife and children. Turley, in his early forties, had moved to New Mexico in 1830, and his two-story, fieldstone-and-adobe-brick compound was at the confluence of the Rio Hondo and Gallinas Creek. It was a huge complex, contained more than sixty thousand square feet,[40] and consisted of a combination distillery, mill, trading post, and home. Turley's Mill was a frequent resting place for mountain men, Indians, New Mexicans, and weary travelers. His whiskey was known far and wide, and customers came from miles around to bargain for the powerful liquor. Like his friend Charles Bent, Turley was married to a New Mexican woman, and the relationship between him and his Indian and New Mexican neighbors had always been one of mutual respect and friendship.[41]

On January 19, when Turley received news of the massacre at nearby Taos, he was hosting a reunion—in fact, a sort of indoors, old-time rendezvous—with several of his mountain men friends from the past. George Ruxton, the English traveler and writer, had visited Taos, as well as Turley's Mill, only a few weeks before the violence and left an account of the hostile action there. He wrote that Turley had been warned of the unrest in the region but had brushed the warnings aside "until one morning a man . . . made his appearance at the gate on horseback, and, hastily informing the inmates of the mill that the New Mexicans had risen and massacred Governor Bent and other Americans, galloped off."[42]

Turley and his guests set about taking security precautions. The gates to the compound were closed, windows to the house and outbuildings were barricaded, and rifles were gathered and made ready. Nine men, including Turley, were at the mill later in the day as a large party of New Mexicans and Indians rode up to the compound and demanded that Turley surrender his American friends. No harm would come to Turley himself, the revolutionaries promised, but according to Ruxton, "To this summons Turley answered that he would never surrender his house nor his men, and that, if they wanted it or them, 'they must take them.'"[43]

The impasse then began. Turley's Mill was admirably situated for defense. According to Ruxton, the main building sat at the foot of a brush-covered slope fed by the stream that had carved the Rio Hondo. In the rear of the property were a still-house, garden, and corral.[44] The odds against the defenders were overwhelming. Several hundred rebels who were poised outside the compound walls readied themselves to attack the grizzled old mountain men inside. Turley would not budge, and soon after he refused to surrender his friends it became apparent to the assailants that there would be no peaceful victory. They attacked.

The struggle continued all day, and as dusk approached, the New Mexican and Indian attackers pulled back to plan how they might finish off the mill and its defenders the next morning. All night long, the vigilant inhabitants of the compound kept busy standing watch and "running balls, cutting patches, and completing the defences [sic] of the building."[45]

Vicious fighting commenced early the next morning, by which time the enemy forces had increased in strength. It was soon discov-

John D. Albert, in a 1901 *Denver Post* photograph, left, survived the assault on Turley's Mill, escaping the building and making his way to Pueblo, Colorado, where he informed mountain man Dick Wootton, right, of the massacre.

ered that during the night, several rebels had occupied part of the courtyard. Skirmishing continued and two defenders were killed as the lengthening day saw the weary Americans run low on ammunition. Some of the outbuildings were then set on fire, and Turley decided that further defense of the compound was futile in the wake of such overwhelming odds.

The survivors inside Turley's Mill discussed the rapidly worsening situation and decided that every man should attempt to escape the compound on his own. As the fighting continued, one by one they attempted freedom, but only three succeeded; the rest were killed inside.[46] Turley, John D. Albert, and Thomas Tobin escaped the mill, but Turley was caught and murdered a few miles away when he revealed himself to a long-time New Mexican friend whom he erroneously believed he could trust. Albert marched night and day until he arrived at the site of present-day Pueblo, Colorado, and informed a group of mountain men there of the massacre. Tobin hastened to Santa Fe, where residents had already heard the grisly details of the killings at Taos and at Turley's Mill.[47]

Mountain man Dick Wootton was at Pueblo when Albert arrived with the sad news of the demise of Turley's Mill. Years later Wootton recalled that many of his dearest friends had been among those killed in Taos and at Turley's. Believing that he "should . . . do something toward securing punishment of their murderers . . . five of us . . . started across the country" to offer whatever assistance they could to American authorities in Taos.[48]

Adding to the chaos and slaughter on that bloody nineteenth day of January 1847, several rebels captured two other mountain men a few miles north of Turley's Mill. The victims, William Harwood and Mark Head, were on their way to Taos on a trading trip when they were overtaken near Rio Colorado (present-day Questa, New Mexico).[49] Ruxton noted that "a Mexican, riding behind Harwood, discharged his gun into his back." Harwood lived only long enough to call out to his partner that he was "finished." Mark Head was killed in a similar fashion, and both men were stripped of their clothes and belongings, "scalped and shockingly mutilated, and their bodies thrown into the bush by the side of the creek to be devoured by the wolves."[50]

The following day, rebels attacked the small village of Mora, about thirty miles north of Vegas. Reports of American casualties there vary. Several Missouri traders, on their way home to Independence, had just reached the area, unaware that the locals had rebelled against their American conquerors. Among those killed at Mora were Romulus E. Culver, a former US superintendent of teamsters, teams, and wagons at Bent's Fort; Benjamin Pruett, the proprietor of Santa Fe's first hotel and a long-time trader and rancher in the region; Lawrence L. Waldo, a brother of Captain David Waldo of the 1st Missouri Volunteers; Lewis Cabanne; Joseph Funk; Ola Ponett; a Mr. Noyes; and a Mr. Valentine.[51] Details of the killings are sketchy and vary depending on the source. One of the most reliable accounts suggests that angry townspeople, whipped into a frenzy by Manuel Cortez, one of the principals of the uprising in Taos, convinced the Americans that they would only be held as prisoners and not killed if they surrendered their weapons. Vastly outnumbered, the traders had no choice but to comply. Minutes later, they all lay dead in an arroyo outside town.[52]

As soon as the news of the various massacres of American citizens reached Colonel Price in Santa Fe, he went into action. Over the next two weeks, he and his staff busied themselves with planning an all-out reprisal against the strongholds of the revolting New Mexicans and Indians. As he planned to depart Santa Fe on this important mission, he must have realized the truth in the words that he would later write to the adjutant general in Washington: "It appeared to be the object of the insurrectionists to put to death every American and every Mexican who had accepted office under the American government."[53]

During the days following the bloodshed at Taos, Turley's Mill, Rio Colorado, and Mora, the bodies of many of the Americans and their allies who were killed were removed to a peaceful plot of land in Taos along the street presently called Paseo del Pueblo Norte. The property was donated by Father Martínez and was first called El Cementerio Militar (Military Cemetery).[54] When the bodies of Kit Carson and his wife, Josefa, were returned from Colorado to their longtime hometown of Taos in 1869 for reburial, its name was changed to the Kit Carson Cemetery, and today it forms part of the Kit Carson State Park.[55]

Charles Bent was not buried in this cemetery. The governor's body was first interred elsewhere in Taos but soon was moved to Fort Marcy in Santa Fe. Later, his remains were removed to the Masonic Cemetery and finally to the National Cemetery, both in Santa Fe.[56] Father Martínez, upon his death in 1867, was buried at his church, Nuestra Señora de Guadalupe near the plaza in Taos, but twenty-four years later his remains were reinterred in Kit Carson Cemetery.[57]

Sheriff Stephen Lee, Circuit Attorney James W. Leal, Prefect Cornelio Vigil, and the young men Narciso Beaubien and Pablo Jaramillo—all murdered at Taos—were buried in El Cementerio Militar. The mountain men killed at Turley's Mill—William Austin, William Hatfield, Joseph Marshall, Peter Robert, Louis Tolque, Albert Turbush, and Simeon Turley—were also interred there in a single mass grave, as were the two mountain men, William Harwood and Mark Head, killed near Rio Colorado.

Within a month, a number of other men—American soldiers and civilians killed in Colonel Price's reprisal on the revolutionaries—would be buried in the military cemetery alongside their countrymen.

Donaciano Vigil, left, the acting governor of New Mexico following the murder of Charles Bent. Colonel Sterling Price, right, 2nd Regiment, Missouri Mounted Volunteers.

Although hostilities and more killings would continue throughout the region for several more months, the fury unleashed by the revolutionaries at Taos, Rio Colorado, and Mora on January 19, 1847, and at Turley's Mill on that day and the next, constituted a major effort on their part to destroy anyone and anything related to the American presence in northern New Mexico. Price, concerned that the capital would be left unprotected from continued outbreaks of violence if he utilized the entire Santa Fe garrison for his strike force against the rebels in Taos, called up other Missouri volunteer and regular army elements from Albuquerque. Major Benjamin Edmonson, of the 2nd Missouri, and Captain John Burgwin, of the 1st Dragoons, quickly led their men north to Santa Fe, with orders for Burgwin to join Price on his march to Taos and for Edmonson to stay in Santa Fe. When Price determined that the garrison at Santa Fe was well secured, he made his final preparations to march out of the capital.[58]

Donaciano Vigil, the acting governor of New Mexico following the murder of Bent, issued a proclamation from Santa Fe on January 22, urging all citizens of the territory to cease their resistance to the Americans. He told them that American troops would leave soon "for the purpose of quelling the disorders of Pablo Montoya, in Taos." Furthermore, he stated, the army would "protect honest and discreet

The primitive road that linked Santa Fe and Taos was still treacherous in the first decade of the twentieth century when this photograph was made. (*Denver Public Library*)

men" while chastising the revolutionaries, and he urged them to heed "the voice of reason" and to "keep yourselves quiet and engaged in your private affairs."[59]

On January 23, Colonel Price left Santa Fe and marched his troops toward Taos. Accompanying him on this mission of reprisal were Companies D, K, L, M, and N, all elements of the 2nd Missouri Volunteers. Also present was the Missouri battalion of infantry under the command of Captain William A. Angney and a company of Santa Fe volunteers commanded by Captain Ceran St. Vrain. Lieutenant A. B. Dyer was placed in command of four mountain howitzers. All told, Colonel Price's effective fighting force numbered 353, all of them dismounted except St. Vrain's volunteers.[60]

The army went north from Santa Fe and onto present-day Old Taos Highway, which merges with present-day US Highway 285/84, then on to Cañada (present-day Santa Cruz).[61] From there, the soldiers would have followed present-day NM Highway 68 to Embudo. From Embudo, Price's troops moved east to Las Trampas, then through Chamisal, then north to Rancho de Taos via present-day NM Highway 518. Merging there with present-day NM 68, the route led into Taos. This thoroughfare was part of the ancient Camino Real that connected Mexico City with Santa Fe and Taos, and the northern section especially was extremely rugged and treacherous.

As late as 1854, several years after Price's march to Taos, local residents were still fighting the tortuous thoroughfare, which they had to navigate to the capital. They petitioned the US Congress to improve the "road from Santa Fe to Don Fernandez." Members of the Legislative Council of New Mexico pointed out in their plea that "the present route [essentially the northern one-half of the present-day High Road to Taos], and that which has always been used for wagons, is . . . almost impassable." On the other hand, according to the petitioners, a pack trail existed from Embudo directly into Taos (present-day NM 68), which American troops had begun using after the Taos Revolt. Furthermore, the trail could be improved for a "small expense" and would cut a great deal of travel time and mileage for travel between the two towns.62 In 1925, when the noted artist Eric Sloane first traveled to Taos as a young man, he found most of the roads in the region to be nothing more than narrow dirt thoroughfares through the mountains.63

A Missouri mounted volunteer.

In 1847, Colonel Price found the region between Santa Fe and Taos to be extremely rugged country, and the winter so far had proven to be particularly brutal. Record snowfall and bitterly cold temperatures had already visited the mountains, and the passes through the highlands, treacherous even in fair weather, were practically impassable. When he traveled the region only weeks earlier, Ruxton declared, "It was a cold, snowy day on which I left Santa Fe, and the mountain, although here of inconsiderable elevation, was difficult to cross on account of the drifts." He reported that the road snaked through an arroyo, surrounded by mountains covered with pine and cedar . . . between high banks now buried in the snow." Even the wildlife was eerily scarce except for a lone gray wolf that, in his haste to escape Ruxton's pack train, fell into a snow drift so deep that he had difficulty extricating himself.64

From Santa Fe, Price and his army traveled only a few miles north toward Taos when, at about 1:30 in the afternoon on the following day, January 24, St. Vrain's advance scouts discovered that the enemy

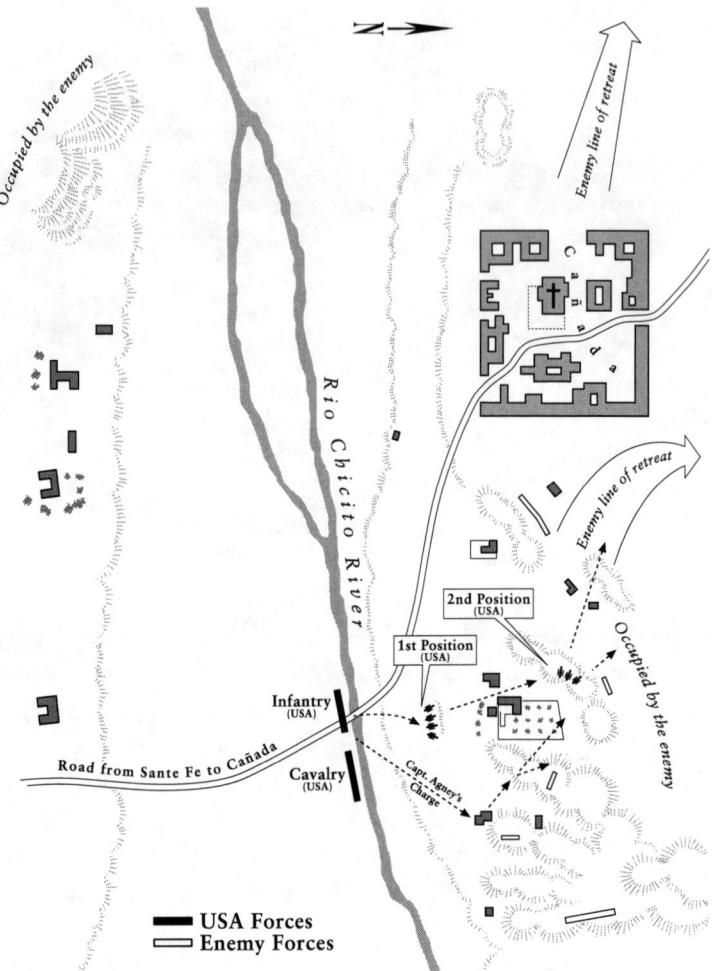

The battle at Cañada based on the official U.S. Army plan.

had fortified the village of Cañada.⁶⁵ Quickly, Price organized his men to attack. The rebels had occupied the highlands overlooking the road that led from the south into town, and the colonel ordered his artillery to shell their positions. The American supply trains lagged behind the troop movement, and when the revolutionaries discovered this, they attempted to cut the wagons off from the rest of the troops but failed in the endeavor.

In his report to the adjutant general, Price wrote that he had his men charge all sectors that were occupied by the rebels. Meanwhile, St. Vrain's mounted men cut off all retreat. The artillery units overran some buildings and the heights beyond them from which the enemy kept up a steady fire. "In a few minutes my troops had dislodged the enemy at all points, and they were flying in every direction," declared Price, adding that it proved impossible to pursue them because of the rugged terrain and because nightfall was rapidly approaching. The enemy had an estimated fifteen hundred troops, of which around forty-five were wounded and thirty-six were killed, including Jesus Tafoya, one of the ringleaders of the earlier revolt in Taos. American losses were two killed and six wounded. On the following morning, the rebels appeared that they would give additional resistance, but after Colonel Price personally led a column in pursuit, they retreated from their positions and left the region.[66]

Five days later, after resting and regrouping at Cañada, Price and his men resumed marching toward Taos. The Americans were now reinforced by Captain Burgwin's company of 1st Dragoons from Albuquerque and another company of Missouri Mounted Volunteers. With his army numbering 479 men, Price continued north along the east bank of the Rio Grande. As the army approached the small village of Embudo, situated along the narrow road that twisted through a deep canyon, the men were confronted by around sixty to eighty guerrillas nestled in the rocks that lined the steep canyon walls. Burgwin was dispatched with 180 men to flush them out. As he proceeded down the canyon, he discovered that enemy forces numbering about six hundred or seven hundred had taken up positions along the steep cliffs of a mesa between the road to Embudo and the river. The countryside was so rough that the movement of wagons and artillery was practically impossible. Price later wrote, "The rapid slopes of the mountains rendered the enemy's position very strong, and its strength was increased by the dense masses of cedar and large fragments of rock which every where offered them shelter." St. Vrain dismounted his men, who climbed the mesa, supported by elements of the 2nd Missouri Volunteers and the 1st Dragoons. "These parties ascended the hills rapidly, and the enemy soon began to retire in the direction of Embudo, bounding along with a speed that defied pursuit," Price wrote.

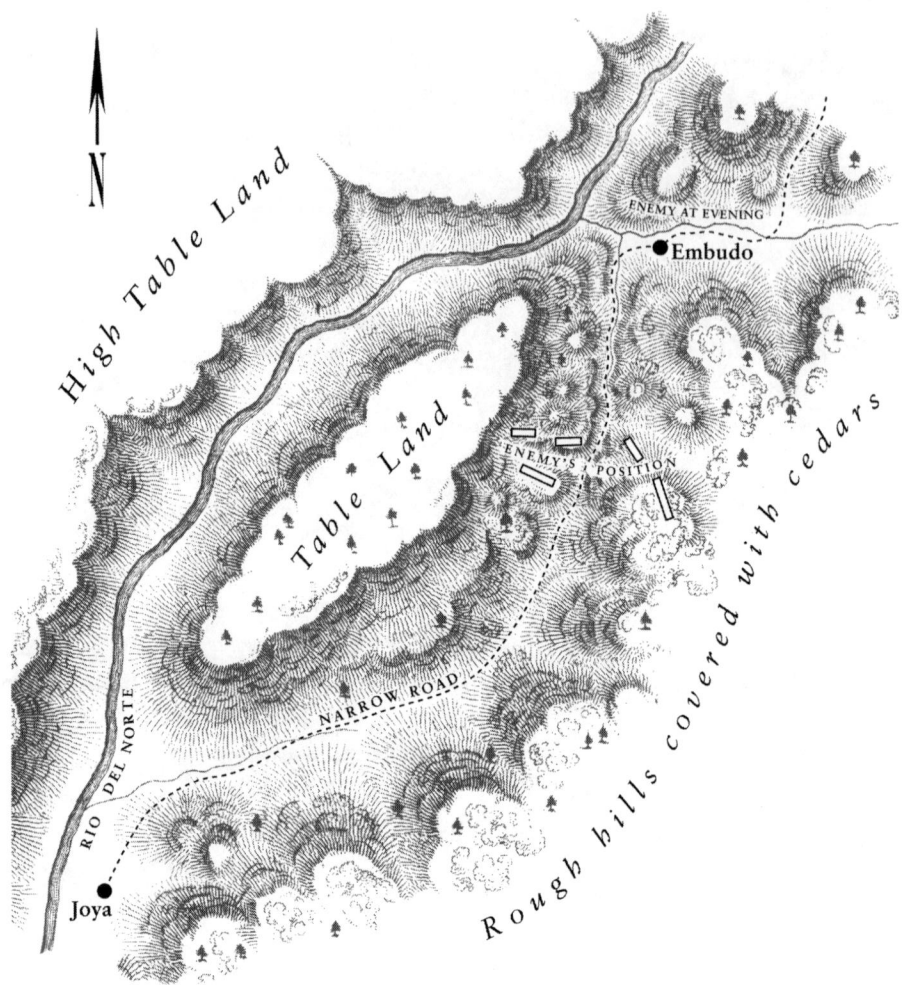

The battle at Embudo based on the official U.S. Army plan.

When Burgwin reached the far side of the defile, he and his men entered the valley in which Embudo was situated. Burgwin regrouped his men "and entered that town without opposition, several persons meeting him with a white flag." Despite the heated fighting at Embudo, only one American was killed and one wounded, compared to twenty enemy killed and sixty wounded.[67]

The battle at Mora.

While Colonel Price and his command were fighting their way up the Rio Grande Valley toward Taos between January 23 and 29, more conflict broke out near the village of Mora, where the Missouri traders had been murdered by local dissidents a few days earlier. Juan de Dios Maes, the *alcalde* of Vegas, had been apprised of the recent outbreak of violence at Taos and the murders of the traders at Mora and was under pressure from the insurrectionists to break his vow of allegiance to the United States and to join the growing number of locals preparing for more violence. Dios Maes refused to renege on his promise and urged the townspeople not to join the rebels.[68]

Anticipating more trouble in the region, Captain Israel R. Hendley, in charge of a grazing detachment at Vegas, reported to Price on January 23 that "the whole population [of the region] appear ripe for the insurrection." He told Price that he intended to attack Mora, which he had learned was occupied by a large number of New Mexican insurgents. He also advised his commander that his men were running low on ammunition and asked to be resupplied at once. He explained, "If you will forward me one or two pieces of artillery, well manned, and plenty of ammunition, I pledge myself to subdue, and keep in check every town this side of the mountains."[69]

Hendley and eighty American troops marched on Mora on January 25 to restore order following the rebels' murder of the Missouri traders there on January 19. Hendley was met by a contingent of 150 to 200 New Mexicans prepared to defend the village. During the next hour or so, Hendley's men and the New Mexicans fought door to door. When the rebels holed up in an old fort, the Americans were unable to dislodge them without artillery. In the effort, however, Hendley was killed and three soldiers were wounded. The New Mexicans suffered fifteen to twenty-five killed and fifteen to seventeen taken prisoner, depending on the source. The remainder of Hendley's command retreated to Vegas, carrying Hendley's body with them.[70]

Sometime during the Mora action in late January, an unfortunate incident occurred that no doubt at the time made American soldiers stationed in the vicinity even less popular than they already were. The exact day of the episode is unknown since it was never reported in the immediate official military reports and correspondence, only surfacing more than seven years later. On June 21, 1854, Thomas Hart Benton, a Missouri congressman and member of the Committee on Military Affairs (and formerly the US senator who had regularly met with President Polk and his cabinet about Mexican-American War matters), reported to the House of Representatives on the matter of a claim filed against the US government. In his declaration, Don Juan Jesus Vigil, an affluent New Mexican farmer who was also a friend of Governor Charles Bent's and possibly an American sympathizer, asserted that during January 1847, troops of Lieutenant Clare Oxley's Missouri volunteers seized several thousand sheep, took into custody the herdsmen who were minding them, and escorted the entire body to Vegas. The herdsmen were detained for over a week, and many of the sheep were butchered for the soldiers' sustenance.

The resulting investigation of Benton's committee revealed that Oxley's orders to apprehend the sheep were issued because of "an erroneous suspicion that the animals were intended for the supply of the enemy." When the herdsmen were finally released from custody, they were allowed to take with them the remainder of the sheep that could be located. The number of animals already lost or disposed of amounted to "upwards of four thousand head."

In view of the circumstances surrounding this episode, Benton's committee unanimously recommended that the US government be "justly bound to make compensation for the amount of the sheep thus seized or converted to their use, except so many as are shown to have been afterwards restored." President Franklin Pierce signed Joint Resolution HR 26 on December 19, 1854.[71]

In retaliation for Hendley's death, his successor, Captain Jesse B. Morin, along with his command and one cannon, proceeded from Santa Fe to Mora on February 1 and leveled the town. Buildings were burned to the ground and fields were destroyed as the town's terrified residents fled to the mountains. Several New Mexicans suspected of being involved with the murder of the Missouri traders were arrested and eventually revealed the locations of the traders' graves.[72]

A second incident, the details of which surfaced more than a decade after its occurrence, was brought to the attention of the House Committee on Military Affairs on May 29, 1858. A claim against the US government brought by the widow of Mora resident Francisco Robaldo requested payment of $30,000 for the destruction by American forces of a large store of grain, corn, and fodder. By virtue of a verbal contract between Robaldo and Captain William M. D. McKissack, the army's quartermaster in late 1846, the claimant's husband promised to furnish up to $50,000 worth of supplies to the army and to store the material in his buildings in Mora. By February 1, 1847, when Captain Morin laid to waste the town and outlying areas, Robaldo had purchased $30,000 worth of commodities for the army's use. Although a thorough investigation found that Morin destroyed Robaldo's property "to prevent such large supplies . . . falling into the hands of the enemy," it also discovered that McKissack refused to reimburse Robaldo for his loss. Robaldo then decided to take his case to Washington, DC, but shortly after arriving in Saint Louis, he committed suicide. A joint congressional resolution approved the payment of the claim.[73]

At about the same time Mora was being razed by Captain Morin, Sterling Price was finally approaching his destination, the recently terrorized village of Taos. Price recalled later, "On the 1st of February, we reached the summit of the Taos mountain which was covered with snow to the depth of two feet."[74] He reported that many of his soldiers were victims of frostbite, having marched for the past two days "in front of the artillery and wagons in order to break a road through the snow."[75]

The American army attack on San Gerónimo de Taos church at Taos Pueblo.

After eleven days of travel over the cold, snowy, rugged countryside of northern New Mexico and following two pitched battles in which several of his men were killed and wounded, Colonel Price and his army finally arrived in Taos on February 3. The Missourian wasted no time getting down to the business that brought him to his destination. He wrote later that the revolutionaries had retreated to Taos Pueblo, a large complex consisting of two separate buildings about three miles out of town. "I found it a place of great strength, being surrounded by adobe walls and strong pickets," he wrote. He estimated that each building might provide quarters for five hundred or six hundred residents and said a large church known to the pueblo residents as San Gerónimo, and to which most of the rebels had fled, occupied one angle of the village. "The town was admirably calculated for defence, every point of the exterior walls and pickets being flanked by some projecting building."[76]

Upon surveying the premises, Price realized that its capture would not be simple. A captain in the Missouri Light Artillery, Woldemar Fischer, described the invulnerability of the pueblo in a letter to the adjutant general, writing that mortars firing a fifty-pound projectile were required to breach the three-foot-thick walls of the various buildings. The twelve-pounder cannons, on the other hand, would be of little use, since their light-weight projectiles would simply pass through the relatively soft consistency of the adobe walls.[77]

At two o'clock on the afternoon of February 3, Price ordered an artillery attack using everything he had on the western flank of the church. The field howitzers and the six-pounder cannon fired round after round at the strong church building from a distance of 250 yards. Nightfall approached rapidly, and the soldiers—cold, tired, and nearly out of ammunition—retired from the battle with little sense of accomplishment.

The Americans were up early the next morning to again attack the pueblo. The howitzers were divided between the commands of Captain Burgwin, who was ordered to a position about 260 yards west of the church, and Lieutenant Dyer, who, with most of the remainder of the army, occupied a spot some 300 yards from the northern wall of the pueblo. Captains St. Vrain and William Slack, along with their mounted volunteers and dragoons, proceeded to the eastern end of the pueblo, with orders to cut down any rebels who tried to escape in that direction.

For two hours, the artillery blasted away at the church, with very little effect. At around 11:00 a.m., Burgwin and two companies of dragoons charged the western wall of the sanctuary, while Captain Angney's infantry and a contingent of Missouri volunteers attempted to breach the northern wall. While the American soldiers hacked away at the church's formidable adobe walls, one of the troops brought up a ladder and set fire to the building's roof. In the confusion, Burgwin was killed. Finally, under cover of the six-pounder cannon firing grapeshot into the pueblo, soldiers cut several small holes into the church's walls and manually threw artillery shells into the building. Then, at about 3:30 p.m., the six-pounder was brought to within sixty yards of the church, and its crew zeroed in on one of the holes in the wall. After ten rounds, the artillery fire enlarged the hole appreciably. The grand finale of the battle for the church was reported by Colonel Price:

> The gun was now run up within ten yards of the wall—a shell was thrown in—three rounds of grape were poured into the breach. The storming party . . . entered and took possession of the church without opposition. . . . A few of the enemy were seen in the gallery where an open door admitted the air, but they retired without firing a gun. The troops left to support the battery on the north were now ordered to charge on that side. The enemy abandoned the western part of the town. Many took refuge in the large houses on

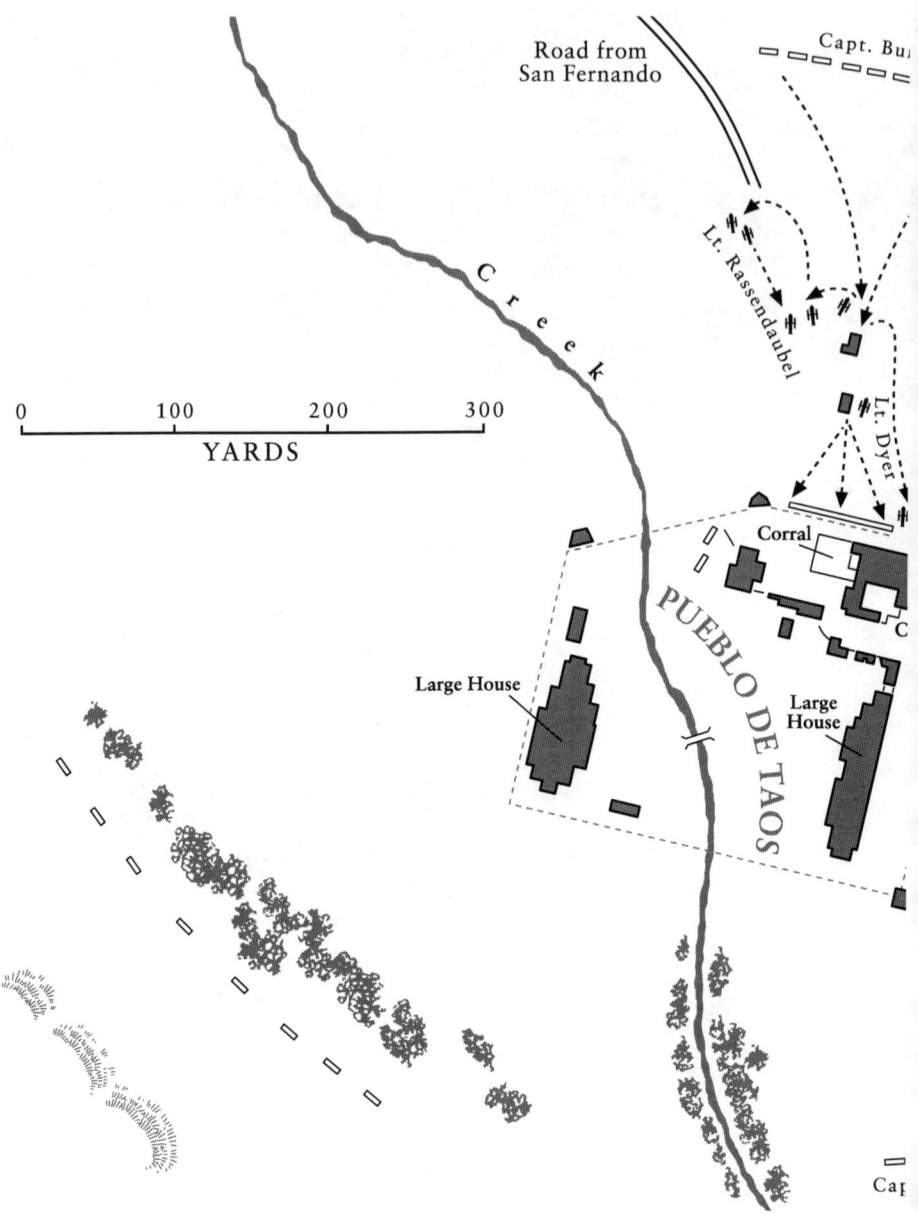

The battle at Taos Pueblo based on the official U.S. Army plan.

## "We Were Without Food and Had No Covering"

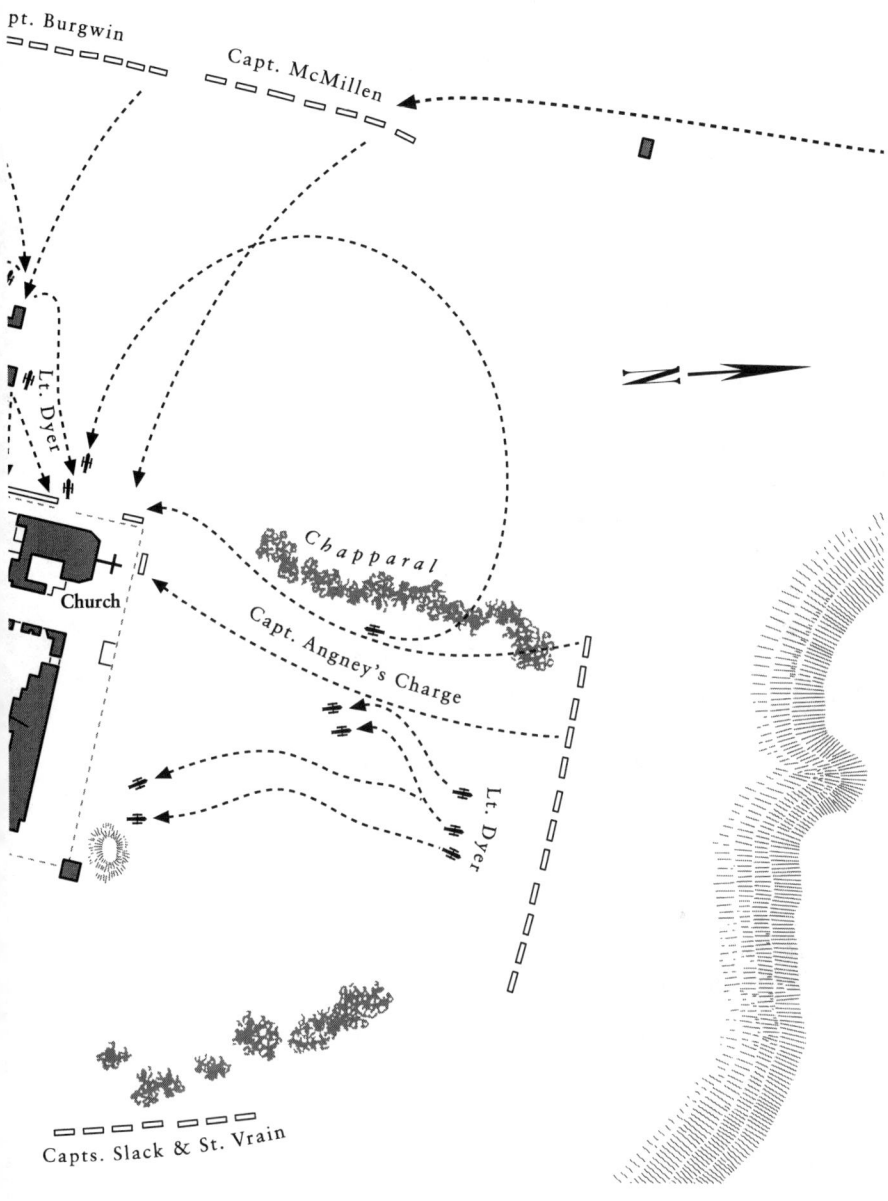

the east, while others endeavored to escape toward the mountains. These latter were pursued by the mounted men under Captains Slack and St. Vrain, who killed fifty-one of them, only two or three escaping.[78]

The American losses at the battle of Taos Pueblo were seven killed and forty-five wounded, many of whom died later. Out of the estimated six hundred or seven hundred of the enemy who participated in the fighting, 154 were killed, including Pablo Chavis, one of the leaders of the revolt. An unknown number of Indians and Mexicans were wounded.[79]

The following day, the Indian residents of Taos Pueblo sued for peace. Price agreed, provided that Tomás Romero (Tomacito), one of the two primary organizers of the revolt, was surrendered to the Americans. As it turned out, both of the instigators, Romero and Pablo Montoya, were captured. On February 6, Montoya was tried and sentenced to hang the next day.[80]

Dick Wootton participated in the battle, and his recollection of the fate of Romero was related in his 1890 biography:

> El Tomacito, the Indian leader, was placed under guard, and we proposed to give him, along with the rest, a formal trial, but a [US] dragoon by the name of Fitzgerald saved us the trouble. Fitzgerald was allowed to go into the room where the Indian was confined, along with others who wanted to take a look at him. The soldier looked at the savage a few minutes, and then quick as a flash, drew a pistol and shot him in the head, killing him instantly. . . . The Indian deserved to be killed, and would have been hanged anyhow, but we objected to the informal manner of his taking off.[81]

Although the next several months would bring more turmoil and bloodshed to northern New Mexico, the successful conquest of Taos Pueblo by Colonel Price's troops provided the death knell for the insurrectionists in the region, as they began to lose their strength and popularity. The uprising had failed in its long-range objective of killing all Americans and New Mexicans with American sympathies, but not without first taking the lives of scores of soldiers and civilians on both sides. The trials and executions of many of the conspirators

Present-day view of the ruins of San Gerónimo de Taos church. (*John Phelan*)

were yet to come, but for all intents and purposes, the decisive victory of the US Army and the Missouri Mounted Volunteers at Taos Pueblo sealed the fate of the joint New Mexican-Indian plans to permanently expel all Americans from New Mexico. In the meantime, the bodies of Governor Bent and Captain Burgwin were returned to Santa Fe for burial on February 13, the ceremonies witnessed by a crowd of thirteen hundred Americans and a large number of New Mexicans.[82]

*Seven*

# "Dead! Dead! Dead!"

## Trial and Execution

O<small>N</small> F<small>EBRUARY</small> 15, 1847, C<small>OLONEL</small> P<small>RICE</small> <small>DISPATCHED A LENGTHY</small> report to the adjutant general in Washington, DC. In the message, he gave a careful and detailed accounting of his and his army's activities since they left Santa Fe in January to quell the revolt at Taos. Price was proud of the officers and men under his command and proclaimed that in the encounters with the revolutionaries at Cañada, Embudo, and Pueblo de Taos, his entire army conducted itself "gallantly." He refrained from commending any one over the other "as such discrimination might operate prejudicially against the just claims of others."[1] When President Polk received the news of Price's victory, he placed great importance on the recent events in New Mexico, recording in his diary that although "the number of troops engaged was comparatively small . . . I consider this victory one of the most signal which has been gained during the war."[2]

Of the captives taken by the American army during the encounters at the three battle sites, many of them were, to use present-day jargon, released on their own recognizance and allowed to return to their homes and families.[3] However, the trial of Pablo Montoya, one of the rebellion's ringleaders, was expedited. On February 6, Price had issued Order No. 115, directing that Montoya be tried in Taos by a drumhead court-martial (a military trial usually held in the field and lacking some of the protections for the rights of the accused) on three counts: that on January 19, 1847, he incited certain Indians and New Mexicans to "rebellious conduct"; that on January 25, he issued a proclamation "exciting the people to rebellion"; and that he encouraged his followers to rob any US wagons en route to Santa Fe that might be carrying public funds. Lieutenant L. J. Easton (or Eastin) served as judge advocate; Captain William Angney, commander of the 2nd Missouri Volunteers infantry battalion, was named president of the court. Other members were Captain Thomas Barbee, 2nd Missouri Volunteers; Captain William Slack, 2nd Missouri Volunteers; Lieutenant Rufus Ingalls, 1st US Dragoons; and Lieutenant White, 2nd Missouri Volunteers.[4]

Montoya pleaded not guilty to the charges, and the panel of army officers was sworn. Lucian Thruston and Thomas Rowland acted as interpreters. The first witness for the prosecution, Jose Maria Sandoval, testified that he had served as Montoya's secretary and that on January 21, 1847, he had transcribed a letter for him addressed to the *alcalde* of Taos Pueblo, in which Montoya revealed that he had "this moment . . . received intelligence of importance, requesting us to be in readiness before the forces of Santa Fe advance and overcome our forces at the different points, Rio Abajo, Cañada, &c." He instructed the *alcalde* to assemble the men of the pueblo to equip themselves "with arms and provisions, that they may leave for Santa Fe with dispatch." The witness testified that Montoya had read the letter and approved it.

He further testified that he had transcribed a second letter for Montoya, which was read, approved, and signed as "Empowered general of the superior command." The letter, written on January 22, authorized the *alcalde* of Taos Pueblo "to cause the people under his command to keep themselves well equipped with arms, with the understanding that they will be chastised who disobey the orders and commands of Señor Alcalde." According to the witness, he transcribed a proclamation on January 25 that was read and approved by Montoya, who noted that he had received news from the "commander of the Mexican forces" that "the war [had] commenced at the Cañada with the foreign army. He [the commander] also states that they [the New Mexicans] have already vanquished them [Price's army]; believing which, honored Mexicans we shall come out triumphant in all our undertaking." Montoya continued:

> Mexican citizens!—Live in the hope that we will yet shout glory hallelujah in our province, and live in the confidence that the Divine Protector of the Indians will never permit his people to be vanquished.—Believing in His powerful assistance, no harm can befall us.
>
> Companions in arms!—I request you to try and make yourselves possessors of the money and effects that they [the Americans] are now taking to Santa Fe in the wagons.—Accomplishing this, you will place it under the strictest orders according to our plan, until it is in my disposal, taking care not to let the people steal it, it being alone for the defence of our sacred country.

The witness concluded his testimony by stating that wherever Montoya traveled, he was always "looked upon . . . as the general commanding the forces."

The prosecution's next witness was Padre Antonio José Martínez, who testified that on the morning of January 19, Montoya and several followers approached him at his home and inquired of the whereabouts of Elliott Lee (Sheriff Lee's brother), whom they accused Martínez of protecting. According to Martínez, the mob was still looking for the sheriff. "My room at that time, was filled with Indians and [New] Mexicans," declared Martínez. "The murder of Governor Bent and others, was the commencement of the revolution." He closed his testimony by revealing that Montoya had initially rejected being appointed general, with the role of restoring "good order among the [New] Mexicans," but later decided to accept the commission.

Elliott Lee was called to the stand next and swore that Montoya had told him on January 20 that he, Montoya, was commander in chief of the New Mexican forces and that he boasted of being "the Santa Anna of the north." Montoya further indicated that he fully intended to retake the territory recently occupied by the American army. According to Lee, Montoya then asked him whether "wagons [were] coming from the states to Santa Fe, with powder, and ball, and money?" Lee told him that it was his understanding that wagons were indeed on the way and that they were carrying upwards of $200,000. Montoya then told Lee that he was dispatching a party to intercept the wagons, which he did. To his dismay, however, the proposed heist of the wagon train failed, and his men returned with only some captured mules and horses. Lee then testified that Montoya left Taos with several troops to confront the Americans but that Montoya doubted that any Americans were left in Santa Fe, since "all of them had been killed."

The prosecution's final witness was Jesus Maria Tafoya, who testified that on January 20, the day Montoya was questioning Elliott Lee about the American wagons, he, Tafoya, was the interpreter for the two men. Tafoya revealed that Montoya told him to tell Lee that "if he did not answer the questions correctly, he had an instrument with which he could cut his throat." Montoya then had Tafoya question Lee about the American wagons, particularly wanting to know "whether there was powder and ball and plenty of money in them." Montoya threatened to capture the wagons and distribute the money among the Taoseños.

Montoya then told Tafoya that only around two hundred American troops were stationed in Santa Fe, mostly "boys," but that was of no concern, "we can kill them all off." Montoya then told the witness that he was "the Santa Anna of the north," the "commander in chief of the forces against the Americans," and that he would remain in Taos "to keep good order."

Montoya was found guilty of all charges. He was sentenced to death by hanging, subject to Colonel Price's consideration. Price reviewed the proceedings, approved them, and confirmed the death penalty to take place on the Taos plaza between 11:00 a.m. and 2:00 p.m. the following day.[5]

About forty of those captured with Montoya following Price's victory at Taos Pueblo were jailed in town to await trial during the spring term of court, due to begin April 5. Several other prisoners were taken directly to Santa Fe and jailed until the US District Court met there in March with Judge Joab Houghton presiding. Twenty-four or more of the Santa Fe suspects were eventually released for "want of testimony."[6]

A little more than a month after Montoya was hanged in Taos, Antonio Maria Trujillo, a high-level member of the rebellion's leadership, and three others were arraigned before a Santa Fe grand jury and charged with treason. In Trujillo's case, the indictment charged that he, as "a citizen of the United States of America," had "disrespect[ed]" his allegiance and "withdraw[n]" the duty and obedience expected of "true and faithful citizen[s]." Furthermore it charged that Trujillo, on January 20, 1847, "and on divers other days, as well before as after, with force and arms," and accompanied by "divers other false traitors . . . did . . . maliciously, wickedly and traitorously levy war against the government of the United States of America."[7]

During the subsequent trial, the US prosecutor, Francis P. Blair, Jr., introduced documents to support the government's case. One item showed that on January 20, 1847, the day after the uprising in Taos, General Jesus Tafoya dispatched a circular letter, countersigned by Trujillo as the rebellion's inspector of arms and commander of militia, to all of the military commanders throughout the region. The rambling message essentially told the officers to prepare themselves and their men for military action and to be "ready for the 22d day of this month." Accompanying the letter were orders from Trujillo to "raise all the forces, together with all the inhabitants that are able to bear arms," explaining that "we have declared war with the American[s] and it is now time that we shall all take our arms in our hands in defense of our abandoned country."[8]

Historian Ralph Emerson Twitchell wrote in 1909 that Trujillo was "promptly found guilty," suggesting that the defense counsel made little progress with refuting the indictment.[9] What the defense did do, however, was raise the question of the legality of the court hearing the case at all. In charging the jurors, Judge Houghton instructed them to disregard any of the defense's arguments that the court did not have the constitutional authority to try a New Mexico citizen for treason.[10]

During Trujillo's sentencing, Houghton faced the convicted man and said, "A jury of twelve citizens, after a patient and careful investigation, pending which all the safeguards of the law, managed by able and indefatigable counsel, have been afforded you, have found you guilty of the high crime of treason." The judge went on to say that Trujillo's "age and gray hairs" had aroused the sympathy of everyone present, but that "not content with the peace and security in which you have lived under the present government, secure in all your personal rights as a citizen," he had given his "name and influence to measures intended to effect universal murder and pillage, the overthrow of the government and one widespread scene of bloodshed in the land." Houghton then ordered Trujillo to "be hanged by the neck till you are dead! dead! dead!" The sentence was ordered to be carried out at 2:00 p.m. on April 16, 1847.[11] The trials of Trujillo's three compatriots—Pantaleón Archuleta, Trinidad Barcelo, and Pedro Vigil—were declared mistrials, with the result that all charges were eventually dropped.[12]

Francis P. Blair, Jr., the American prosecutor at the Taos trials.

Following Trujillo's trial, an appeal was sent to President Polk, signed by the presiding judge, the associate judge, the prosecuting attorney, the defense counsel, and most of the jurors, recommending the convicted man be pardoned on account of his "age and infirmity."[13] In a letter to Secretary of State Buchanan written in late March, acting governor Vigil opined that "though feeling assured that the accused had had a fair trial and had been justly sentenced and legally convicted, I still feel justified in granting the prayer of the petition, signed as it was by the court and the jury before whom he was tried and convicted."[14] On June 11, Secretary of War Marcy wrote Colonel Price in Santa Fe that after reviewing the court's recommendations, "the President sincerely hopes that the life of Antonio Maria Trujillo may be spared . . . [and] he leaves the case of Trujillo to your disposal."[15] According to Senator Thomas Hart Benton, Price, or perhaps a subordinate, solved the problem of Trujillo's pardon by simply letting him go free.[16]

On April 1, prosecutor Francis Blair, Jr. wrote to John Y. Mason, the attorney general of the United States, requesting his counsel about the legality of US courts trying citizens of New Mexico for treason. Blair reviewed with Mason the matter of Trujillo's defense argument that the court lacked jurisdiction to hear such treason cases, based on the unconstitutionality of trying "any *native* inhabitant of New

Mexico for the crime of treason against the government of the United States, until by actual treaty with Mexico he became a citizen." Judge Houghton's charge to the jury to disregard the arguments of the defense, according to Blair, left "only the evidence and the facts upon which to make its verdict."[17]

Blair's letter to Mason was referred to Secretary of War Marcy, with the comments that he Mason "would give an official opinion upon the questions presented, if, as is the legal course, it should be requested; but the error in the designation of the offence was too clear to admit of doubt, and it is only in cases of doubt that resort can be had to the Attorney General for his opinion."[18] On June 26, Marcy then advised Price in Santa Fe that New Mexico did not become "by the mere act of conquest" permanently attached to the United States, and its citizens did not automatically become American citizens. While the inhabitants of an occupied region might owe obedience to their conquerors and be liable for prosecution of crimes such as murder, Marcy wrote, "it is not the proper use of legal terms to say that their offence was treason committed against the United States."[19] Marcy also referred Price to his opinion on the same matter sent on January 11, 1847,[20] to General Kearny in California, with a copy to the "commanding officer at Santa Fe, with instructions to conform his conduct to the views herein presented." Fearful that Price never saw the January 11 document, Marcy sent him another copy with his June 26 dispatch. The absence of a reply from Kearny to Marcy's January letter might indicate that he never received the message, or, if he did, failed to forward it to Price at Santa Fe, thinking the colonel would receive the copy referred to in Marcy's transmittal. Whatever the reason, Marcy's directives were obviously not heeded, and charges of treason were filed against several defendants.

As winter turned into spring, Taos was astir with talk of the upcoming trials for those arrested during the rebellion and their possible outcomes. Although affairs in town had returned to near normal following the sound defeat of the rebels at the Pueblo, many New Mexicans and Taos Indians were justifiably concerned about the fates of their friends and neighbors being tried in the totally unfamiliar American court system. As would soon be demonstrated, the trials

Charles H. Beaubien, left, chief judge at the Taos trials, and and Ceran St. Vrain, right, business partner of Charles Bent and participant in the American army attack on Taos Pueblo.

and sentencing of the captured revolutionaries served only to provide additional fodder for some disgruntled local agitators who perceived the legal proceedings as just another American-orchestrated exercise to extinguish all native claims to New Mexico. Indeed, it took little imagination on anyone's part to accurately predict the outcome of many of the hearings, since the juries were composed of either Americans or New Mexicans with American loyalties.[21]

Much of what is known today about the trials at Taos is derived from the original court minutes, rediscovered in the early 1920s and published in the *New Mexico Historical Journal* in 1926, and the book *Wah-To-Yah and the Taos Trail*, written by Lewis H. Garrard and published in 1850. Garrard, not yet twenty years old, had joined a trading caravan earlier at Westport Landing, Missouri, bound for Bent's Fort on the Arkansas River. When he arrived at the fort, he stayed for several weeks before being recruited by William Bent to go to Taos to avenge the recent murder of his brother, Charles.[22] Garrard attended most of the proceedings and subsequent hangings of the convicted rebels.

The Taos grand jury and criminal trial proceedings reveal a system that was a far cry from present-day judicial ethics, decorum, and jury selection. Presiding over the court was Judge Charles H. Beaubien, who was the father of Narciso Beaubien, one of those murdered at Taos on January 19. Joab Houghton—a New York native and chief justice of the three district courts established by the Americans in occupied New Mexico—served as an associate judge. The prosecuting attorney was Francis Blair, Jr. Both his assistant and the counsel for the defense were American army privates, selected because of their legal backgrounds in civilian life. Ceran St. Vrain, Charles Bent's old partner—and also a son-in-law of Judge Beaubien's and a brother-in-law of the murdered Narciso Beaubien's—was the official interpreter for the proceedings, and Bent's younger brother, George, was appointed foreman of the grand jury. One of the grand jurymen was Elliott Lee, a brother of Sheriff Stephen Lee, who was also killed during the Taos mayhem. Lucien Maxwell, another son-in-law of Charles Beaubien's and brother-in-law of Narciso Beaubien's, as well as the future heir to his father-in-law's sprawling land grant in northern New Mexico, served on the trial jury. Several other members of the trial juries—among them Charles Town, Jean-Baptiste Chalifoux, Antoine Ledoux, and Charles Autobees—were American or French fur trappers who had frequented Taos and in some cases made their homes there for years.[23] One can only imagine the feelings of futility and despair that the accused and their families must have felt when they became aware of the structure of the court that held their destinies.

The Circuit Court for the Northern District of New Mexico held its proceedings in Taos from Monday, April 5, until Saturday, April 24, 1847, and testimony for the accused New Mexicans and Taos Indians captured in the recent uprising was heard from April 5 until Tuesday, April 13. During the morning of the first day, the marshal issued the list of grand jurors: George Bent, James S. Barry, Joseph M. Graham, Antonio Ortiz, Jose Gregory Martínez, Miguel Sanchez, Elliott Lee, Mariano Martin, Matias Vigil, Gabriel Vigil, Santiago Martínez (a younger brother of Padre Martínez's, who was suspected by many of being a leader in the Taos uprising), Ventura Martínez, Jose Cordoval, Felipe Romero, Ramonde Cordoval, Antonio Medina, Jose Angel Vigil, Antonio Jose Bingo, and Jean Bennette Valdez, all but four of them New Mexicans. Court was adjourned until 9:00 a.m. the next day, and the grand jury retired to chambers to consider the upcoming cases.

On the following day, Tuesday, April 6, the court convened at 9:00 a.m. to consider the indictment of José Manuel Garcia for murder. The defense counsel reported that he was not ready for trial and petitioned the court to adjourn until the afternoon, a request the judge granted. When the court reconvened, the accused pleaded not guilty, and a panel of twelve jurors was appointed to hear the case. Testimony was given, and the accused was found guilty as charged. A death sentence was recommended. The next day, April 7, Judge Beaubien announced his decision: "That on Friday next the 9th Inst. he be taken from the Jail of said County to the place of execution and between the hours of ten o'clock in the forenoon and two o'clock in the afternoon and hang him said José Manuel Garcia by the neck until he is dead."24

That same day, the court heard the case for murder against Pedro Lucero, Manuel Antonio Romero, Juan Ramón Trujillo, and Isidor (Ysidro) Romero, all four of whom pleaded not guilty. The jury was sworn, and the defense counsel immediately petitioned the court to dismiss the indictment, a motion the judge overruled. After hearing the evidence, the jury returned a guilty verdict for all four defendants. The men were all sentenced to be hanged on the following Friday between 10:00 a.m. and 2:00 p.m.25

Rounding out the court's work for April 7, the grand jury returned an indictment for treason against Hipólito (Polo) Salazar. The defendant pleaded not guilty, the testimony was heard by the trial jury, Salazar was found guilty as charged, and the jury recommended the death penalty. The next day, April 8, Salazar was formally sentenced to be hanged on the following Friday. Also on the eighth, the grand jury indicted five additional men for murder: Francisco Naranjo, José Gabriel Romero, Juan Domingo Martin, Juan Antonio Lucero, and El Cuervo. The five defendants pleaded not guilty and were bound over for trial. They were tried the same day and found guilty as charged. The judge remanded the five convicted men to jail to await formal sentencing.26

On Friday, April 9, four New Mexicans—Manuel Miera, Manuel Sandoval, Rafael Tafoya, and Juan Pacheco—who earlier had been indicted by the grand jury for murder, pleaded not guilty, and their trials were set for the next day. Another defendant, Francisco Rivole (or Revali), also pleaded not guilty to the indictment of treason. Rivole's counsel requested a postponement for his client's trial until the following Monday. The motion was granted, and court adjourned until the next day.

When court reconvened Saturday morning, the counsel for the five men (in the court minutes, these men are identified as "Indians") convicted of murder the previous Thursday—Naranjo, Romero, Martin, Lucero, and El Cuervo—asked the court to order a new trial for his clients. Judge Beaubien overruled the motion and sentenced the convicted men to be hanged on Friday, April 30. Also during Saturday's session, the four men who were in court the previous day—Miera, Sandoval, Tafoya, and Pacheco—were tried and found guilty as charged. They were sentenced to be hanged on April 30.[27]

On Monday morning, April 12, the grand jury indicted someone named Asencio for murder. The accused pleaded not guilty, and a trial jury was chosen. Testimony was heard, the jury returned a not guilty verdict, and the defendant was released from custody.

The treason trial for Francisco Rivole, postponed from the previous Friday, was also held on April 12, and he was found not guilty and released.[28] Also on the twelfth, the case against Juan Antonio Avila, indicted for murder, was deferred until the following day. Avila and his counsel were back in court at 9:00 a.m. Tuesday. The trial jury was selected, testimony was heard, and the defendant was found guilty as charged. Avila was sentenced to be hanged on May 7. Treason charges against Varua Tafoya, Felipe Tafoya, and Pablo Guerrera were dropped without being prosecuted.[29]

The burial services for several of the New Mexicans hanged at Taos were conducted by Padre Antonio José Martínez, and their interment took place in the cemetery of Martínez's parish church, Nuestra Señora de Guadalupe, on the western side of the plaza in Taos. They were Hipólito Salazar, José Manuel Garcia, Manuel Sandoval, Rafael Tofoya, Ysidro Antonio Romero, Manuel Antonio Romero, and Juan Ramon Trujillo.[30] Around the turn of the twentieth century, the original Guadalupe church was replaced by a second sanctuary, which in turn was destroyed by fire in 1961. Then a third church replaced the second one, not on the same site but across the street. The church's original site was paved over for a strip mall and parking lot, and all evidence of the graves of those hanged at Taos in 1847 was lost.[31] The bodies of the five Indians executed during the Taos trials—Francisco Naranjo, José Gabriel Romero, Juan Domingo Martin, Juan Antonio Lucero, and El Cuervo—were carried back to Taos Pueblo for burial amid the ruins of San Gerónimo de Taos (Saint Jerome of Taos) Church, recently destroyed by Price's troops.[32]

In contrast to the official court records, Lewis Garrard's accounts of the Taos trials and executions provide a totally different view of the harsh reality of the American judicial system and its impact on the natives of northern New Mexico. Compared to the insensitive language recorded at the trials, his comments are those of a young, innocent American, gone from home for the first time and little informed in the ways of world as it was and not as it should have been. While attending one of the trials in the jam-packed courtroom, he observed that Judges Beaubien and Houghton were on the bench when the accused—"ill-favored, half-scared, sullen fellows"—were brought before them. The mixed trial jury of New Mexicans and Americans had been impaneled, and they all watched the indicted men. Garrard, with as much empathy for the witnesses called to testify as for the accused, revealed that they "touched their lips to the Bible, on taking the oath . . . with . . . a combination of reverential awe for the book and the fear of *los Americanos*. . . . The poor things were as much frightened as the prisoners at the bar."[33]

Although feeling compassion for the families of those Americans and New Mexicans who were massacred by the rebels during the assaults on Taos, Turley's Mill, Rio Colorado, and Mora, Garrard leaves his reader with the impression that he was equally as sympathetic with the culprits, who, after all, were only defending their homeland. His scathing words leave no doubt that he clearly appreciated and understood both sides of the issue. His remarks relative to the treason charge against one of the accused were especially poignant:

> It certainly did appear to be a great assumption on the part of the Americans to conquer a country and then arraign the revolting inhabitants for treason. American judges sat on the bench, New Mexicans and Americans filled the jury box, and an American soldiery guarded the halls. Verily, a strange mixture of violence and justice—a strange middle ground between the martial and common law.[34]

During one particular trial, the outcome was practically guaranteed. After the jury declared a guilty verdict against one defendant tried for treason, Garrard displayed maturity far beyond his years when he wrote:

> Treason, indeed! What did the poor devil know about his new allegiance? . . . I left the room, sick at heart. Justice! Out upon the word, when its distorted meaning is the warrant for murdering those who defend to the last their country and their homes.[35]

So far, the Taos trials, sentencing hearings, and executions had left the residents of the town and the nearby pueblo shaken. Rightfully indignant, but with a fear of further reprisal, most of the population simply dejectedly took the matter in stride—except Father Martínez. Not a man to mince words, he wrote a letter to his friend Manuel Alvarez, the American consul in Santa Fe, on April 12, while the trials were winding down and all the executions had not yet taken place. "Carlos Beaubien and his associates, the Judges of the crime [the Taos Revolt], are trying to kill all the people of Taos," he lamented. He then told Alvarez that he was also making known his feelings about the rapid-fire trials and executions to Colonel Price and asked for his friend's intervention with the colonel on his behalf.[36]

In his letter to Price, dated the same day, Martínez called the trials "a frightful proceeding" and suggested that the scandal and resentment they were causing might even lead to "a new and obstinate movement . . . becoming worse each day." He apprised Price that the language barrier was causing a problem since none of the defendants spoke or understood English. He also told the colonel that the defense lawyers were demanding immediate payment for their services from their clients, who were poor and had no means of raising funds. Lastly, the agitated, but polite, padre took a shot at the jurors, whom he termed "a class of ignorant men . . . tainted with passion."[37]

During one of the trials, Maria Ignacia Jaramillo Bent, Josefa Jaramillo Carson, and Rumalda Luna Boggs attended the proceedings. Lewis H. Garrard was there and reported:

> The courtroom was a small, oblong apartment, dimly lighted by two narrow windows; a thin railing kept the bystanders from contact with the functionaries. The prisoners faced the judges, and the three witnesses (Senoras Bent, Boggs, and Carson) were close to them on a bench by the wall. When Mrs. Bent gave in her testi-

mony, the eyes of the culprits were fixed sternly upon her; on pointing out the Indian who killed the Governor, not a muscle of the chief's face twitched or betrayed agitation, though he was aware her evidence unmistakenly sealed his death warrant—he sat with lips gently closed, eyes earnestly centered on her, without a show of malice or hatred—an almost sublime spectacle of Indian fortitude and of the severe mastery to which the emotions can be subjected. Truly, it was a noble example of Indian stoicism.[38]

And so, during three weeks in April 1847, when the days showed signs of returning warmth, and snow in the mountains was beginning to melt, yielding life-saving moisture to the dormant pasturelands of the high desert, final judgment was passed on the convicted leaders of the Taos Revolt. If neither the speed nor the results of the trials surprised anyone in Taos, then neither should have the alacrity with which the Americans pursued the executions of those convicted. Hangings held on April 9, April 30, and May 7 took the lives of seventeen men. During the latter executions, the sheriff couldn't find enough rope and had to borrow several rawhide lariats from Lewis Garrard and his friends and some picket cords from a teamster. Garrard helped soap the makeshift leather lariats to make them softer, then went to the sheriff's office and observed the prisoners. "These men were the condemned," he commented. "In two short hours, they hung lifeless on the gallows."[39]

The gallows, consisting of a scaffold of two upright posts with a crossbar connecting them, was about 150 yards from the jailhouse. As the condemned approached their destiny, they "marched slowly, with down-cast eyes, arms tied behind, and bare heads, with the exception of white cotton caps stuck on the back part, to be pulled over the face as the last ceremony."[40]

The American army took no chances. In one hanging incident described by Garrard, he related that soldiers positioned themselves on the roof of the jail and aimed the mountain howitzer that had been used in the battle at Taos Pueblo at the gallows. A soldier stood erect over the fuse with a lighted match in his hand. Two hundred and thirty American soldiers marched down the street in front of the jail in a show of force. The sheriff and his assistant placed the nooses around the prisoners' necks as officials balanced the men on a board that stretched across a wagon drawn by two mules. Garrard watched as the proceeding drew to a close, later observing that the convicted men talked quietly to their families. One of the convicted admitted that their crimes of murder deserved the death penalty, and then all uttered "earnest appeals, which I could but imperfectly comprehend, [but] the words 'mi padre, mi madre'—'my father, my mother'—could be distinguished." The man at this hanging, convicted of treason, especially impressed Garrard, demonstrating a "spirit of martyrdom worthy to the cause for which he died—the liberty of his country; and, instead of the cringing, contemptible recantation of the others, his speech was firm asseverations of his own innocence, the unjustness of his trial, and the arbitrary conduct of his murderers."[41]

The command was at last given. The mules struggled to pull the combined weight of the wagon and the men poised on its platform. "Bidding each other 'adios,' with a hope of meeting in Heaven,"[42] the accused swayed back and forth in the dry, gentle breeze. After the men had swung lifelessly for forty minutes, they were cut down. The military guard was dismissed, and the sad spectators slowly returned to their homes. Weeping relatives claimed the bodies, which Garrard helped cut down from the scaffold. It was "a most unpleasant business, too, for the cold, clammy skins and dead weight were revolting to the touch," he wrote.[43]

The repulsive task at hand now done, Garrard and his friends marched off to the local cantina and lost themselves in drink. It was all in a day's work, he kept telling himself. Writing about the event three years later in his book, he wondered, "Who would blame a man for making a temporary sacrifice of himself on Bacchus, on such an occasion?"[44]

In summer 1848, after the Taos trials had been over for more than a year, President Polk was still haunted by the treason issue. A congressional resolution was sent to the president asking him if the charge of treason against Mexican nationals during the aftermath of the revolt had resulted in execution. Polk replied on July 24 that it was true that certain New Mexican citizens, who previously had "submitted to our authority," had fomented "insurrection" and killed soldiers and civilians alike. Ringleaders of the revolt were arrested, tried, found guilty, and "condemned by a tribunal invested with civil and criminal jurisdiction, which had been established . . . by the military officer in command." Polk wrote that while there was no doubt that the accused, once tried and found guilty of the charges brought against them, "deserved the punishment inflicted upon them," the prosecution of them for "treason against the United States" was erroneous. He added that the entire matter had been addressed by Secretary of War Marcy in a letter to Colonel Sterling Price "in command in New Mexico," dated June 26, 1847.[45] Attached to Polk's response to Congress was a copy of Marcy's January 11, 1847, dispatch (sent before the Taos trials and erroneous convictions) treating the same subject and addressed to General Kearny, with a copy to Colonel Price in Santa Fe.[46]

As affairs turned out, the treason charges were indeed illegal on the premise that one cannot commit treason against a country of which he is not a citizen. A ruling from the US Supreme Court on an 1850 case (*Fleming v. Page*) with its roots in the Mexican-American War underlined the illegality of some of the previous Taos proceedings as far as the treason charges were concerned. In the case, Justice Roger B. Taney wrote his opinion that:

> A war . . . declared by Congress can never be presumed to be waged for the purpose of conquest, or the acquisition of territory, nor does the law declaring the war imply an authority to the President to enlarge the limits of the United States by subjugating the enemy's country. . . . This can be done only by the treaty making power, or the legislative authority, and is not a part of the power conferred upon the President by the declaration of war. . . . The relation in which the conquered territory [Mexico] stood to the United States while it was occupied by their arms did not depend on the laws of nations but upon our own constitution and acts of Congress. . . . The inhabitants were still foreigners and enemies, and owed to the United States nothing more than submission and obedience, sometimes called temporary allegiance, which is due from a conquered enemy when he surrenders to a force which he is unable to resist.[47]

Unfortunately for Hipólito Salazar, the Taoseño hanged for treason following his trial in early 1847, Justice Taney's ruling came three years too late.

*Eight*

# "The New Mexicans Entertain Deadly Hatred against Americans"

## Hostilities Continue

A LTHOUGH NEW MEXICANS RETURNED TO SOME DEGREE OF normalcy following the execution of the last of the Taos insurgents on May 7, 1847, Colonel Price still had ample reason to be less than optimistic about affairs in the region. An especially thorny issue was the continuing questionable conduct of his command. During May, a writer sent the following comments back East:

> One thing must be done speedily. This military mob must be relieved, or we must be relieved of them soon: they become more lawless and insubordinate every day. By the instructions lately received here, all the officers created under the government for this territory are declared temporary—to continue only until such time as the country shall be declared annexed, or its possession shall be renounced.[1]

A second unresolved issue, at least from the New Mexican standpoint, was the fact that the occupying American military leadership had failed to live up to a very important promise made to the natives by General Kearny. Practically everywhere the general spoke the previous year when he invaded New Mexico, he had vowed to his listeners to provide American protection from raids by the warring Navajo, Apache, and Ute tribes. However, despite a few early forays into Indian territory in September and October 1846, attacks by the powerful Indian tribes continued to plague the rural villages throughout the area.[2]

The army's largest operation occurred during late October 1846, when Colonel Alexander Doniphan and a contingent of the 1st Missouri Mounted Volunteers penetrated deep into Navajo country to negotiate an end to the tribe's continuous raids. Doniphan split his command into three elements and personally led one of them up the Rio Puerco to its headwaters. Major William Gilpin took two hundred troopers from Abiquiu and marched up the Rio Chama, across the Continental Divide, to the valley of the San Juan River. Captain John W. Reid and thirty soldiers marched cross-country straight into Navajo territory. By late November, about five hundred Navajos had assembled at Ojo del Oso in the heart of their homeland to hear what the Americans had to say.

The Navajos' spokesman was a young chief named Sarcilla Largo (or Zarcillos Largos). He told Doniphan that "he was gratified to learn the views of the Americans" and that "he admired their spirit and enterprise, but detested the Mexicans." When Doniphan explained to him that the New Mexicans had surrendered and that the entire region was now under US rule, Largo scolded the Americans. He told Doniphan that his tribe had warred against the New Mexican villages for years and that they had killed many and had captured many more. "We had just cause for all this," he declared, adding that the Americans, in their recent warfare with the region's inhabitants, had "captured them, the very thing we have been attempting to do for so many years." Continuing, Largo expressed bewilderment with American military policy:

> You now turn upon us for attempting to do what you have done yourselves. We cannot see why you have cause of quarrel with us for fighting the New Mexicans on the west, while you do the same thing on the east. Look how matters stand. This is our war. We

have more right to complain of you interfering in our war, than you have to quarrel with us for continuing a war we had begun long before you got here. If you will act justly, you will allow us to settle our own differences.³

On November 22, when Doniphan explained to the Navajos that any future warfare against the New Mexicans by the tribe would be considered war against the United States, Largo and other leaders signed a treaty, agreeing to a "firm and lasting peace and amity . . . between the American people and the Navajo tribe of Indians."⁴

This important treaty notwithstanding, the Navajos continued to be troublesome. According to a letter dated March 26, 1847, written by Donaciano Vigil, New Mexico's governor since the death of Charles Bent, American authorities had done little to allay the natives' fears of Navajo depredations. In the message to Secretary of State Buchanan, Vigil related that Colonel Price had been assured by the Navajos that they would release all prisoners and livestock secured in recent raids. However, he also confided in Buchanan that since the Navajos continued to make daily raids on the local villages, he personally doubted that any quick resolution to the problem would be forthcoming. He expressed hope that the army would soon recover the property and kidnapped prisoners taken by the Indians and that some sort of "future respect" among the Navajos for the American government could be obtained. Vigil ended his message with the concern that if the raids in the region were not halted immediately, the inaction would be looked upon by the natives as evidence that Kearny's promises were hollow and that they had been "shamefully violated and disregarded."⁵

The lack of manpower also posed a serious problem to American authorities in Santa Fe. Enlistments were ending for many of the volunteers, and replacements were difficult to obtain. Governor Vigil urged Secretary Buchanan to replace the volunteer force with regular troops as soon as possible, citing reasons of "greater economy, expediency, and efficiency."⁶ As late as the following July, Price was still echoing Vigil's apprehensions about a volunteer army in which many of its soldiers' enlistments had terminated, writing that his forces had been so much reduced that he was compelled to utilize what troops he had to protect Santa Fe.⁷

Colonel Alexander Doniphan with Navajo chief Sarcilla Largo.

During late spring and early summer, Price was faced with still more problems as fighting between New Mexicans and their Indian allies, led by the Taos revolutionary Manuel Cortéz, and units of the American army erupted in the region east of Santa Fe. By late May, Cortéz had assembled three hundred to four hundred New Mexicans and Cheyenne and Apache Indians at the confluence of the Mora and Canadian rivers, intent on raiding the surrounding countryside.[8] On May 20, Captain Benjamin Robinson's grazing party of Missouri Mounted Volunteers camped near Wagon Mound was attacked. The marauders made off with about two hundred fifty horses and wounded three soldiers, one of them fatally. When Major B. B. Edmonson, commander at Vegas, received information of the attack, he at once took a detachment of seventy-five to eighty men, with himself in command, to Robinson's relief. Arriving on May 24, Edmonson learned that on the previous day, a twelve-vehicle wagon train belonging to American settlers had been attacked by Indians. The wagons were still filled with their cargo, but the sixty to seventy oxen used to pull them had been slaughtered by the tribesmen.[9]

The region was reconnoitered on May 25, and on the next day, Edmonson—accompanied by Captains John Holloway and Robinson and Lieutenants Robert T. Brown and Richard Smith Elliott and their commands—descended into a deep canyon of the Canadian River, where they soon confronted the enemy. "The hills around us were by this time literally covered with Indians and [New] Mexicans, who . . . opened a fire upon us from every point occupied by them," Edmonson later wrote in his report. By sunset, most of the troops were running low on ammunition, and when they attempted to evacuate their positions, they were fired on. Two Americans were wounded, and several of the horses were killed. Five of the enemy were killed, and an unknown number were wounded. Edmonson and his command reached the top of the canyon and relative safety just as darkness was approaching. During the entire engagement, one American, Private Edward G. Whitworth,[10] was killed and three were slightly wounded. The enemy's loss—out of a total of four hundred to six hundred men—was forty-one killed and an unknown number wounded.

On the next day, although practically out of ammunition, Edmonson led his command back into the canyon, where they discovered that all of the enemy forces had fled in haste, leaving much of their supplies, equipment, and horses behind, "not taking time to scalp or strip our man lost in the action, as is their custom." The Americans followed the fleeing marauders far out onto the plains until it became necessary to return to camp due to the lack of supplies and the condition of the horses.[11]

In late June, several army horses in the Vegas region belonging to Major Edmonson's command were stolen by a group of insurrectionists. Lieutenant Brown, accompanied by Privates James M. McClanahan and Charles Quisenbury (or Quesenberry) and a New Mexican guide, located the animals a few miles southeast of Vegas near the village of Los Valles de Agustin. When the soldiers attempted to reclaim the horses, the rebels fell upon them and killed all four men. A few days later, a New Mexican woman reported to authorities in Vegas that the entire party had been killed by the rebels and their bodies burned. Later, when three New Mexicans were brought in for questioning, they confirmed that the four men had met their fates as feared.[12]

On July 5, Edmonson formed a detail of thirty-three infantrymen, twenty-nine cavalrymen, and one mountain howitzer and descended on Los Valles. The battle lasted only 15 minutes, during which time ten New Mexicans were killed, fifty prisoners were taken, and the town was burned. No Americans were killed or wounded. Lieutenant Brown's body was discovered—not burned after all—as were the ashes of his three companions. The prisoners were taken to Santa Fe and tried by a military court, where six of them—Jose Tomas Duran,

The American army attack on Los Valles.

George Rodriges (Rodriguez), Manuel Saens, and brothers Pedro, Carpio, and Deonicio Martin—were found guilty of murder and hanged on August 3.[13]

Early July saw yet another move on American forces in the region: Captain Jesse Morin's company of Missouri volunteers was attacked at Cieneguilla, a small village on the road to Taos between Santa Fe and Embudo. The fierce action occurred a couple of hours before dawn when around two hundred New Mexicans and Pueblo Indians killed five soldiers—Lieutenant John Larkin and Privates W. Owens (or Owen), J. A. Wright, W. S. Mason, and A. S. Wilkinson—and wounded nine others. Captain Samuel Shepherd, of Lieutenant Colonel David Willock's command at Taos, pursued, but to no avail.[14] An exasperated Price warned in his letter of July 20 to the adjutant general, "Rumors of insurrections are rife, and it is said that a large force is approaching from the direction of Chihuahua [but] I am unable to determine whether these rumors are true or false."[15]

During this entire period, hostile Indians, in some instances agitated by New Mexican rebels, were raising havoc with American wagon trains, both government and civilian, approaching Santa Fe from the United States. As early as spring 1847, according to Private John Hughes of the 1st Missouri Volunteers, "Pawnees and Comanches infested the Santa Fe road [and] committed repeated depredations on the government trains, fearlessly attacked the escorts, killed and drove off great numbers of horses, mules and oxen, belonging to the government, and in several instances, overpowered, and slew, or captured many of our people."[16]

On June 22, a wagon train was attacked on the Arkansas River and eighty yoke of oxen were slaughtered in the presence of the teamsters who were too few to resist. Four days later, Lieutenant John Love, commanding officer of Company B, 1st US Dragoons, was escorting a government train carrying about $350,000 when it was attacked in the same neighborhood by about five hundred Indians, thought to be of the Osage or Pawnee tribe. The raiders frightened one hundred fifty oxen into desperation and stampeded them across the prairie. Some of Love's men gave chase, only to be ambushed when one hundred Indians attacked them. The soldiers finally escaped through the ranks of Indians, killing twenty-five and wounding around fifty. Love's detail lost eleven killed and wounded.[17] The terrifying incident prompted the young lieutenant to flaunt the army's rigid chain of command process and write directly to Adjutant General Roger Jones in Washington. In his letter, dated June 17, 1847, Love suggested to Jones, "The only way, then, sir, to insure safety to public property on this road [the Santa Fe Trail], is, in my opinion, to station about 300 mounted men at Pawnee Fork, 300 near the crossing of Arkansas, and 300 more at or near the upper Cimeron spring." He added that although the soldiers should be permanently assigned at these three places, they should "scour the country in all directions, and at least keep the Indians in check, or they cannot catch them."[18]

With the continuation of the hit-and-run tactics by the roving bands of Indians and insurgents, Price was concerned about his army's position, so remotely located in enemy territory with little hope of relief. The United States was still at war with Mexico, and, regardless of the presence of American forces in the region, many natives still maintained a fierce loyalty to their country. Price cautioned the adjutant general that it was "certain that the New Mexicans entertain deadly hatred against Americans, and that they will cut off small parties of the latter whenever they think they can escape detection."[19]

*Nine*

# Causes and Consequences

## Attempting an Interpretation

MANY WRITERS OF THE HUNDREDS OF BOOKS PUBLISHED SINCE the Mexican-American War fail to mention the unpleasantness at Taos and its aftermath. Of those who do, few make much effort to posit definitive reasons for its origin, or to attempt to identify those responsible for its occurrence, or to tackle its more complex issues, or to delve into its consequences. Content to gloss over the entire episode in two or three pages, covering the battles and recounting those people killed and wounded, they quickly move on to other aspects of the war. Since the revolt occurred far from the major conflicts in Mexico, it is often considered to have been but a mere blip on the radar screen and one that lacks merit for serious discussion.

However, the Taos affair did generate several issues that require edification and explanation. A few writers have provided a degree of insight into the revolt, and some of their findings lend credence to certain conclusions and theories. This information is explored and synthesized here in an effort to arrive at plausible answers to several quandaries that have never been fully explained, for instance: the reasons for the Taos Revolt occurring in the first place, Padre Antonio José Martínez's role in the incident, and the Polk administration's monumental error in prematurely declaring territorial status for New Mexico.

*What Caused the Taos Revolt of 1847?*

When the Mexican-American War began in 1846, the phrase Manifest Destiny had been in general use in the United States for only a year. However, its premise that the millions of white, Anglo residents in the nation had the sole right to exclusively settle the continent—unopposed by anyone and unobstructed by anything—all the way to the Pacific Ocean was already immensely popular and had been for a number of years. In the seven decades since its founding, the United States had grown into an international power, had twice defeated the British Empire in war, and progressively settled the continent from the Atlantic Ocean to the Mississippi River. The northern section of the country was an industrial power on a par with most of the much older nations in Europe, while many of the southern states nurtured a slave-based agricultural economy that flourished.

In order to continue this progress, however, obstacles standing in the way had to be dealt with. America's Indian inhabitants had to be systematically removed from their ancestral homelands to make room for white settlement. During 1838–39, in an early example of misguided federal policy that would plague tribe after tribe for the next half century and more, around eighteen thousand Cherokee Indian men, women, and children were forced by seven thousand US Army troops under the command of General Winfield Scott from their Southern Appalachian Mountain homes in Tennessee, North Carolina, and Georgia to new lands in the trans-Mississippi West.[1] The Trail of Tears was the consequence of the Indian Removal Act of 1830, orchestrated by President Andrew Jackson, to transplant several tribes of southeastern Indians out of reach of the expansion of the white population taking place east of the Mississippi. The federal government's efforts were precipitated, in part at least, by the discovery of gold in 1828 on Cherokee land in Georgia. The effects of the removal on the Cherokees were devastating: estimates vary between four thousand and eight thousand deaths[2] along the way, most caused by hunger, disease, and the elements.

Fifty years after the event, eighty-year-old John G. Burnett, who in his youth was a young army private escorting a detachment of Cherokees on their long journey west, recalled his thoughts of the horrible experience:

Murder is murder, and somebody must answer. Somebody must explain the streams of blood that flowed in the Indian country in the summer of 1838. Somebody must explain the four-thousand silent graves that mark the trail of the Cherokees to their exile. I wish I could forget it all, but the picture of six-hundred-and-forty-five wagons lumbering over the frozen ground with their cargo of suffering humanity still lingers in my memory.[3]

Despite the uproar by hundreds of thousands of sensitive Americans, north and south, who vigorously protested the Removal Act and the eventual forced expulsion of thousands of Cherokee, Chickasaw, Choctaw, Creek, and Seminole Indians from their homelands, hundreds of thousands of others looked on the legislation and its results as a necessity that had to be dealt with, and sooner, rather than later.

In a sense, the Taos Revolt was a microcosm of the Trail of Tears. The Mexican-American War provided a ready vehicle for the United States to seize a massive piece of real estate from its neighbors to the south. Because American traders had already frequented the northern reaches of Mexico for twenty-five years, the occupation of New Mexico was a natural course to follow when the war began. The takeover was performed without much difficulty. Many of the natives were already friendly because of amicable trading experiences. Somehow, in the whole scheme of things, the American government hoped to end up with New Mexico as a territory.

As the war continued, Manifest Destiny became a full-blown concept grasped by millions of Americans. In order to ensure a successful drive to the Pacific, however, many issues had to be considered, not the least of which was the assurance that a virtually unlimited expanse of land was available for national expansion and that the existing claimants to the land must be expelled from it. Acquisition of New Mexico and the bestowal of territorial status would provide a much-desired American military presence in the all-important region of the present-day Southwest while at the same time allowing for the gradual acculturation of the New Mexicans. There was only one problem with this scenario: Like the Cherokees in the previous decade, the New Mexicans and their Indian neighbors had different ideas. In Taos and the surrounding countryside, they resisted the

American invasion, much as the Cherokees refused to obey the federally imposed Removal Act.

The occupation of New Mexico (and California, which is another story) was a contentious topic back East. Party-line loyalties were evident throughout the war, with Polk's Democratic allies supporting him every step of the way while the Whig opposition bitterly criticized all aspects of the war effort, notwithstanding the fact that the two top field commanders, Generals Winfield Scott and Zachary Taylor, were fellow Whigs.

It is difficult for twentieth and twenty-first century Americans to comprehend the mind-set of first- and second-generation residents of the United States. The philosophical, moral, and religious mores of our forebears, along with their humanitarian awareness, were molded from living a precarious existence on a raw, unforgiving frontier. Their understanding (or misunderstanding), reactions, and attitudes toward neighboring cultures were crucial to their survival and could make the difference between life and death. There is no doubt that in the early years of the nation, racial prejudices ran high. For the first several decades of immigration to the United States, the newcomers were overwhelmingly northern and western Europeans with a definite bias against immigrants from other parts of the world. By the middle of the nineteenth century, even fellow southern and eastern European neighbors—those from Italy, Spain, Russia, and the Baltic states, and Jews from everywhere—were discriminated against. Always at the bottom of the ladder were blacks and American Indians.

Just as many earlier colonial Americans despised Indians and drove several tribes into extinction, so did many mid-nineteenth-century residents harbor ill feelings against many of their neighbors who displayed differences from them. As relations with Hispanics in the newfound lands of Texas and the southwest became commonplace, the prejudices extended to them, and by the time the Mexican-American War came along, many Americans' feelings toward New Mexicans were ones of superiority.

President Polk and his Democratic Party allies foresaw tremendous value in the United States acquiring the present-day American Southwest and California. There is no doubt that American imperialism was a significant factor in the decision to enter the conflict with Mexico. Considering the political smugness and vainglory of

Americans and their government during this so-called National Era, augmented by the racial attitudes of many white US citizens, it should come as no surprise that most Americans foresaw a short-lived conflict with their "inferior" neighbors to the south.

Historian George I. Sánchez, with a keen view of his land and his people as they were in the 1930s, has poignantly described the role of the New Mexican as he was in the days of the Great Depression and as his forebears faced the reality of the Mexican-American War ninety years earlier:

> Far removed from the currents of civilization, the New Mexican has been forced to live in a world of his own making—a world in which only what is is real. Compelled to identify himself with the region, he has learned to accept the rigors of time and clime with a patience that borders on fatalism. The experience of three hundred years has taught him the futility of relying on the promise of a new day. Projected reforms are meaningless and uninteresting in the light of that experience. During that period he has also learned to adapt himself to his environment and to meet, and to expect, the vicissitudes of time and tide patiently and stolidly. In those three hundred years he developed a way of life suited to the region, an economy adjusted to his basic needs.
>
> This economy, this way of life, took into consideration the region and the people as they were and as they had been through many generations. It did not provide for major changes and did not anticipate the effects of new culture contacts and conflicts. The New Mexican was prepared to survive in the New Mexico of the [Spanish] Conquest. He was not prepared to set forth along new cultural paths, under a new economy, and under a foreign [American] mode of administration.
>
> To the New Mexican, only the struggle for survival was real. New methods, new ideas, new horizons were incomprehensible because they were shockingly out of keeping with his experience of long standing. The rhythm of centuries had set a persistent tempo to New Mexican life. It was folly to expect that, by the magic stroke of a pen upon a treaty, the New Mexican should become an American citizen overnight.[4]

Arguably, the most elementary explanation for nationalistic uprisings might simply be mankind's primal instinct to resist any effort by foreigners to invade, conquer, or dominate one's home territory. A review of world history during the last millennium yields many such examples. Despite a number of Crusades mounted by European Christians between 1095 and 1291 to rescue the Holy Land from Muslims, multiple invading armies encountered steady and continuous opposition until they at last retreated to their homelands in ultimate defeat (and with Jerusalem still in the possession of the Saracens). The World War II era was full of similar examples wherein protectors of the home turf caused all manner of havoc to invaders with dreams of domination; e.g., during Nazi Germany's occupation of Austria in 1938 and of Poland the following year. The Soviet Union's takeover of Hungary in 1956, and its ill-fated occupation of Afghanistan from 1979–1989, were likewise met with savage and deadly opposition from the defenders. And the US-supported Bay of Pigs debacle in Cuba in 1961, and America's continuing Middle Eastern experiences clearly demonstrate that defense of one's own country provides all of the ingredients for major civilian unrest and political violence.

When one's homeland is invaded by a foreign military force, the event is often accompanied by another adverse effect: the objectionable and sometimes criminal conduct of the occupiers toward the native population. Tragedies demonstrating man's inhumanity to man occur in all conflicts—whether they be between individuals, groups, or nations—and they provide ample proof that warring factions bring out the worst characteristics in all parties. Although Americans would like to believe that the United States—born out of concerns for liberty, justice, humaneness, and respect for all peoples—would never permit the mistreatment of innocent civilians by its military forces, the opposite is unfortunately true.

During the Mexican-American War, the ranks of the US Army included, in addition to its regular members, large numbers of nonprofessional volunteers, most of whom lacked the rigid code of conduct and discipline associated with regular troops. The volunteer units were raised by the states following a call to action by the secretary of war to the governors. The civilians who responded included farmers, merchants, miners, laborers, the unemployed, and others, most with no prior military preparation or experience. Although the recruits received several weeks of drill and instruction before they departed for the war zone, their training provided them with minimal skills to face what lay ahead. In most cases the volunteers happily joined their state's ranks believing they were off to some gala affair that would provide them with fame, more money than they could make in civilian life, and maybe even a temporary escape from troubles at home. The carefree attitudes of many volunteers, at least those who served as troops of occupation rather than glory-gaining combat heroes, were quickly relegated to boredom.

Historian Richard Bruce Winders writes in his book *Mr. Polk's Army*, "Crimes committed against Mexicans and fellow Americans marred the record of the volunteers in the Mexican War."[5] But in defense of these volunteers, who certainly offended many New Mexicans with their drunkenness and ill behavior, it is a fact that local residents also sometimes acted in a disgraceful manner.

Even before Kearny's occupation of Santa Fe, affairs between the Americans who resided in or frequented northern New Mexico and the local citizens were sometimes less than cordial. A case in point occurred during early May 1846, when Frank Blair, Jr., who in a few months would be appointed US district attorney for New Mexico, and George Bent, the brother of the soon-to-be murdered Governor Charles Bent, were mercilessly beaten on the streets of Taos by villagers for no apparent reason other than that they were in the wrong place at the wrong time. The incident was witnessed by two brothers of Father Martínez's, yet New Mexican authorities failed to make any immediate arrests. Both Americans were confined to George Bent's house in Taos, where they slowly recuperated. Some of the attackers were finally arrested but soon escaped from jail.[6]

Many of the American soldiers stationed in northern New Mexico prior to the Taos Revolt were members of the 2nd Missouri Volunteers, commanded by Colonel Sterling Price and serving a one-year enlistment. Augmenting Price's men were a few units of General Kearny's 1st US Dragoons left behind in Santa Fe when Kearny departed for California with the rest of the regiment. Later, following the revolt and Price's defeat of the New Mexicans and Indians at Taos Pueblo and other actions, more volunteers arrived from Illinois, these to serve for the duration of the war. Other than being involved in the battles fought in northern New Mexico that focused on the Taos Revolt and its aftermath, most volunteers served as occupation troops minding the store until civil government could be implemented.

Winders places the attitudes and rationale of many volunteers in proper perspective when he writes:

> Volunteers certainly were made differently from the regulars of the Old Establishment. Reared in Jacksonian America, the former clung tightly to the privileges they had known in civilian life. The melding of democratic institutions and the army never was completed, as the "citizen" never really became transformed into the "soldier." Although volunteers were hard fighters when called to battle, their staunch defense of their "rights" made them difficult to control in camp and on the march.[7]

Referencing a few contemporary incidents that occurred in New Mexico during the war confirms not only the independence of volunteer soldiers and the difficulty sometimes encountered in controlling them, but also the mixed feelings many natives felt toward all Americans. George Ruxton, the English traveler to the American West during this period, left several interesting inferences about New Mexican-American relationships. By no means was Ruxton an admirer of New Mexicans:

> A want of honourable principle, and consummate duplicity and treachery, characterize all their dealings. Liars by nature, they are treacherous and faithless to their friends, cowardly and cringing to their enemies; cruel, as all cowards are, they unite savage ferocity with their want of animal courage; as an example of which, their recent massacre of Governor Bent and other Americans may be given—one of a hundred instances.[8]

At the same time, Ruxton admitted his admiration for certain American traits when he wrote:

Faults the Americans have—and who have not? But they are, I maintain, failings of the head and not the heart, which nowhere beats warmer, or in a more genuine spirit of kindness and affection, than in the bosom of a citizen of the United States.[9]

Yet Ruxton discovered an undercurrent of animosity toward Americans by New Mexicans even before the revolt at Taos. Writing of an incident that occurred just days prior to the uprising, he revealed that on one cold evening while sharing a meal with a New Mexican family, "The patrona [lady of the house] . . . seemed rather shy of me at first, until, in the course of conversation, she discovered that I was an Englishman. 'Gracias a Dios,' she exclaimed, 'a Christian will sleep with us to-night, and not an American!'"[10] Ruxton found that wherever he traveled in New Mexico, he sensed

> that the most bitter feeling and most determined hostility existed against the Americans, who certainly in Santa Fe and elsewhere have not been very anxious to conciliate the people, but by their bullying and overbearing demeanour towards them, have in a great measure been the cause of this hatred which shortly after broke out in an organized rising of the northern part of the province, and occasioned great loss of life to both parties.[11]

Ruxton also criticized the American soldiers' appearance and conduct when he once called them "the dirtiest, rowdiest crew I have ever seen collected together."[12] However, in defense of the volunteers, the Englishman admitted that Santa Fe was full of negative influences, particularly gambling and drinking, not compatible with the troops' well being.[13]

Other contemporaries commented on American soldiers' indulgence in liquor and the resultant mischief. Private Philip Gooch Ferguson wrote in his diary that on September 2, 1846, when three companies of volunteers left Santa Fe bound for Navajo country to enforce an earlier treaty between the tribe and Colonel Doniphan, "Nearly every man left drunk," and he described them as "a very wild and reckless set."[14]

Even following the revolt and its aftermath, attempts by army authorities to improve discipline and curtail drunkenness among

American soldiers failed, prompting Secretary of War Marcy to send a dispatch to Colonel Price in Santa Fe. Marcy wrote:

> You will, I trust, excuse an allusion to another subject not officially before me; I mean the state of discipline among our troops at Santa Fé. Though I am very far from giving credence to the newspaper accounts in relation to it, they ought not to pass entirely unnoticed, and may be permitted to prompt caution on that point.
>
> As commanding officer you cannot err, in an isolated situation like yours, in enforcing the most rigid rules of discipline. The welfare of the men composing your command, as well as its safety and the interest of your country, committed to your custody, require that the most careful attention should be given to this important matter.[15]

Headlines of an August 1847 issue of *Niles' National Register* apprised readers back East of post-revolt events when it reported, "Santa Fe, New Mexico, Aug, 13, 1847: All is hubbub and confusion here, discharged volunteers are leaving, drunk, and volunteers not discharged are remaining drunk."[16] The heavy drinking among American soldiers, both before and after the revolt, wearied their officers, and during late September 1847, the commandant of the 9th Military District with headquarters in Santa Fe prohibited the sale of liquor to any American serviceman.[17]

Another factor negatively affected the morale and well-being of the volunteer soldiers during the war. Regardless of their combat prowess, in many instances they failed to garner the respect of the regular army officers. Nor were they treated with the same sense of dignity and professionalism as members of the regular army. For example, early in the conflict, Colonel William Bowen Campbell—a former congressman who, following the conflict, was elected the last Whig governor of Tennessee—commanded the 1st Tennessee Volunteer Regiment (called the "Bloody First"), an exceptionally efficient unit that saw its share of hostilities at the Battle of Monterrey, Mexico, in September 1846. From New Orleans, fresh on his way to Matamoras, Mexico, in June 1846, an enthusiastic Campbell wrote, "My regiment is said here to be the finest looking Regt. that has passed here en route to Genl. Taylor. I hope they will give a good account of themselves on the Rio Grande."[18] By the end of 1846, however, following the Bloody First's intensive combat at Monterrey, which resulted in an alarmingly high casualty rate, Campbell had lost a great deal of enthusiasm over the status and treatment of the volunteer army. "I would willingly continue in the army had I a permanent command and of the rank I think I am entitled to, but I know Mr. Polk would not appoint me to any thing and I will not engage in the volunteer services," he wrote, acknowledging a sad, but true, understanding of the role that party politics played in the assignment of key military personnel. Praising his own regiment for possessing "fine character" and "good demeanor," Campbell admitted that it "is far behind the regular Corps, in drill and neatness and economy, etc." Ruefully he added that "it is an impossible task to drill and discipline an army of volunteers like the Regular Army."[19]

Beyond the invader-versus-invaded and soldiers-behaving-badly issues, the origin of the Taos Revolt can possibly be linked to other factors. In his book *Forgotten People*, George Sánchez described the age-old autonomy and self-determination of New Mexicans in general and Taoseños and the neighboring Taos Indians in particular, as well as their propensity to agitation and rebellion:

> The people of Taos have [always] been a restless people. Far removed from the center of government in colonial days, they have long been accustomed to the independence of the frontier. That independence and restlessness has often been manifested—in the search for lands, in conflicts with the Indians, in dealings with the authorities of government. Probably no section of the state has witnessed as many revolts, plots, and counterplots, as have been staged in Taos. Here was hatched the plan which culminated in the Pueblo Revolt of 1680, the colonists of Taos feeling the first bloody blow of that great gamble for freedom by the Pueblos. . . . In 1837, a group of Taos Indians and New Mexicans marched on Santa Fe and 'elected' José Gonzales . . . to succeed Governor Pérez, who was murdered in the revolt. In 1847, revolt was again plotted by taoseños [and] Indians . . . [seeking] to restore the province to Mexico shortly after the American Occupation.[20]

Historian Janet Lecompte has also made a case that New Mexico and New Mexicans of the mid-nineteenth century were no strangers to turmoil and rebellion. Of the 1837 Chimayo Rebellion referred to above (which in many ways resembled the Taos Revolt ten years later, except that both parties in the 1837 ordeal were New Mexicans), she wrote, "The rebels . . . had many complaints, especially regarding the neglect of Mother Mexico."[21] She quotes that a contemporary writer who identified himself only as "a former member of the government, now retired"[22] wrote in 1837, "New Mexico, abandoned since the beginning of independence [1821], appeared to have no other relation to the rest of the Republic than a common origin, language, and customs."[23] Discussing the frequent attacks by neighboring Indians, the writer revealed that the central government paid no attention to the New Mexicans' ordeals and furnished neither manpower, arms, nor ammunition to resist the raiders. "The poverty of this period was such that the few foot soldiers in service were discharged, and various respectable citizens who were convinced that the ruin of the territory was inevitable, petitioned the governor for passports to move with their families to California," he wrote.[24] Donaciano Vigil's letter of June 18, 1846, to New Mexican assembly members urging them to petition the Mexican congress for permission to import arms and ammunition with which to combat marauding Indians seems to confirm the fact that New Mexicans were treated like stepchildren by an uninterested, uncaring central government in Mexico City.[25]

Upon the arrival in Santa Fe of General Kearny's Army of the West in August 1846, Acting governor Juan Bautista Vigil y Alarid also alluded to the estranged relationship of his province with Mexico City in his speech on the plaza in response to Kearny's address:

> Do not find it strange if there has been no manifestation of joy and enthusiasm in seeing this city occupied by your military forces. To us the power of the Mexican Republic is dead. No matter what her condition, she was our mother. What child will not shed abundant tears at the tomb of his parents? I might indicate some of the causes for her misfortune, but domestic troubles should not be made public. It is sufficient to say that civil war is the cursed source of that deadly poison which has spread over one of the grandest and greatest countries that has ever been created.[26]

During Franklin Roosevelt's New Deal years, workers for the Federal Writers Project interviewed people all over the country to gather their life stories, ancestral histories, and local folklore. Luis Martínez was one of the New Mexicans interviewed, and in March 1936, he recounted the history of the Taos Revolt as passed down through his family. He dictated close to two thousand words in which he said that because of the ill manner in which the Mexican government had treated New Mexicans, a large majority of them, "especially those of Santa Fe and vicinities, accepted the order of destiny" and approved of the American occupation. Not so for the residents of Mora, Vegas, and Taos according to the writer. Taos particularly had "a population whose temper, even to this day, puts them in the category of the rough and ready, fire-eating element." All that was needed for an outbreak to occur in the three towns during late 1846 and early 1847 was "leadership," which was quickly supplied by Diego Archuleta.[27]

According to Luis Martínez, Archuleta's plan consisted of a pincer movement wherein a large Mexican army, moving from the south toward Santa Fe, would rendezvous with "the masses" in the north. Part of the northern group consisted of large numbers of Indians from Taos Pueblos, whom Archuleta allowed "to partake plentifully of liquor, which turned them into real savages." When the Indians "ran out of control" from their overindulgence of alcohol, the scene was set for "the butchery at Taos and the Rio Hondo." Martínez stated that after the war was over and the peace treaty was signed, Archuleta repeatedly maintained that "his intention was to make prisoners of war of the Americans in Taos and to furnish his forces with the necessary provisions from the stores owned by some of the Americans." When the attack on Taos came, the out-of-control Taos Indians "disobeyed all orders and the massacre ensued."[28]

Archuleta's claims that the revolt's original goal was the arrest of the Americans in Taos, as opposed to their outright murder, are supported by another early writer, E. Bennett Burton, who presented a paper about the uprising in the magazine *Old Santa Fe* in 1913. Without attribution to a source, Burton wrote that during the height of the ordeal at Governor Bent's house, as Bent was in his final death throes, a New Mexican named Buenaventura Lobato, who later admitted being a leader of the rebellion, "entered the room and seeing what they [the rebels] were doing, cried: 'I did not tell you to kill him, but only to take him prisoner!'"[29] Burton further states that Mrs. Bent and others present during the governor's murder took refuge in the home of Mrs. Juana Catalina Valdez-Lobato, but he fails to quote a source for this information, nor does he write whether the two Lobatos were related.[30] This incident is counter to what Richard Smith Elliott wrote in his column to the Saint Louis *Weekly Reveille* on February 15, 1847, in which he stated that before the Indians killed Charles Bent, they "told him they did not intend to leave an American alive in New Mexico."[31] Of course, if most of the attackers were heavily influenced by alcohol, their revised intent may have been to kill, rather than to capture, all of the Americans, counter to Lobato's orders. So did the rebellion's leaders really plan for it to be a peaceful one, only to be compromised and thrust into a full-blown massacre by inebriated participants?

Other sources introduce yet another possible motive for the rebellion. It will be recalled that at the trial of Pablo Montoya, Elliott Lee, a survivor of the Taos killings, testified that Montoya had told him that he was commander in chief of the New Mexican forces and that he was planning to retake the region from the American army. During the conversation, Montoya expressed keen interest whether a wagon train carrying "powder, and ball, and money" was expected to soon arrive from the United States. Lee told Montoya that wagons carrying $200,000 were, indeed, due from the States soon. Montoya then told Lee that he intended sending men to intercept the money, but the mission apparently failed and his force returned with only mules and horses. During the same trial, Jesus Maria Tofoya testified that he had served as interpreter for the Lee-Montoya conversation and confirmed Lee's testimony, adding that Montoya told him that he would capture the wagons and distribute the money to the Taoseños.[32] Both Lee and Tofoya swore that their conversation with Montoya occurred on January 20, the day following the violence in Taos. Did Montoya's interest in robbing the US wagon train in order to finance his troops reflect preknowledge of the money-bearing wagons and thus provide a reason for the revolt? Or did he realize that the originally planned peaceful revolt in which the Americans would be arrested and not killed had gone terribly awry, so he ordered the rebels to intercept the pay wagons as an after-the-fact decision, since the point of no return had been reached?

Historian Thomas E. Chávez suggests a factor that may also have figured in the fomentation of the Taos Revolt: "Most of the killing in the Taos area was done by Indians from the Taos Pueblo, who did not revolt out of any deep sense of loyalty to Mexico but out of a bitter feeling of revenge."[33] Chávez relates that four years before the rebellion, several Taos Indians had been conscripted by Governor Manuel Armijo to rendezvous with a New Mexican militia company to escort a large wagon train (fifty-two of the wagons were owned by Armijo) to Santa Fe. Along the Cimarron Cutoff of the Santa Fe Trail, a party of Texans attacked the New Mexicans, killing eighteen, all of them Taos Indians. Chávez continues:

> For Taos Pueblo, the defeat was a bitter loss that became the major factor in their participation in the revolt of 1847. The Taos Indians blamed the deaths of their brethren on the Texans, who were Anglo-Americans, and they apparently accepted the Mexican chauvinists' line: All Americans were in collusion with Texas, and Mexicans and Indians shared a common threat from the United States and Texas.[34]

If Chávez is correct in his assessment, then Taos Indians might have been the fomenters of the uprising or been whipped into a frenzy by New Mexicans with a similar agenda.

So, was the primary reason for the Taos Revolt the eruption of an intense hatred for the American army, which had brashly occupied the region, demanded allegiance of its leaders and citizens, and declared that the inhabitants were no longer a part of Mexico but now a territory of the United States? Did drunken and sometimes abusive American soldiers, who under different circumstances might have been considered liberating saviors, alienate the already tentative local population? Was the revolt hatched out of the New Mexicans' pessimistic view of "Mother Mexico," based on their recent inability to obtain weapons and other essentials for defense against marauding Indians? Was it assumed among the natives that despite the American army's invasion, their region would once again be left without support from Mexico City? Or, did the revolt occur because of a combination of these and other factors, all of them, no doubt, occupying prominent places in the minds of the bitter and perplexed New Mexican and Taos Indian leaders?

*What Was Padre Antonio José Martínez's Role in the Taos Revolt?*
As challenging as the quest for the origins of the Taos Revolt is the search to determine Padre Antonio José Martínez's role in the planning and organization of the rebellion (if he did have a role), his support for the uprising after it began (if he did provide support), and his true feelings toward the invading Americans. An enduring myth surrounding the revolt alleges that Martínez was the uprising's primary architect or, if he was not an organizer, at the very least he played an important role in the affair. However, a review of the most relevant documents—both official and unofficial—published during the first year following the revolt fails to validate that claim.

Within three days of Governor Charles Bent's murder on January 19, 1847, his successor, the acting governor, Donaciano Vigil, distributed a circular to "the territory and its inhabitants." In this document, Vigil proclaimed that the "popular insurrection" was led by Pablo Montoya and Manuel Cortez and promised, "To-day, or tomorrow, a respectable body of troops will commence their march, for the purpose of quelling the disorders of Pablo Montoya, in Taos."[35]

On January 25, Vigil released a second circular, in which he told readers, "The gang of Pablo Montoya and Cortez, in Taos, infatuated, in consequence of having sacrificed to their caprice his excellency, the governor, and other peaceable citizens, and commenced their great work of plunder" had been routed by "government" (i.e., American) forces at La Cañada and that many had been killed and taken prisoner.[36]

In a third circular, dated February 12, and written more than a week after Colonel Price had defeated the main body of insurgents at Taos Pueblo, Vigil related that a few Indians in Taos had identified

Diego Archuleta as "the individual who, before flying from the country, aided by the so-called Generals Pablo Montoya, Manuel Cortés [Cortez], Jesus Tafoya, and Pablo Chávez, instigated them [the Indians] to the insurrection and proceedings which they carried into execution." Vigil further stated that the individuals listed in the circular were, "so far as now known, the chiefs of this band of murderers and thieves."[37]

On February 15, a broadside circular published by the Government Printing Office in Santa Fe recounted Price's reprisal on the instigators, although it does not reveal the names of the revolt's organizers.[38] Also on February 15, Colonel Price sent the adjutant general in Washington, DC, a detailed accounting of the recent military action in Taos and the surrounding region. In the letter, Price states, "The principal leaders in this insurrection were [Jesus] Tafoya, Pablo Chavis [Chávez], Pablo Montoya, [Manuel] Cortez, and Tomas [Romero], a Pueblo Indian. Of these, Tafoya was killed at Cañada; Chavis [Chávez] was killed at [Taos] Pueblo; Montoya was hanged at Don Fernando [Taos] on the 7th instant, and Tomas was shot by a private while in the guardroom at the latter town. Cortez is still at large."[39]

The following day, Vigil wrote to Secretary of State James Buchanan but didn't name names and listed only four principals, revealing that "two were slain in battle [Chávez and Tafoya]; one was taken and hanged under sentence of a court-martial [Montoya]; one survives, and has not yet been taken [Cortez]." Vigil was apparently unaware that Tomas had already been shot and killed while a prisoner.[40]

Rounding out the year 1847, a series of newspaper articles[41] and three full-length books were published, all of them carrying accounts of the Taos Revolt.

*The Conquest of California and New Mexico* was written by James M. Cutts, who although not an eyewitness to the events he described nevertheless made extensive use of a vast array of government documentation available to him as a high-ranking official at the Treasury Department in Washington. In the book, Cutts makes no personal observation about whom the uprising's ringleaders might have been. *Doniphan's Expedition; Containing an Account of the Conquest of New Mexico*, was the product of John T. Hughes, a member of Colonel Doniphan's 1st Regiment of Missouri Volunteers.

Hughes lists "Generals [Tomás] Ortiz, Lafoya [Jesus Tafoya], [Pablo] Chávez, and [Pablo] Montoya" as the primary culprits.[42] *Adventures in Mexico and the Rocky Mountains* was published in London by George F. Ruxton (the New York edition was issued the following year), who had left Taos only days before the rebellion occurred. Ruxton, who received the news of the incident at Pueblo Fort (present-day Pueblo, Colorado) mentioned the Taos incident briefly but left a detailed accounting of the murders of Harwood and Markhead, as well as the siege at Turley's Mill. He did not identify the attackers other than as "New Mexicans and Pueblo Indians."[43]

Also published in 1847 was the book *A Campaign in New Mexico*, by Frank S. Edwards, also a member of the 1st Regiment of Missouri Volunteers. Containing only a couple of passing comments about the Taos uprising and listing no names of conspirators, its only interest is a recounting of Edwards's spurious theory that he did not "consider that the murder of Governor Bent was caused by the insurrection at Taos, but rather that this occurrence was used as a cloak to cover what was, undoubtedly, an act of private malice, instigated by his wife."[44] Newspaper correspondent Richard Smith Elliott filed his reports to the Saint Louis *Weekly Reveille* beginning in September 1846, and continued until summer 1847. His dispatch covering the revolt reported that Padre Martínez sheltered Elliott Lee, the sheriff's brother, as well as a number of other victims who fled to his house for protection against the revolutionaries.[45]

In summary, seven men are mentioned in the above documentation as organizers of the Taos uprising: Diego Archuleta, Tomás Ortiz, Jesus Tafoya, Pablo Chávez, Pablo Montoya, Manuel Cortez, and Tomas Romero. In none of the accounts reviewed here—the majority of them published within a year of the uprising and originating from the pens of five Americans, one New Mexican, and one Englishman, each of whom was in a position to know—is Padre Martínez mentioned as a principal of the Taos Revolt.

In 1857, W. H. H. Davis, who was interim governor of New Mexico Territory for a brief time during 1856–57, published *El Gringo: New Mexico and Her People*, in which he accused (with no authority cited) Padre Martínez of explicit involvement in the Taos Revolt:

A large body of the rebels, composed mainly of Pueblo Indians, and incited to the act by Priest Martínez and others, attacked his [Governor Bent's] residence, and murdered him and several others in cold blood.[46]

During the 1880s, three additional books were published with references to the uprising, but none sheds light on either the origins of the revolt or of Padre Martínez's role (if any) in the incident.[47] But another book, dictated by the famed mulatto mountain man James P. Beckwourth and published a decade after the revolt, tells a different story. Beckwourth claims he had just arrived in Santa Fe when Colonel Price received news of the revolt from an Indian runner from a village between Santa Fe and Taos. The Indian recounted the story of the outbreak and further told his listeners that Santa Fe was to be attacked in a similar fashion, "of which . . . full information could be obtained by the arrest of a Mexican who was then conveying a letter from the priest in Taos [Martínez?] to the priest in Santa Fé."[48] Unfortunately, the runner eluded capture and escaped. Price then commenced assembling his force for the march on Taos.

Sixty-one years after the revolt, Father W. J. Howlett of Colorado, in his 1908 biography of Joseph Projectus Machebeuf, the bishop of Denver, reintroduced the long-deceased Martínez into the literature of the rebellion. Howlett wrote:

> It was said that he [Martínez] had much to do with the uprising of the Indians and [New] Mexicans at Taos when Governor Bent and about fifteen Americans and their [New] Mexican sympathizers were massacred on January 19, 1847. He at least shared with the Indians and [New] Mexicans in hatred for the Americans and in their ignorance of events and conditions outside of their little valley. They imagined that they were but beginning a patriotic war which would result in freeing their country from the foreigner, who was supposed to be an enemy to their race and to their religion. The suspicion is probably well founded, although the U.S. Government did not find Father Martínez guilty of direct complicity in the unfortunate insurrection.[49]

Thomas J. Steele writes that Howlett commissioned Father Gabriel Ussel—a French padre who served as pastor at Taos for seventeen years beginning in early 1859 and who, no doubt, rubbed elbows with many of the participants in the rebellion—to write a "memoir" of the incident. Howlett then used Ussel's memoir for his own Machebeuf biography. Later, Willa Cather was influenced by Howlett's book for her novel *Death Comes for the Archbishop*.[50]

Although Ralph Emerson Twitchell, an early twentieth century New Mexico historian and writer, does not mention Howlett in his own 1909 book about the American occupation of New Mexico, it seems highly likely that he would have had access to Howlett's volume. Twitchell wrote, with little or no accreditation:

> The home of Fr. Antonio Jose Martínez was generally regarded as the headquarters for the insurrectionists prior to the uprising and until after the assassination of Governor Bent. His [Martínez's] power over his parishioners was absolute and his hatred of Americans and American institutions was recognized by all. This fact was regarded by such men as Governor Bent, Colonel Saint Vrain and Col. Kit Carson as ample proof of his complicity in the revolution. His brother, Captain Pascual Martínez, had been in command of a company of soldiers under Governor Armijo, prior to the coming of General Kearny, and there are persons still living who are authority for the statement that he [Pascual Martínez] actively participated in the uprising at the instigation of his brother, the priest.

Elsewhere in his book, Twitchell continues his accusations of Martínez's involvement with the rebels, writing that, "Fr. Antonio Jose Martínez . . . was regarded by many as one of the chief authors of the revolution" and that,

> No one, except those who were actually engaged as principals in the insurrection, knew positively just what part Fr. Martínez took in the uprising. He was a very crafty man and the American authorities never could affirmatively fix upon him any active participation, although in later years there were many native citizens, who had been identified with the movement, who did not hesitate to declare that they had been guided by his counsel and advice.[51]

Even more damning to the padre than the unattributed words of Howlett and Twitchell were those written in the early twentieth century by the woman who has been heralded as one of the premier American novelists of all time. In 1922, Willa Cather, a Virginia-born, Nebraska-raised writer, was awarded the Pulitzer Prize in fiction for her book *One of Ours*, set during the Great War in Europe. The prestigious award solidified the not-yet-fifty-year-old Cather's permanent place among American novelists. Five years after receiving the Pulitzer, Cather published another novel, *Death Comes for the Archbishop*. Set in New Mexico, it depicts the checkered and contentious relationship between Padre Antonio José Martínez and his younger, newly arrived superior, Bishop Jean Marie Latour, a French churchman based on the life of the real Archbishop Juan Bautista Lamy, the builder of Saint Francis Cathedral in downtown Santa Fe. In her novel, Cather clearly takes the side of the Frenchman over that of the New Mexican and in so doing paints an overwhelmingly negative and unfounded portrait of Martínez.

Cather spent considerable time in New Mexico researching her book and even interviewed such local literati as Mabel Dodge Luhan and Mary Austin.[52] Although Cather clearly wrote her tome as fiction, she used Martínez's correct name throughout, while giving fictitious names to many of the other characters, including the book's protagonist, Latour. Cather's contentious characterizations of the Taos priest besmirched his reputation in 1927, and they continue to do so today. The book has never been out of print, and as late as 2005, *Time* magazine named it one of the best English-language novels since 1923.[53]

Although no evidence existed at the time her book was published that Martínez was unequivocally linked to the organization of the Taos Revolt, Cather's scathing, fictional depiction of an actual historical individual and his connection with a real historical incident quickly passed into the realm of reality for many readers. Here is a short excerpt:

> It was common talk that Padre Martínez had instigated the revolt of the Taos Indians . . . when Bent, the American Governor, and a dozen other white men were murdered and scalped. Seven of the Taos Indians had been tried before a military court and hanged for

the murder, but no attempt had been made to call the plotting priest to account. Indeed, Padre Martínez had managed to profit considerably by the affair.

The Indians who were sentenced to death had sent for their Padre and begged him to get them out of the trouble he had got them into. Martínez promised to save their lives if they would deed him their lands, near the pueblo. This they did, and after the conveyance was properly executed the Padre troubled himself no more about the matter, but went to pay a visit at his native town of Abiquiu. In his absence the seven Indians were hanged on the appointed day. Martínez now cultivated their fertile farms, which made him quite the richest man in the parish.[54]

Even Cather's physical descriptions of Martínez—he was a "dark" priest; he possessed a "swarthy" body; his teeth were "long, yellow" and "too large—distinctly vulgar," were controversial and unfounded.[55] She wrote, "His mouth was the very assertion of violent, uncurbed passions and tyrannical self-will; the full lips thrust out and taut, like the flesh of animals distended by fear or desire."[56]

The late University of New Mexico English professor Patricia Clark Smith has written:

> Since 1927, many people in the United States and abroad have derived their ideas about the Southwest and its native cultures largely from her [Cather] enduringly popular novel, and few people outside the Southwest know anything at all about Padre Martínez and the "American" conquest of New Mexico except by way of Cather. What Cather knew, how she knew it, what use she chose to make of that knowledge, and why she chose to use it as she did . . . are important matters.[57]

Although Cather had written the final chapters of *Death Comes for the Archbishop* in Mary Austin's Santa Fe home, Austin's pointed criticism of Cather's depiction of Southwestern culture and characters came across clearly when she wrote,

> Cather had given her allegiance to the French blood of the Archbishop; she had sympathized with his desire to build a French

cathedral [Saint Francis] in a Spanish town. It was a calamity to the local culture. We have never gotten over it.[58]

The release of Cather's book in 1927 coincided with the overwhelming success of a touring service operated out of Santa Fe called the Indian Detours. It was the brainchild of R. Hunter Clarkson, an employee of Fred Harvey's, the noted hotelier and restaurateur whose facilities followed the Santa Fe Railroad throughout much of the Southwest. Harvey eagerly embraced Clarkson's dreams of implementing a transportation company that would offer guided, chauffeured trips across New Mexico in luxurious Harveycars and specially designed tour coaches accommodating as many as twenty-six passengers. Announced during the 1925 tourist season, the Indian Detours was a joint venture of the Fred Harvey Company and the Santa Fe Railroad and offered the first tours beginning in 1926.[59]

The Indian Detours operated for several years until, like much of the rest of the leisure industry in the United States, its economic success was compromised by the rapidly approaching Depression. During the mid- to late-1920s, though, at the height of its popularity, it introduced thousands of individual tourists and scores of chartered tour groups to the grandeur and magnificence of New Mexico. One of the most popular destinations was Taos, and the rich heritage of the town and the nearby pueblo fascinated eager visitors, who listened intently as tour guides reeled off tales from the past. *Death Comes for the Archbishop* was enjoying a tremendous popularity at the time, and it seems reasonable to assume that tour guides referenced the book frequently. Who knows how many wide-eyed visitors received their first impression of Martínez from the tour guides' interpretation of the fiction spun by Cather?

Searching further, one finds a few additional inferences that shed some light on the possible involvement, or lack thereof, of Martínez in the Taos Revolt. Captain Henry Smith Turner, adjutant to General Kearny's Army of the West, wrote in his journal on August 24, 1846, just days following the army's occupation of Santa Fe:

> A deputation of Indian Pueblos, conducted by their curé [Martínez?] have an interview with the General. The curé appeared much agitated—it having been reported [that] he encouraged resistance to the U.S. troops on hearing of their approach.[60]

Elsewhere in his journal, Turner describes Kearny's attendance with his staff at mass in the local church. He displays displeasure with the officiating vicar, whom the captain calls "a large, fat looking man," who in reality was Father Juan Felipe Ortiz, an older half-brother of Tomás Ortiz's, one of the Taos Revolt's ringleaders. Of the priesthood in general, he complains that "it seems a desecration of the temple of God, that such men should be permitted to officiate as priests." Yet in the same journal entry, Turner admits that the priests "may not be so abandoned as they are said to be—the reports we receive are from ignorant Americans generally, with whom want of veracity and violent prejudice are the conspicuous traits of character." He then laments, "A truthful American is rarely seen here."[61]

Several writers have opined that Martínez lent the printing press that he had owned and operated in Taos since the mid-1830s to General Kearny for the printing of *Laws of the Territory of New Mexico* and that the gesture reflected the padre's nonhostile attitude toward the American occupation. However, differences of opinion exist about the ownership of the press. John Hughes, the volunteer with Colonel Doniphan (the compiler of the *Laws*), wrote that the press was located "in the capital," presumably meaning that the machinery was in place when the army arrived. According to Hughes, it was used for "printing public laws, notices, advertisements, proclamations, manifestos, pronunciamentos and other high-sounding Mexican documents, in the form of pamphlets and handbills."[62] This could have been the same press brought to New Mexico from Missouri over the Santa Fe Trail by Josiah Gregg in 1834.[63] Another authority, however, suggests that the Santa Fe press had been brought to the city from Mexico in 1834 by Ramón Abréu.[64] This version of the press's original ownership also relates that Padre Martínez purchased it in 1835 and removed it to his hometown of Taos.[65] Supposedly, eleven years later, when Kearny offered to buy the press for US government use, the padre returned it to Santa Fe as a loan to the army, then brought it back to Taos after Kearny had printed *Laws*.[66] Regardless of the press's convoluted history, one fact is certain: an American employee of Governor Bent's, Oliver Perry Hovey, was hired on October 7, 1846, to print and deliver five hundred copies of *Laws* at a cost of

$1,705. Hovey reportedly received $150 as a first payment. After Bent was assassinated, Hovey waited twelve more years to receive the balance due.[67]

*The Question of Territorial Status for Occupied New Mexico and Its Impact on the Taos Treason Trials.*
The *American Heritage Dictionary of the English Language* defines *treason* as a "violation of allegiance toward one's own sovereign or country: especially the betrayal of one's own country by waging war against it or by consciously and purposely acting to aid its enemies." The same dictionary defines *traitor* as one "who betrays his country" or "one who has committed treason."

Considering these two definitions, it becomes clear that individuals in America's past such as Benedict Arnold, James Wilkinson, and Aaron Burr were, indeed, traitors guilty of planning and perpetrating treasonous acts that aided the nation's enemies (Arnold) or other countries with different agendas than those of the United States (Wilkinson and Burr). What is by no means clear is why any New Mexicans or Taos Indians who participated in the Taos Revolt were tried for treason. Murder, yes—but treason?

The hasty American declaration of territorial status for New Mexico upon the occupying Army of the West's arrival in Santa Fe in August 1846, an action lacking approval by Congress, caused President Polk a great deal of consternation and initiated some rapid backpedaling from his administration. Despite the fact that the issue received a fair amount of press at the time, especially in Whig newspapers and journals, its relevance was overshadowed by the frenzy of America's war mentality and, over the years, has become largely lost in the haze of history.

Polk served fourteen years in the US House representing Tennessee, from March 4, 1825, to March 4, 1839. He was speaker of the House during his last two terms, from December 7, 1835, to March 4, 1839 (during the 24th and 25th Congresses). Considering his experience as a multiterm congressman and speaker prior to becoming president, Polk surely would have been familiar with the strict requirements for the admission of new territories and states to the Union. In fact, during his tenure as speaker, he oversaw two new approvals of territorial status—Wisconsin Territory on April 20, 1836, and Iowa Territory on June 12, 1838—as well as the admission of two new states—Arkansas on June 15, 1836, and Michigan on January 26, 1837.

The involvement of Congress with the creation of territories reaches back to the very foundation of the United States, predating by two months the enactment of the US Constitution. The Northwest Ordinance, approved by Congress on July 13, 1787, established the "Territory of the United States northwest of the River Ohio" (the Northwest Territory) and legislated, by precedent, rules and regulations for future territorial creation, including the appointment of governors, secretaries, and general officers of the militia.[68] When the Constitution was ratified and made effective in June 1788, it declared additionally, "The Congress shall have Power to dispose of and make all needful Rules and Regulations respecting the Territory . . . belonging to the United States."[69]

On the other hand, Colonel (later General) Stephen Watts Kearny was a strict military man who, no doubt, possessed limited knowledge about the legal requirements for recognizing and admitting new territories into the Union. At the beginning of the war, Secretary of War William Marcy directed him to march to New Mexico and California and to "establish temporary civil government therein" and

> assure the people of those provinces that it is the wish and design of the United States to provide for them a free government, with the least possible delay, similar to that which exists in our Territories. They will then be called on to exercise the right of freemen in electing their own representatives to the territorial legislature.[70]

No doubt Kearny, with the clear backing of the president and the secretary of war, assumed he had the authority to perform the duties assigned to him. He therefore accepted his orders as gospel and pursued them with little thought that they might be illegal.

Kearny's various speeches and proclamations made to the New Mexican people during the process of occupying Santa Fe in August 1846 are laden with references leaving no doubt that the American army intended to permanently acquire the entire region for the United

States. "It is the wish and intention of the United States to provide for New Mexico a free government, with the least possible delay, similar to those in the United States; and the people of New Mexico will then be called on to exercise the rights of freemen in electing their own representatives to the Territorial legislature," he declared, echoing the words of Marcy's earlier dispatch to him. Then in words that could hardly be misunderstood, he said, "The United States hereby absolves all persons residing within the boundaries of New Mexico from any further allegiance to the republic of Mexico, and hereby claims them as citizens of the United States."[71] Two days later, Kearny sent the adjutant general a copy of the proclamation, summarizing that it claimed "the whole of New Mexico, with its then boundaries, as a territory of the United States of America, and taking it under our protection."[72]

By late September or early October, Polk had received Kearny's reports of his actions in New Mexico. One wonders what the president thought when he read the news of Kearny's absolution of Mexican citizenship for New Mexicans and his declaration bestowing American citizenship on them in its place. It should have come as no surprise, since Kearny carried out his orders exactly as issued. Polk apparently understood the circumstances and the impact of what he read, because on October 2 he wrote to his brother:

> Despatches have been received from Genl Kearney to day, that on the 18th of August he took possession of Santa Fe without firing a gun, had hoisted the flag of the U. States, and proclaimed the province of New Mexico of which Santa Fe is the capital to be a part of the U. States. . . . So that you see that although there may not have been much fighting we will soon be in undisputed possession of valuable provinces, and will hold them until a just and honorable peace is concluded.[73]

Some of the headaches that this issue caused Polk and his cabinet were recounted in chapter 5. And, although Polk denied in his congressional report of late 1846 that any harm appeared to have been done by Kearny's misunderstanding of his orders (or Washington's misuse of authority), that innocence did not last. During the Taos trials of April 1847, one rebel was hanged for treason, either out of ignorance on the part of US Army and trial court officials or in direct violation of Secretary Marcy's rebuke of January 11, 1847, to General Kearny, a copy of which was sent to "the commanding officer in Santa Fe," that is, Colonel Price.[74] Of course, by the time Price received his copy of the dispatch, he was well on his way to prosecute the attack on Taos Pueblo and subdue the rebellion. Marcy reiterated the same information to Price in a dispatch dated June 26, 1847, but by then the revolt was essentially over, and the sentences imposed on the revolutionaries had been carried out.[75]

Of all the American writers who attempted to explain the Taos Revolt and its resulting embarrassment to the Polk administration, L. Bradford Prince perhaps best understood the complexity of the political scene in New Mexico, as well as the treason issue, when he wrote that Americans should

> remember in judging of the acts of those days, that the people were [New] Mexicans, and their territory a part of the Republic of Mexico, which had been invaded by an American army and was being held by force of arms; and that so long as the war continue[d] it was simply an act of patriotism, from their point of view, to drive from their soil these invaders of the country, or to destroy them from the face of the earth. What afterwards, when they had accepted American citizenship, would have been treason and rebellion, at that time, while war was raging between the two countries, was for them, as Mexican citizens held under foreign military control, a natural manifestation of love of country. . . . A Mexican citizen could not commit treason against the United States; and this should be carefully borne in mind, in reading and judging of the events connected with the American occupation and the revolt of 1847; and it is also to be noted that those who were most patriotic [New] Mexicans . . . have been among the most valuable and loyal American citizens in civil affairs, in Indian wars, and the war of the Rebellion, since the treaty of peace transferred their allegiance.[76]

For whatever reason or reasons—be it a misinterpretation of President Polk's orders to Kearny and other commanders or a serious flaw in Polk's orders from the very beginning—mistakes were made that had dire and everlasting effects on residents of New Mexico, both Hispanos and Taos Indians.

# EPILOGUE

SUMMER AND FALL 1847 WITNESSED SEVERAL THOUSAND NEWLY volunteered soldiers either being mustered into their units at Fort Leavenworth or, having dispensed with that task, traveling along the Santa Fe Trail, bound for New Mexico.[1] They were members of the 3rd Regiment of Missouri Mounted Volunteers, commanded by Colonel John Ralls,[2] and the 1st Regiment of Illinois Volunteers, commanded by Colonel Edward W. B. Newby.[3] The two regiments were to relieve the soldiers in New Mexico whose enlistments had either expired or were about to expire.

New Mexico's first newspaper, the *Santa Fe Republican*, was established at about the same time by two privates of the 1st Missouri Volunteers, Oliver Perry Hovey and Edward T. Davis. It was launched on September 10, 1847, and the editors promised to "make it a News Paper in which every thing of interest to the public will be noticed, for the public good and not for private or party purposes."[4] As of the date of the first issue, the newspaper reported that the American military presence in New Mexico stood at a total force of thirty-three hundred men and consisted of three companies (three hundred men) of the regular dragoons, four companies of revolunteered Missourians (four hundred men), and the rest divided between mounted and infantry companies of the Missouri and Illinois volunteers.[5]

By late summer 1847, signs of unrest began to reappear among the residents of Taos. The *Republican* reported that Judge Charles Beaubien had raised concerns that roving bands of Jicarilla Apaches and "disaffected [New] Mexicans" had caused frightened villagers to be fearful of "depredations" and the theft of their cattle. The Taoseños had requested military assistance, and according to the newspaper, "we hear that several companies will go."6 However, dissatisfied New Mexicans and Indians were not the only issues that the military command at Santa Fe was worried about. The town was bulging with American servicemen, a few regulars, but mostly volunteers from Missouri and Illinois. On September 24, Colonel Newby, who in the temporary absence of Colonel Price was serving as commandant of the 9th Military Department with headquarters in the capital city, issued his Order No. 10. Newby complained that despite "repeated and strenuous efforts" of commanders, "a woeful want of sobriety, good order and subordination yet prevails at this post." If not corrected immediately, Newby feared that "fatal disease and lasting disgrace" could play havoc with his command. The colonel ordered that only with the permission of a regimental or battalion commander could any person sell or furnish any US soldier with "intoxicating drinks of any description." Furthermore, "Fandango, Ball or Dance" would not be permitted without proper permission and the payment of five dollars, to be used to benefit disabled and ill soldiers.7

During late summer and early fall, plans were also being laid in Santa Fe to organize some form of civil government for New Mexico to take the reins once the war was over and the official military occupation ended. According to *Laws of the Territory of New Mexico*, promulgated by General Kearny in October 1846, elections for a US congressional delegate and members of the territorial general assembly were to be held on August 2, 1847. The duly elected delegates to the assembly would meet in Santa Fe the following December 6 and on the first Monday in December every two years hence. The assembly would consist of two chambers, a legislative council and a house of representatives. House members were to be elected every two years and council members every four years. Members of both chambers would elect their own speakers. The division of New Mexico into counties would be the responsibility of the general assembly, but until its members directed otherwise, the county structure as it existed under a Mexican decree issued June 17, 1844, would remain in force, consisting of Santa Fe, San Miguel del Bado, Rio Arriba, Valencia, Taos, Santa Ana, and Bernalillo Counties.[8]

When the called assembly met in December, the house of representatives elected as its speaker William Z. Angney, the former commander of the Missouri volunteer infantry battalion. The legislative council elected Antonio Sandoval as its speaker, or president, as he was called. Governor Donaciano Vigil spoke to the assembly and reviewed the state of affairs in New Mexico, challenging the legislators to provide for the needs of all the people with particular emphasis on education. Pointing out that only one public school existed in the entire territory, he asked, "The world at large is advancing and how can we profit by the advance unless the people are educated?"[9]

This first assembly also called for a convention to be held in Santa Fe in October 1848 to discuss the issues involved in becoming a full-fledged territory of the United States. General Winfield Scott and his army had captured Mexico City on September 14, 1847, and on February 2, 1848, the Treaty of Guadalupe Hidalgo was signed between the United States and Mexico and soon ratified by both countries, thus officially ending the Mexican-American War. The meeting called for by the general assembly occurred October 10, 1848, and its members elected Reverend Antonio José Martínez president.[10] The upshot of the gathering was to petition Congress to grant New Mexico territorial status with all of the protections that went with it, to deny the introduction of slavery into the territory, and to allow New Mexico one delegate in Congress.[11]

Congress failed to act on the 1848 petition, so beginning September 24, 1849, a second convention, again with Martínez serving as president, met in Santa Fe with the mission of once again petitioning Congress for territorial status. Members elected Hugh N. Smith, a citizen of Santa Fe, as their delegate to Congress and enclosed with their entreaty a constitution to be presented to Congress for approval. In the event the granting of a territorial government was not feasible, Smith was given authority to accept a state government.[12]

On February 27, 1850, before Smith arrived in the nation's capital, one Enrique Sanchez and "other citizens and residents of the territory and valley of the Rio Grande" appealed to Congress that "all of the country east of the Rio Grande and south of the line of New Mexico, distinct from the former province of Texas, be erected into a territorial government, and that it be called the 'Territory of the Rio Grande.'" Signed by fifty-eight residents of the valley, it, too, was doomed to failure.[13]

During spring 1850, the Elections Committee of the US House received New Mexico's 1849 request for the seating of Hugh Smith as a delegate and the region's admittance to the Union as a territory. On April 4, after deliberation, the request was sent to the full House with the recommendation that "it is inexpedient to admit Hugh N. Smith, esq., to a seat in this House as a delegate from New Mexico," based on the fact that New Mexico was not yet a territory and that it was impossible to admit anyone representing a region that is "unknown to the laws of the United States." New Mexico was "as much unknown to our laws as is the Great Salt Lake valley, or the territory west of Minnesota," the report declared. "There is now no such Territory, no such government as New Mexico having a legal being." Smith returned to Santa Fe empty-handed.[14]

Back in New Mexico, on May 25, yet another convention met in Santa Fe with the mission of framing a state constitution and calling for it to be approved or disapproved by the voters the following June 20. A governor, lieutenant governor, delegate to Congress, and members of the state legislature would also be elected at the same time, with all elected officials to convene in Santa Fe on July 1.[15] When the polls closed on June 20, the vote on the new constitution was 8,371 for versus 39 against. Henry Connelly, a Santa Fe physician and businessman who later served as New Mexico Territory's governor during the Civil War, was elected governor, and Manuel Alvárez, the former American consul in Santa Fe, won the lieutenant governor's seat.[16]

During the first meeting of this first "state" legislature that began on July 1, 1850, Richard H. Weightman, the former commander of a Saint Louis company of artillery in the Missouri Volunteers, was selected to represent New Mexico in the US Senate, and W. S. Masservy, who later served as New Mexico Territory's secretary, was chosen to take a seat in the House. The two men traveled to Washington, DC, to plead their cases before Congress for New

Mexico statehood and their own appointments as senator and representative.[17] Weightman arrived in the capital during the fall and was joined by Masservy sometime later. Weightman delivered copies of the constitution and other relevant documents to President Millard Fillmore, and the president presented them to Congress on September 9.[18]

Likely unknown to Weightman or to the average New Mexican resident, Congress had been wrestling since the first of the year with one of the most controversial pieces of legislation ever heard before that body, the Compromise of 1850. Introduced by Henry Clay on January 29, 1850, the proposed legislation was so complex and fraught with such hotly debated issues as the organization of new territories, the exclusion of slavery in such new territories, and the prohibition of slavery in the District of Columbia that it required being broken down into several parts. The resolution that interested New Mexicans was the Texas and New Mexico Act, which would clarify once and for all the issue of the contested land east of the Rio Grande claimed by Texas (for which the state of Texas would be paid $10 million by the federal government for the relinquished property). As part of the package, the Territory of New Mexico would be officially organized and accepted into the Union. The act was approved September 9, 1850 (the same day Fillmore delivered Weightman's documents to Congress) to become effective March 3, 1851.[19]

The passage of the Compromise of 1850 effectively ended the push for state government (versus territorial government) for New Mexico. James S. Calhoun, the former Indian agent at Santa Fe, was nominated to be territorial governor by Fillmore on December 23, 1850, and was confirmed January 7, 1851.[20] Secretary of State Daniel Webster advised Calhoun of his appointment on January 9,[21] and he officially took office March 3.[22]

The years between the American occupation of New Mexico and the granting of full territorial status to the region were burdened not just by political affairs and the push for official territorial or state recognition. Although New Mexicans had shown minimal interest in continuing the rebellion and had posed little additional resistance since late 1847, several of the regional Indian tribes continued their harassment of local farmers and herdsmen by regularly raiding Hispano villages, as well as army facilities. Several US Army posts were established across northern New Mexico during the period, including the post of Taos in October 1847; the post at Vegas in February 1848; the post of Abiquiu in April 1849; and the post at Rayado in May 1850.[23]

By summer 1849, Calhoun had arrived in Santa Fe to take over the office of Indian agent for New Mexico. He had served as a captain in a Georgia volunteer regiment during the late war and was appointed to his post by President Zachary Taylor.[24] He wasted no time getting to work, and on September 9, he; Colonel J. M. Washington, who had succeeded Donaciano Vigil as civil governor; head chief Mariana Martínez; and other Navajo leaders signed a treaty at Canyon de Chelly between the US government and the Navajo tribe. In the treaty, the Navajos acknowledged the jurisdiction of the US government, pledged to cease hostilities, promised to surrender all American and New Mexican captives and all stolen property, guaranteed US citizens free and safe passage through Navajo territory, and promised to allow the construction of US military posts and trading houses on Navajo land. The US government promised to arrest, prosecute, and punish any person subject to the laws of the United States who killed, robbed, or abused any member of the Navajo tribe. In consideration of the Navajos' promise to abide by the treaty, the United States promised to "grant to said Indians such donations, presents, and implements and adopt such other liberal and humane measures as said Government may deem meet and proper."[25] The treaty was short-lived. By the following June, Navajos were reported to be raiding pueblos on the west side of the Rio Grande, causing their residents to live "in a constant state of excitement."[26] On July 15, Calhoun reported to Commissioner of Indian Affairs Orlando Brown that "Navajos have driven off Stock in large numbers, west of the Rio del Norte, and seized a few captives."[27]

In October 1849, a particularly troubling incident occurred near Point of Rocks, located on the Cimarron Route of the Santa Fe Trail in present-day Colfax County. As a Santa Fe merchant named James M. White and his entourage, which included his wife and small daughter, were on their way home from Missouri, their wagon train was attacked by Jicarilla Apaches. All were killed except Mrs. White, a black servant, and the little girl, all of whom were taken captive.[28] News eventually reached military authorities that a large band of Jicarilla Apaches had frequented the area in which the massacre had occurred, and a contingent of US soldiers led by Kit Carson came upon the place in late November. Despite Carson's advice to attack the Apaches immediately, the troops' commander, Major William N. Grier, delayed. When the charge was ultimately issued against the Jicarilla band, its members killed Mrs. White and fled, leaving her mutilated body behind.[29] Neither pitiful entreaties by the uncle of the White daughter to Secretary of the Interior A. H. H. Stuart,[30] nor any other move made by authorities could persuade the Apaches to release her or the servant. Neither was ever heard from again.[31]

If the residents of northern New Mexico—Hispano and Pueblo—believed that the official bestowal of US territorial status on their homeland in early 1851 would immediately alleviate their years of struggle and strife with either the temporary military government or the incursions of the various marauding Indian tribes, they were sorely mistaken. Within three weeks of assuming office, Governor Calhoun advised Luke Lea, the commissioner of Indian affairs in Washington, that the Navajos and Jicarilla Apaches continued to make numerous depredations upon New Mexicans and Pueblo Indians. "The people of this Territory are without the means of self protection, the Territorial Treasury is a blank, and the protection of persons and property depend solely upon the action of the Government of the United States," Calhoun wrote.[32]

With his letter, Calhoun also enclosed for the commissioner's review a proclamation that he had issued a few days prior, calling for "all able-bodied male citizens of the Territory, capable of bearing arms, [to form a] Volunteer Corps to protect their families, property and homes." He told his readers that such volunteers would be allowed to dispose of any captured property from the hostile tribes according to law, but also warned them not to use their positions "as a pretext for any depredations upon or invasion of the property of the peaceable citizens of N. Mexico."[33] At least one New Mexican volunteer took Calhoun up on his call for troops. Before the ink was dry on the governor's proclamation, Manuel Chaves issued a statement of his own at Santa Fe, declaring that he proposed to raise six hundred men, divided into six companies, to "pursue the Navajo Nation to their extinction or complete surrender." He asked the US government to furnish him with one hundred mules, to be returned at the end of the campaign, and six hundred rifles with sufficient ammunition, the rifles also to be returned after the hostilities. Chaves stated that his men would expect no monetary compensation for their efforts, but he requested that they have the right to dispose of all prisoners, livestock, and other property they might capture. While the volunteers would not report to the US Army or be commanded by its officers, they would "always be ready to obey the orders of the Civil Government of the Territory of New Mexico."[34] A search of Calhoun's papers fails to reveal that Chaves's offer was ever accepted.

At the same time, the governor sent messages to the leaders of the area pueblos, authorizing their residents to forcibly resist any invasion of their homeland by Navajos. He also gave them permission to dispose of, according to their custom, any confiscated animals and other property captured from the raiders.[35]

A frustrated Calhoun continued to make his entreaties known to Washington. On March 29, he wrote directly to President Fillmore, asking for assistance. "If we had the use of one thousand stand of arms at this time, we could effectually check depredations that are being daily committed in our very midst," he pleaded.[36] Two days later, Calhoun dispatched a letter to Secretary of the Interior Stuart. In order to protect the citizenry, reprisal expeditions must be made against "our wild and savage neighbors," he wrote, adding that the territory desperately needed all manner of arms and ammunition to combat the hostile Indians. "Has Congress provided the means to aid us?" he inquired.[37]

On May 1, Calhoun wrote to Commissioner Lea that fifteen Indians, suspected to be Apaches, attacked a party of five Americans and three New Mexicans at a place Calhoun identified as "the Dead Man's Spring, in the Tornado, north of Doñana," killing one of the Americans.[38] On June 11, Judge Beaubien alerted the governor to his suspicions that "a rebellion against the constituted United States authorities is in contemplation among the Lower class of the inhabitants of the country [county] of Taos."[39] Major John Monroe, Governor Washington's successor as civil governor and now commandant of all New Mexico military forces, disagreed with Beaubien's assessment in a letter to Adjutant General Roger Jones dated June 30.[40]

From Calhoun's first days in office as governor, his time was spent arguing with Washington officials for money, arms, and ammunition with which to fight the Indians and keeping those Indians from attacking the far-flung New Mexican villages and pueblos. His correspondence reveals that he was in constant communication with the commissioner of Indian affairs, the secretary of the interior, his various military commanders in New Mexico, and even the president of the United States. And he was not a little concerned about the possibility of another uprising among the residents.

In mid-1852, Calhoun died on the Santa Fe Trail en route to Independence, Missouri, with plans to later confer with government officials in Washington. New Mexicans had to wait sixty more years before their homeland was granted statehood. In the meantime, the territory's leaders and citizens wrestled with the consequences of the Taos Revolt of 1847, a sad legacy that would not be soon forgotten. New Mexico would continue to have problems all the way into the early twentieth century, when the Taos Indians again threatened rebellion and army troops were placed on alert.[41]

Over the years, the populations of the territory's three diverse and sometimes alienated cultures—Indian, Hispano, and Anglo—slowly but surely galvanized themselves into the proud people they are today.

# Appendix A

## Chronology of Events Surrounding the American Occupation of New Mexico in 1846 and the Taos Revolt of 1847

### 1846

May 13. The United States declares war on Mexico almost three weeks after Mexican soldiers cross the Rio Grande and kill eleven American troops. Secretary of War William L. Marcy advises Colonel Stephen Watts Kearny, commander of the 1st Regiment of Dragoons at Fort Leavenworth, that war has been declared with Mexico. Marcy asks Governor John C. Edwards of Missouri to raise a regiment, consisting of eight companies of mounted volunteers and two companies of volunteer artillery. Adjutant General Roger Jones advises Kearny that a mounted force, probably under Kearny's command, will soon be organized and dispatched to occupy Santa Fe and New Mexico.

May 14. Jones confirms to Kearny that the colonel will personally command the army to be sent to New Mexico.

May 30. President James K. Polk and his cabinet adopt the strategic plan that Kearny will follow on his journey to Santa Fe. Following the occupation of New Mexico, Kearny and most of his army will continue to California, weather permitting.

June 3. Marcy advises Kearny that the command to occupy New Mexico and California is his. Marcy also tells Kearny about the raising of the Mormon Battalion, a military unit to consist of Mormon emigrants crossing the Great Plains on their way to the Great Salt Lake.

June 18. All volunteer forces from Missouri gather at Fort Leavenworth. Alexander W. Doniphan, a well-known lawyer, is elected colonel and commander of the 1st Missouri Mounted Volunteers.

June 19. Kearny orders Captain James Allen to visit the Mormon camps and recruit four or five companies of volunteers to accompany him to California.

June 29. Kearny begins moving various units of his Army of the West, approximately 1,658 men, from Fort Leavenworth toward Santa Fe.

July 16. The newly recruited Mormon Battalion musters in at Council Bluffs, Iowa Territory, and soon marches to Fort Leavenworth for training.

Late July. Lead elements of the Army of the West approach Bent's Fort on the Arkansas River.

July 31. At Bent's Fort, Kearny drafts a proclamation announcing the imminent occupation of New Mexico by the American army and distributes copies to the Mexican populace as he proceeds to Santa Fe.

August 1. From Bent's Fort, Kearny dispatches James Wiley Magoffin, a respected Missouri trader, to Santa Fe to parley with Governor Manuel Armijo and to attempt to negotiate a peaceful surrender of the city and the rest of New Mexico.

August 2. The Army of the West breaks camp at Bent's Fort and begins the final leg of its journey to Santa Fe.

August 6. Lead elements of Kearny's army approach Raton Pass. The crossing is made with difficulty the following day.

August 8. As Kearny continues toward Santa Fe, Armijo issues a proclamation in which he urges his subjects to hear "the signal of alarm which must prepare us for battle."

August 10. An escaped American from Taos reports to Kearny that Armijo has assembled a large force of Mexicans and Indians to resist him.

August 11. Several Mexican civilians are captured by Kearny's army and have on their persons copies of a call to arms issued by the prefect of Taos, based on Armijo's proclamation.

August 12. Magoffin, escorted by Captain Philip St. George Cooke, enters Santa Fe. Magoffin secretly meets with Armijo and persuades him not to resist the American occupation. Magoffin leads Armijo's second in command, Diego Archuleta, to believe that the Americans have no interest in that part of New Mexico lying west of the Rio Grande.

August 13. Another American enters Kearny's camp with additional reports of native unrest and information that Armijo is gathering a large army at Apache Canyon a few miles east of Santa Fe.

August 14. As extra precautions are taken among the American troops, Kearny receives a letter from Armijo exclaiming, "If you take the country, it will be because you prove strongest in battle." Kearny's army camps on the outskirts of Vegas (present-day Las Vegas, New Mexico).

August 15. Kearny receives orders that he has been promoted to brigadier general. He rides into Vegas and, from the roof of one of the buildings on the plaza, proclaims that New Mexico is now part of the United States.

Mid-Aug.. The first units of Colonel Sterling Price's newly organized 2nd Missouri Mounted Volunteers depart Fort Leavenworth for Santa Fe.

August 16. The Army of the West rides into San Miguel, where Kearny delivers a speech similar to the one given at Vegas.

August 17. Rumors reach the American camp that the soldiers at Apache Canyon under the command of Armijo have abandoned their positions.

August 18. As Apache Canyon is approached, the American soldiers, unaware of the earlier secret negotiations between Magoffin and Armijo, are ecstatic when they find that the enemy has fled. At noon, two New Mexican officials tell Kearny that the way to Santa Fe is clear and that he will meet no resistance. Advance elements of the army enter Santa Fe at 3 p.m., with the remainder arriving around six. As dusk approaches, the American colors are run up the flagstaff in the plaza opposite the Palace of the Governors.

August 19. Kearny assembles the citizens of Santa Fe in the Plaza and delivers an address similar to the ones given at Vegas and San Miguel. Lieutenant Governor Vigil y Alarid makes a speech in which he accepts the US occupation.

August 22. Kearny issues a proclamation to the people of Santa Fe in which he leaves no doubt that it is the American plan to occupy all of New Mexico, including the west bank of the Rio Grande. He sends a dispatch to General Jonathan E. Wool in Chihuahua, Mexico, that the occupation of New Mexico has been accomplished peacefully and without bloodshed.

August 23. Construction begins on Fort Marcy. The structure will be built on a prominence overlooking Santa Fe.

Sept. 2. On the basis of a rumor that Armijo is approaching with an army to retake Santa Fe, Kearny and a sizable force of dragoons head south out of Santa Fe to meet the New Mexicans and to survey the surrounding countryside.

Sept. 4. With his army in the neighborhood of present-day Bernallio, Kearny learns that the reports about the New Mexican buildup are false. He continues his tour.

Sept. 11. Kearny and his dragoons return to Santa Fe.

Sept. 15. Kearny sends a small party to Taos to reconnoiter the land and determine the condition of the road connecting Taos with Santa Fe.

Sept. 16. In a dispatch to the adjutant general in Washington, DC, Kearny assures army officials that everything is peaceful in Santa Fe.

Sept. 22. Kearny appoints Charles Bent as the governor of New Mexico. Donaciano Vigil, a cousin of the former lieutenant governor's, is named secretary of the territory. Kearny sends a copy of his *Laws of the Territory of New Mexico*, which will be formally published the following month, to officials in Washington.

Sept. 25. Kearny, with three hundred of his 1st US Dragoons, leaves Santa Fe for the second phase of his mission, the occupation of California. Left behind are Doniphan and the 1st Missouri Mounted Volunteers. A few scattered units of the 1st Dragoons also remain.

Sept. 28. Advance units of the 2nd Missouri Mounted Volunteers arrive in Santa Fe.

Oct. 26. Doniphan and most of the remaining 1st Missouri Mounted Volunteers leave Santa Fe to report to General Wool in Mexico.

December. Army officials in Santa Fe receive reports of an impending revolt. The rumor mill has it that Governor Bent, newly arrived Colonel Sterling Price, and many other Americans are to be killed. Authorities act quickly, and the rebellion is aborted during the closing days of the month. Bent issues a proclamation imploring Mexican residents to refrain from participating in revolutionary activities.

Dec. 15. In Washington, members of the House of Representatives petition President Polk to produce all documents relative to the "establishment or organization" by American authority of any civil government in any part of Mexico occupied by American military forces.

Dec. 22. Polk responds to the congressional request.

Dec. 26. The failure of the rumored revolt in Santa Fe, prompts Bent to dispatch details of the aborted uprising to Secretary of State James Buchanan.

1847

Jan. 11. Following Polk's verbal exchange with the House, Secretary of War Marcy mildly rebukes Kearny for overstepping his authority in granting citizenship to the inhabitants of conquered New Mexico.

Jan. 14. Bent leaves Santa Fe for his home in Taos. With him are the new sheriff, Stephen Lee; the circuit attorney, James W. Leal; and a prefect, Cornelio Vigil.

Jan. 19. During the early morning hours, Bent is awakened at his home and brutally murdered by New Mexican and Indian dissidents. The three companions with him on the trip to Taos are murdered as well, in addition to two other citizens, Narciso Beaubien and Pablo Jaramillo. Rebels at Arroyo Hondo, a few miles north of Taos, attack Simeon Turley's mill and distillery and, over a two-day period, kill all but two of the defenders. At Rio Colorado, revolutionaries kill two mountain men.

Jan. 20. At Mora, several Missouri traders are murdered by another group of rebels. News of the uprising at Taos reaches Price in Santa Fe. He quickly formulates plans to attack the rebels on their own turf.

Jan. 22. Acting Governor Vigil issues a proclamation from Santa Fe urging all citizens to cease their resistance to the American occupation.

Jan. 23. Price leaves Santa Fe with a contingent of 2nd Missouri Mounted Volunteers, Captain Ceran St. Vrain's mounted Santa Fe volunteers, the Missouri battalion of infantry, and four mountain howitzers, to be met on the road to Taos by Captain John H. K. Burgwin and his Company G of the 1st US Dragoons. They all head for the revolutionaries' stronghold at Taos.

Jan. 24. Price and his small army successfully rout a much larger force of rebels at the village of Cañada. Jesus Tafoya, one of the rebel ringleaders, is killed.

Jan. 25. Captain I. R. Hendley and eighty soldiers march on Mora. Hendley is killed in the ensuing battle. Americans are forced to retreat when they are unable to dislodge the rebels from an old fort.

Jan. 29. Following the battle at Cañada, Price's command meets a large enemy force near the village of Embudo. The Americans defeat the New Mexicans.

Feb. 1. In retaliation for the death of Captain Hendley at Mora, Captain Jesse B. Morin levels the town with cannon fire.

Feb. 3. Price and his command reach Taos. Finding that the enemy is holed up in the Taos Pueblo about three miles north of town, they proceed there and begin to shell the Indian village. Nightfall cuts the action short, and the Americans retire for the evening.

Feb. 4. After several hours of heavy artillery fire, Price's men finally breach the thick walls of the pueblo church. As rebels attempt to escape the village, they are cut down by St. Vrain's volunteers.

Feb. 5. Leaders of the rebels sue for peace.

Feb. 6. Pablo Montoya, one of the revolutionary leaders, is tried by court-martial in Taos and hanged the following day.

March 26. Governor Vigil, in a letter to Secretary of State Buchanan, complains that Kearny's promises of American protection from the hostile Navajos have not been forthcoming.

April 5. The trials for the imprisoned revolutionaries begin in Taos. The court is presided over by Judge Charles H. Beaubien, the father of one of the men killed in the Taos Revolt on January 19.

April 9. Executions of the Taos rebels who were convicted begin.

April 13. The Taos trials end. The final tally: fifteen of the sixteen men accused of murder are convicted and sentenced to hang. Of the five men tried for treason, one is found guilty and sentenced to hang.

April 30. More hangings take place in Taos.

May 7. The last of the executions of the Taos revolutionaries occurs.

May 20. Captain Benjamin F. Robinson and his detachment of Missouri Mounted Volunteers are attacked while grazing near Wagon Mound. The Americans lose one man killed, two wounded, and about two hundred fifty horses stolen.

May 26. Major B. B. Edmonson, commander of the army contingent at Vegas, after a long pursuit, finds the attackers of Robinson's party on the Canadian River. A battle ensues in which one American and forty-one enemy are killed.

Late June. Several army horses grazing in the Vegas area are stolen, prompting Lieutenant R. T. Brown of the 2nd Missouri Mounted Volunteers to give pursuit. Although the stolen horses and the New Mexicans who took them are found, Brown and his three companions are killed.

July 5. Edmonson attacks Los Valles de Agustin, the New Mexican village where the stolen horses are located. Edmonson's troops destroy the town.

Early July. Captain Morin's company of Missouri mounted volunteers is attacked near Cieneguilla; five men are killed and nine wounded. All army property, including the horses, is stolen. Private John T. Hughes, who would go on to author a comprehensive history of Doniphan's 1st Missouri Mounted Volunteers, writes that this attack occurred on July 9; Price writes July 6.

July 20. Price writes to the adjutant general in Washington, "Rumors of insurrection are rife."

August 3. Several New Mexicans captured at Los Valles in early July are hanged at Fort Marcy in Santa Fe.

Sept. 14. General Winfield Scott captures Mexico City, essentially ending hostilities between American and Mexican forces.

1848

Feb. 2. The Treaty of Guadalupe Hidalgo, officially ending the Mexican-American War, is signed between representatives of the United States and Mexico.

July 4. The treaty is proclaimed after being ratified, with amendments, by the US Senate on March 10 and signed by President Polk on March 16 and by the Mexican government on May 30.

# Appendix B

## General Stephen Watts Kearny's August 19, 1846, Address to the People of Santa Fe

New Mexicans! We have come amongst you to take possession of New Mexico, which we do in the name of the government of the United States. We have come with peaceable intentions and kind feelings toward you all. We come as friends, to better your condition and make you a part of the Republic of the United States. We mean not to murder you, or rob you of your property. Your families shall be free from molestation; your women secure from violence. My soldiers will take nothing from you but what they pay you for. In taking possession of New Mexico we do not mean to take away your religion from you. Religion and government have no connection in our country. There, all religions are equal; one has no preference over another; the Catholic and Protestant are esteemed alike.

Every man has a right to serve God according to his heart. When a man dies, he must render to his God an account of his acts here on earth, whether they be good or bad. In our government all men are equal. We esteem the most peaceable man, the best man. I advise you to attend to your domestic pursuits—cultivate industry—be peaceable and obedient to the laws. Do not resort to violent means to correct abuses. I do hereby proclaim that, being in possession of Santa Fé, I am therefore virtually in possession of all New Mexico. Armijo is no longer your governor. His power is departed. But he will return and be as one of you. When he shall return you are not to molest him. You are no longer Mexican subjects; you are now become American citizens, subject only to the laws of the United States. A change of government has taken place in New Mexico, and you no longer owe allegiance to the Mexican government. I do hereby proclaim my intention to establish in this Department a civil government, on a republican basis, similar to those of our own States. It is my intention, also, to continue in office those by whom you have been governed, except the governor, and such other persons as I shall appoint to office by virtue of the authority vested in me. I am your governor—henceforward look to me for protection.

Source: John T. Hughes, *Doniphan's Expedition; Containing an Account of the Conquest of New Mexico* (Cincinnati: J. A. & U. P. James, 1850), 79–80.

# Appendix C

## Governor Juan Bautista Vigil y Alarid's August 19, 1846, Response to General Kearny's Address

General:

The address which you have just delivered, in which you announce that you have taken possession of this great country in the name of the United States of America, gives us some idea of the wonderful future that awaits us. It is not for us to determine the boundaries of nations. The cabinets of Mexico and Washington will arrange these differences. It is for us to obey and respect the established authorities, no matter what may be our private opinions.

The inhabitants of this Department humbly and honorably present their loyalty and allegiance to the government of North America. No one in this world can successfully resist the power of him who is stronger.

Do not find it strange if there has been no manifestation of joy and enthusiasm in seeing this city occupied by your military forces. To us the power of the Mexican Republic is dead. No matter what her condition, she was our mother. What child will not shed abundant tears at the tomb of his parents? I might indicate some of the causes for her misfortunes, but domestic troubles should not be made public. It is sufficient to say that civil war is the cursed source of that deadly poison which has spread over one of the grandest and greatest countries that has ever been created.

To-day we belong to a great and powerful nation. Its flag, with its stars and stripes, covers the horizon of New Mexico, and its brilliant light shall grow like good seed well cultivated. We are cognizant of your kindness, of your courtesy and that of your accommodating officers and of the strict discipline of your troops; we know that we belong to the Republic that owes its origin to the immortal Washington, whom all civilized nations admire and respect. How different would be our situation had we been invaded by European nations! We are aware of the unfortunate condition of the Poles.*

In the name, then, of the entire Department, I swear obedience to the Northern Republic and I tender my respect to its laws and authority.

Juan Bautista Vigil y Alarid<br>Governor.

*Vigil y Alarid's reference to "the unfortunate condition of the Poles" refers to an abortive uprising in Poland against the central government that was planned to begin nationwide on February 21, 1846. The scheme was betrayed two weeks before launch, and 254 of the would-be participants were arrested and charged with high treason. Trials were held in late 1847, resulting in the acquittal of 134. Death sentences were pronounced for eight, including Ludwik Mieroslawski, the leader of the failed uprising. The rest of the defendants were sentenced to prison. Early in 1848, the king of Prussia commuted all death sentences and released all those imprisoned.

Source: Ralph Emerson Twitchell, *The History of the Military Occupation of the Territory of New Mexico from 1846 to 1848* (Denver: Smith-Brooks, 1909), 74–75.

# Appendix D

## General Stephen Watts Kearny's August 22, 1846, Proclamation to the People of Santa Fe

As by the act of the republic of Mexico, a state of war exists between that government and the United States; and as the undersigned, at the head of his troops, on the 18th instant, took possession of Santa Fé, the capital of the department of New Mexico, he now announces his intention to hold the department, with its original boundaries, (on both sides of the Del Norte,) as part of the United States, and under the name of "the Territory of New Mexico."

The undersigned has come to New Mexico with a strong military force, and an equally strong one is following close in his rear. He has more troops than necessary to put down any opposition that can possibly be brought against him, and therefore it would be but folly or madness for any dissatisfied or discontented persons to think of resisting him.

The undersigned has instructions from his government to respect the religious institutions of New Mexico—to protect the property of the church—to cause the worship of those belonging to it to be undisturbed, and their religious rights in the implicit manner preserved to them—also to protect the persons and property of all quiet and peaceable inhabitants within its boundaries against their enemies, the Eutaws, the Navajoes and others; and when he assures all that it will be his pleasure, as well as his duty, to comply with those instructions, he calls upon them to exert themselves in preserving order, in promoting concord, and in maintaining the authority and efficacy of the laws. And he requires of those who have left their homes and taken up arms against the troops of the United States to return forthwith to them, or else they will be considered as enemies and traitors, subjecting their persons to punishment and their property to seizure and confiscation for the benefit of the public treasury.

It is the wish and intention of the United States to provide for New Mexico a free government, with the least possible delay, similar to those in the United States; and the people of New Mexico will then be called on to exercise the rights of freemen in electing their own representatives to the Territorial legislature. But until this can be done, the laws hitherto in existence will be continued until changed or modified by competent authority; and those persons holding office will continue in the same for the present, provided they will consider themselves good citizens and are willing to take the oath of allegiance to the United States.

The United States hereby absolves all persons residing within the boundaries of New Mexico from any further allegiance to the republic of Mexico, and hereby claims them as citizens of the United States. Those who remain quiet and peaceable will be considered good citizens and receive protection—those who are found in arms, or instigating others against the United States, will be considered as traitors, and treated accordingly.

Don Manuel Armijo, the late governor of this department has fled from it: the undersigned has taken possession of it without firing a gun, or spilling a single drop of blood, in which he truly rejoices, and for the present will be considered as governor of the Territory.

Given at Santa Fé, the capital of the Territory of New Mexico, this 22d day of August, 1846, and in the 71st year of the independence of the United States.

S. W. KEARNY,
Brigadier General U. S. Army.

By the Governor:
Juan Bautista Vigil y Alarid.

Source: James K. Polk, *Message from the President of the United States,* HED 19 (Washington, DC: 29th Cong., 2nd sess., 1846), 20–21.

# Appendix E

## A Description of New Mexico in 1846

New Mexico contains, according to the last census, made a few years since, 100,000 inhabitants. It is divided into three departments—the northern, middle, and southeastern. These are again sub-divided into counties, and the counties into townships. The lower or southern division is incomparably the richest, containing 48,000 inhabitants, many of whom are wealthy and in possession of farms, stock, and gold dust.

New Mexico, although its soil is barren, and its resources limited, unless the gold mines should, as is probable, be more extensively developed hereafter, and the culture of the grape enlarged, is, from its position, in a commercial and military aspect, an all-important military possession for the United States. The road from Santa Fé to Fort Leavenworth presents few obstacles for a railway, and, if it continues as good to the Pacific, will be one of the routes to be considered, over which the United States will pass immense quantities of merchandise into what may become, in time, the rich and populous States of Sonora, Durango, and Southern California.

As a military position, it is important and necessary. The mountain fastnesses have long been the retreating places of the warlike parties of Indians and robbers, who sally out to intercept our caravans moving over the different lines of travel to the Pacific.

The latitude of Santa Fé . . . is N. 35° 44' 06." The longitude . . . from the meridian of Fort Leavenworth is 7h. 04m. 05s5.

The place of observation was the court near the northeast corner of the public square. . . .

The mean of all the barometric readings at Santa Fé indicates, as the height of this point above the sea, 6,846 feet, and the neighboring peaks to the north are many thousand feet higher.

Source: Lieut. Col. W. H. Emory, *Notes of a Military Reconnoissance, from Fort Leavenworth, in Missouri, to San Diego, in California, Including Part of the Arkansas, Del Norte, and Gila Rivers,* HED 41 (Washington, DC: 30th Cong., 1st sess., 1848), 35–36.

# Appendix F

## A Description of Taos and Vicinity in 1847

The name Taos, originally given to the region of country embracing the head waters of a river of the same name, has long since, by universal custom, been applied to the particular settlement of San Fernandez. This town is situated at the junction of the two principal forks of the "Rio de Taos," and 4 or 5 miles from the western base of the Rocky mountain range. Like most of the New Mexican towns it consists of a collection of mud houses, built around a miserable square or plaza. It contains a mixed population of 700 or 800 souls, and, besides being the capital of the northeastern department, possesses little to interest the traveller.

Three miles to the southeast is another town, of about equal pretensions, called "Rancho de Taos;" whilst at about the same distance to the northeast is the celebrated "Pueblo de Taos." This village, interesting in itself as a curious relic of the Aztecan age, is rendered still more so by the recent tragic scenes that have been enacted within its walls. One of the northern forks of the Taos river, on issuing from the mountains, forms a delightful nook, which the Indians early selected as a permanent residence. By gradual improvement, from year to year, it has finally become one of the most formidable of the artificial strongholds of New Mexico. On each side of the little mountain stream is one of those immense "adobe" structures, which rises by successive steps until an irregular pyramidal building, seven stories high, presents an almost impregnable tower. These, with the church and some few scattering houses, make up the village. The whole is surrounded by an adobe wall, strengthened in some places by rough palisades, the different parts so arranged, for mutual defence, as to have elicited much admiration for the skill of the untaught engineers. . . .

Built of "adobes," a material almost impenetrable by shot, having no external entrance except through the roof, which must be reached by moveable ladders, each story smaller than the one below, irregular in its plan, and the whole judiciously pierced with loop-holes for defence, the combination presents a system of fortification peculiarly *sui generis* [unique].

These three towns constitute the principal settlements in the valley, though there are some scattering houses along the water courses. The valley may be eight or nine miles in length from east to west, and some seven or eight miles in width from north to south, embracing about sixty square miles. Only a small portion of this is under cultivation, or indeed ever can be, as no rain falls here except during the wet season. It is necessary to irrigate all the cultivated land, and the small supply of water fixes a limit, and that a very narrow one, to all the tillable land. In point of soil, the valley of Taos compares favorably with other portions of New Mexico; and though snow is to be seen in every month of the year, on the neighboring mountains, wheat and corn ripen very well on the plains. These last are the staple productions of the country; though beans, pumpkins, melons, and red pepper, are raised to some extent. The hills are covered with very good grass, which furnishes subsistence to herds of cattle and horses, as well as to fine flocks of sheep and goats. In them lie the principal wealth of the inhabitants.

Taos is, by nature, almost isolated from the remainder of New Mexico. On the east rise the high peaks of the main Rocky mountain chain, whilst a spur of the same range puts out on the south quite to the banks of the Rio del Norte. On the north and west are the high bluffs which mark the beginning of the extensive "llanos," or table lands. A wagon road of some difficulty has been opened through the southern spur, which leads to Santa Fé, though the communication is usually kept up by the shorter mule road, over the highest point of the spur.

Source: J. W. Abert, *Report of Lieut. J. W. Abert, of His Examination of New Mexico in the Years 1846–'47*, SED 23 (Washington, DC: 30th Cong., 1st sess., 1848), 40–42. This description of Taos was written by Lieutenant William G. Peck, another topographical engineer who accompanied Kearny's expedition with Abert.

# Appendix G

## List of American, New Mexican, and Indian Casualties of the Taos Revolt and its Aftermath

A complete list of all the victims of the Taos Revolt and its fallout does not exist. Below are the names of the known casualties, as well as the known numbers of casualties although names are unknown. While the enumeration of the American casualties is fairly complete, the fate of scores of New Mexicans and Taos Indians involved in the incident have, no doubt, become lost in antiquity.

Murdered at Don Fernando de Taos on January 19, 1847
1. Charles Bent, governor
2. Stephen Lee, sheriff
3. James W. Leal, circuit attorney
4. Cornelio Vigil, prefect
5. Narciso Beaubien, son of Judge Charles Beaubien
6. Pablo Jaramillo, brother of Mrs. Charles Bent

Killed in combat at Arroyo Hondo on January 19 and 20, 1847
1. Simeon Turley
2. Albert Turbush (or Cooper)
3. William Hatfield
4. Louis Tolque
5. Peter Roberts
6. Joseph Marshall
7. William Austin

An unknown number of Taos Indians and New Mexicans were killed and wounded.

Murdered near Rio Colorado on January 19, 1847
1. Mark Head
2. William Harwood

Murdered at Mora on January 20, 1847
1. Romulus E. Culver

2. Lawrence L. Waldo
3. Benjamin Pruett
4. Lewis Cabanne
5. Joseph Funk
6. Ola Ponett
7. Mr. Noyes
8. Mr. Valentine

Killed/Wounded at the Battle of La Cañada, January 24, 1847
Americans Killed
1. Pvt. Graham
2. G. Messersmith, teamster
Americans Wounded
1. 1st Lt. Irvine
2. 1st Sgt. Henry Caspers
3. Pvt. Adam Aulman
4. Pvt. John Pace
5. Pvt. Gotfried Metzger
6. Pvt. Murphy
Thirty-six New Mexicans and Taos Indians were killed and forty-five wounded. Among the dead was one of the rebellion's ringleaders, Jesus Tafoya.

Killed/Wounded at the Battle of Mora, January 25, 1847
American Killed
1. Capt. Israel Hendley
Americans Wounded
Three men, names unknown
Twenty-five Taos Indians and New Mexicans were killed.

Killed/Wounded at the Battle of Embudo, January 29, 1847
American Killed
1. Pvt. Papin
American Wounded
1. Dick Green, black servant of Governor Charles Bent
Twenty Taos Indians and New Mexicans were killed and sixty were wounded.

Killed/Wounded at the Battle of Pueblo de Taos, February 3–4, 1847

Americans Killed
1. 1st Sgt. G. B. Ross
2. Pvt. Brooks
3. Pvt. Beebee
4. Pvt. Levicy
5. Pvt. Huntsecker
6. Sgt. Hart
7. Mr. Atkins, teamster

Americans Wounded
1. Pvt. Robert C. Bower (died later in February of wounds received at Taos)
2. Capt. Samuel H. McMillin
3. Pvt. Henry Fender (died February 10, 1847, of wounds received at Taos)
4. Pvt. George W. Johnson (medically discharged April 2, 1847, of wounds received at Taos)
5. Pvt. Robert Heart (or Hewitt) (or Heurt)
6. Pvt. George W. Howser
7. Pvt. William Ducoing
8. 1st Sgt. Alfred L. Caldwell (died February 7, 1847, of wounds received at Taos)
9. 3rd Cpl. James W. Jones (medically discharged at Santa Fe)
10. Pvt. James T. Austin
11. Pvt. Samuel Lewis
12. 1st Lt. Thomas G. West
13. Pvt. James H. Calloway
14. Pvt. John Nagel (medically discharged on April 12, 1847, for "gunshot wounds."
15. Pvt. John J. Sights
16. 2nd Lt. John Mansfield
17. Pvt. Jacob Moon (or Noon)
18. Pvt. William Gibbons
19. Capt. John H. K. Burgwin (died February 7, 1847, of wounds received at Taos)
20. Sgt. I. (or J.) Vanroe
21. Cpl. C. Ingleman

## Appendix G: Casualties of the Taos Revolt

22. Pvt. I. L. (or J. L.) Linneman
23. Pvt. S. Blodget
24. Pvt. S. W. Craine (or Crain)
25. Pvt. R. Deets
26. Pvt. G. F. (or G. T.) Lickenbergh
27. Pvt. J. Truax (died of wounds received at Taos)
28. Pvt. Hagenbach
29. Pvt. Anderson
30. Pvt. Beach
31. Pvt. Hutton
32. Pvt. Hillerman
33. Pvt. Walker
34. Pvt. Schender (or Schneider) (or Scheider) (died of wounds received at Taos)
35. Pvt. Shay
36. Pvt. Near
37. Pvt. Bremen
38. Pvt. Frederick U. Bielfeldt
39. Pvt. Michael Jod
40. Pvt. Henry Kahn (or Koehn)
41. Lt. Vincent Van Valkenberg (died of wounds received at Taos)
42. Sgt. William H. Ferguson
43. Sgt. A. B. Aull
44. Pvt. George Gold
45. Pvt. Mitchell

Taos Indians and New Mexicans killed totaled 154, with an unknown number wounded. Among the dead was one of the uprising's leaders, Pablo Chávez.

New Mexicans and Taos Indians Hanged in Taos by American Authorities

| | Date Executed |
|---|---|
| 1. Pablo Montoya | Feb. 7, 1847 |
| 2. Hipólito Salazar | April 9, 1847 |
| 3. José Manuel Garcia | April 9, 1847 |
| 4. Pedro Lucero | April 9, 1847 |
| 5. Ysidro Antonio Romero | April 9, 1847 |
| 6. Manuel Antonio Romero | April 9, 1847 |

7. Juan Ramon Trujillo — April 9, 1847
8. Manuel Sandoval — April 30, 1847
9. Manuel Miera — April 30, 1847
10. Juan Pacheco — April 30, 1847
11. Rafael Tafoya — April 30, 1847
12. Francisco Naranjo — April 30, 1847
13. José Gabriel Romero — April 30, 1847
14. Juan Domingo Martin — April 30, 1847
15. Juan Antonio Lucero — April 30, 1847
16. El Cuervo — April 30, 1847
17. Juan Antonio Avila — May 7, 1847

While incarcerated in the Taos jail in February 1847, Tomás (Tomasito) Romero was shot to death by an American soldier.

Killed/Wounded at Wagon Mound, May 20, 1847
One American was killed and two were wounded, names unknown.

Killed/Wounded at the Battle on the Canadian River (called at the time the Battle of Red River Cañon), May 26, 1847
Americans Killed
1. Private Edward G. Whitworth
Americans Wounded
Several, names unknown
Forty-one Taos Indians and New Mexicans were killed and an unknown number wounded.

Killed near Vegas, late June 1847
1. Lt. Robert T. Brown
2. Pvt. James M. McClanahan
3. Pvt. Charles Quisenbury (or Quesenberry)
4. A New Mexican guide, name unknown

Killed at the Battle of Los Valles, July 5, 1847
Ten Taos Indians and New Mexicans were killed.

Killed/Wounded at Cieneguilla, New Mexico, July 6 (or 9), 1847
Americans Killed
1. Lt. Larkin

2. W. Owens
3. J. A. Wright
4. W. S. Mason
5. Wilkinson

Americans Wounded
Nine, names unknown

Captured at Los Valles and executed at Fort Marcy in Santa Fe on August 3, 1847, for the murders of Lt. Robert T. Brown, Pvt. James M. McClanahan, Pvt. Charles Quisenbury (or Quesenberry), and the New Mexican guide near Vegas in late June 1847.

1. Jose Tomas Duran
2. George Rodriguez
3. Manuel Saens
4. Pedro Martin
5. Carpio Martin
6. Deonicio Martin

Sources: Ralph Emerson Twitchell, *The History of the Military Occupation of the Territory of New Mexico from 1846 to 1851* (Denver: Smith-Brooks, 1909), 146; John T. Hughes, *Doniphan's Expedition; Containing an Account of the Conquest of New Mexico* (Cincinnati: J. A. & U. P. James, 1850), 393n403; "Colonel Price's Report," February 15, 1847, in *Report of the Secretary of War*, HED 8 (Washington, DC: 30th Cong., 1st sess., 1848), 527–530; *Niles National Register* 72 (Apr. 24, 1847): 128; *Niles National Register* 73 (Oct. 2, 1847): 76; Government Proclamation, Santa Fe, February 15, 1847, in *Insurrection against the Military Government in New Mexico and California, 1847 and 1848*, Sen. Doc. 442 (Washington, DC: 56th Cong., 1st sess., 1900), 24–26; James W. Goodrich, "Revolt at Mora, 1847," *New Mexico Historical Review* 47, no. 1 (Jan. 1972): 51; Mark L. Gardner and Marc Simmons, eds., *The Mexican War Correspondence of Richard Smith Elliott* (Norman: University of Oklahoma Press, 1997), 139–155.

# Appendix H

## The Taos Revolt in the Performing Arts and Literature

It is possible that in October 2007, more Americans (at least theatergoers) became aware of the Taos Revolt of 1847 than at any other time since the long-ago rebellion occurred. That's because a New York actors' group revived and presented a seventy-five-year-old stage play by Pulitzer Prize-winning playwright Maxwell Anderson.

*Night over Taos: A Play in Three Acts* loosely concerns itself with the revolt, but it primarily focuses on one of the ringleaders, Pablo Montoya, described by one of the play's reviewers as "a sort of non-leftist Fidel Castro/Che Guevara of 1847."[1] The play opens at Montoya's residence, where some of his family and friends are in mourning, incorrectly assuming he has been killed by the Americans. The killings at Taos, which resulted in the murders of Governor Charles Bent and others, have already occurred, and the community is fearful of the American reprisal that is yet to come. Federico, Montoya's son (actually, Montoya had no son named Federico),[2] predicts the doom that will befall the village when he exclaims,

> The United States has formally taken over
> This region of ours, and sent a governor. . . .
> We killed him and killed every northerner we could find
> Along with him in Taos. Now vengeance may be
> Delayed sometimes . . . bad weather can block the roads
> And even cool the blood, but a governor
> Was killed, and that's a first-rate challenge to
> The northerners' sovereignty![3]

Of course, the ever-present subplots exist, including one that pits Montoya against his younger son, Felipe (Montoya had no son named Felipe, either),[4] over their mutual love of eighteen-year-old Diana, who is apparently an American captive. In the meantime, it becomes clear that Montoya's present wife, Josefa (in the play she is his third wife and not the mother of the two sons; in reality, Montoya's wife and mother of his three sons and two daughters was named Maria Teresa, and the couple was married in 1816),[5] hates her husband, and the audience learns at about the same time that Federico wants her for himself.

In the end, Montoya kills Federico, comes to grips with his own mortality and the passing of the old days, and poisons himself, uttering his last words to Felipe and Diana, who have by then become a couple:

> Taos, a little island of things that were,
> Sinks among things that are. The north will win.
> Taos is dead. You told me this before,
> But I wouldn't believe it. I believe it now.
> Yes, and it's right. It's right
> Because what wins is right.[6]

*Night over Taos* was originally presented at the 48th Street Theater in New York the night of March 9, 1932. It was directed by the legendary actor, writer, producer, and director Lee Strasberg, who later would tutor such Broadway and Hollywood luminaries as Paul Newman, James Dean, Geraldine Page, Marilyn Monroe, Dustin Hoffman, and Jack Nicholson. Despite the presence in the production of several rising actors—Franchot Tone, Burgess Meredith, Stella and Luther Adler, and Morris Carnovsky, among others—the play was performed only thirteen times before being consigned to the depths of ignominy.

The 2007 version of *Night over Taos* ran from October 1–20 at Theater for the New City on First Avenue in New York. Directed by Estelle Parsons, an actress who won an Academy Award for her performance in *Bonnie and Clyde*, the play featured a cast of twenty-five, all but three of whom were Hispano. The production ran for two hours and forty-five minutes in three acts and received mixed reviews, ranging from, "The play requires the viewers to sort out a great many roles that often have very few lines,"[7] to, "This revival . . . . both captures the socially relevant style of the '30s theater and demonstrates why [Maxwell] Anderson now seems so plodding and preachy."[8]

*Night over Taos* has little relevancy to the actual Taos Revolt. It's soap-opera-like qualities appeal more to those seeking entertainment than to history lovers. It would be interesting to be able to interview Anderson and ask him how he arrived at such a little-known event in American history to incorporate into an off-Broadway production. The fact that the event, albeit in fictional form, was the subject of a stage play eighty-five years after its incidence and then that same lost play was resurrected seventy-five years following its premier is phenomenal.

The New York theater was not the first vehicle to popularize the Taos Revolt, however. That was done by actor, playwright, and newspaper journalist Joseph M. Field. Field was an owner of the Saint Louis *Weekly Reveille*, and from time to time he contributed articles to the newspaper using the pseudonym Everpoint. Within one month of the killings in Taos and Colonel Sterling Price's swift retaliation on Taos Pueblo, Field wrote and published a lengthy article for his newspaper, "Taos, A Romance of the Massacre." The article was issued as a booklet bearing the same name later in the year. The piece is a highly fictionalized account of the episode, quite obviously written to entertain as much as to inform. Fictionalization aside, however, it is interesting that Field's Missouri readers—and by extension Eastern readers—would be as familiar with affairs in faraway New Mexico as they apparently were. In the historical background material Field provided in his article, he wrote:

> New Mexico has been rendered so familiar to readers, generally, that we may be spared detailed descriptions in our story, either of town or country. Even in the case of the valley of Taos we need do no more than to give such outlines and bearings as an interest in the fate of some of those whom we mention may render desirable.[9]

In the mid-1980s, Albuquerque historian and poet E. A. Mares wrote a one-act, one-person play designed around three principals: Padre Antonio José Martínez; his nemesis later in life, Archbishop Jean Baptiste Lamy; and twentieth-century novelist Willa Cather, who, more than any other person, maligned Martínez to generations of worldwide readers. Mares played Martínez, while vacant chairs represented the other two characters. By asking the invisible Cather and Lamy pointed questions and supplying his own comment, Mares (Martínez) hoped to enlighten modern-day generations of the erroneous conceptions that have revolved around Martínez since the Taos Revolt.[10]

# NOTES

## Prologue

1. For a brief biography of Bent, see Harold H. Dunham, "Charles Bent," in LeRoy R. Hafen, ed., *The Mountain Men and the Fur Trade of the Far West* (Spokane: Arthur H. Clark, 2002), 2:27-48. For a history of the fur-trading empire that Bent and his brothers established on the southern Great Plains, see David Lavender, *Bent's Fort* (Garden City, NY: Doubleday, 1954). An interesting aside in Bent's family history reveals that he was a great-uncle of the eminent Western artist Charles Marion Russell. See Louis Chapin, *Charles M. Russell: Paintings of the Old West* (New York: Crown, 1978), 7, and Frederic G. Renner, *Charles M. Russell* (New York: Harry N. Abrams, 1974), 19.

## Chapter One: Gone to Texas

1. Bernard L. Fontana, *Entrada: The Legacy of Spain & Mexico in the United States* (Tucson: Southwest Parks and Monuments Association, 1994), 191-92.
2. Hubert Howe Bancroft, *History of Arizona and New Mexico 1530-1888* (San Francisco: History Company, 1889), 308-9; Louise Barry, *The Beginning of the West* (Topeka: Kansas State Historical Society, 1972), 98-99; Fontana, *Entrada*, 191; David J. Weber, *The Mexican Frontier, 1821-1846: The American Southwest Under Mexico* (Albuquerque: University of New Mexico Press, 1993), 1-14. In late February 1821, Mexico, under the leadership of Agustín de Iturbide, declared its independence from Spain, although the news only reached the frontiers of New Mexico during the following September. Iturbide visualized the new country operating as an empire, much like Spain had. However, within three years, it had become the Estados Unidos Mexicanos—the United States of Mexico—with a new constitution that defined within its borders nineteen states and four territories, one of the territories being New Mexico.
3. For more about the Austin colonizing scheme, see Ron Tyler, Douglas E. Barnett, and Roy R. Barkley, eds., *The New Handbook of Texas*, 6 vols. (Austin: Texas State Historical Association, 1996), available online at www.tshaonline.org/handbook. For a recent work on Stephen Austin, see Gregg Cantrell, *Stephen F. Austin: Empresario of Texas* (New Haven: Yale University Press, 2001). For an older, but still useful, biography of Austin,

see Eugene C. Barker, *The Life of Stephen F. Austin* (Nashville: Cokesbury, 1925). Moses Austin's biography can be found in David B. Gracy, *Moses Austin, His Life* (San Antonio: Trinity University Press, 1987).
4. The Fredonian revolution is covered at length in William Campbell Binkley, *The Texas Revolution* (Austin: Texas State Historical Association, 1979).
5. William Campbell Binkley, *The Expansionist Movement in Texas, 1836-1850* (Berkeley: University of California Press, 1925), 13-14.
6. Andrew Jackson to John Overton, June 8, 1829. Quoted in Robert V. Remini, *Andrew Jackson and the Course of American Democracy* (New York: Harper & Row, 1981), 2:202.
7. Binkley, *Expansionist Movement*, 14.
8. Gene Brack, *Mexico Views Manifest Destiny* (Albuquerque: University of New Mexico Press, 1975). Quoted in Jeff Long, *Duel of Eagles* (New York: William Morrow, 1990), 16-17.
9. José María Sánches, "A Trip to Texas in 1828," *Southwestern Historical Quarterly* 29, no. 4 (1926). Quoted in Long, *Duel of Eagles*, 18.
10. Sean Wilentz, *Andrew Jackson* (New York: Times Books, 2005), 143.
11. Literature about the fight for Texas independence and the pivotal fall of the Alamo is plentiful. See especially H. W. Brands, *Lone Star Nation: The Epic Story of the Battle for Texas Independence* (New York: Doubleday, 2004); James Donovan, *The Blood of Heroes* (Boston: Little, Brown, 2012); William Groneman III, *Eyewitness to the Alamo* (Plano, TX: Republic of Texas Press, 2001); Stephen L. Hardin, *Texian Iliad: A Military History of the Texas Revolution* (Austin: University of Texas Press, 1996); Long, *Duel of Eagles*; Walter Lord, *A Time to Stand* (Lincoln: University of Nebraska Press, 1978); Lon Tinkle, *13 Days to Glory* (College Station: Texas A & M University Press, 1996).
12. Binkley, *Expansionist Movement*, 16-42; *The American Heritage Pictorial Atlas of United States History* (New York: American Heritage, 1966), 161-63; Mark J. Stegmaier, *Texas, New Mexico, and the Compromise of 1850* (Kent, OH: Kent State University Press, 1996), 5.
13. *Austin City Gazette*, April 28, 1841, quoted in Noel M. Loomis, *The Texan-Santa Fé Pioneers* (Norman: University of Oklahoma Press, 1958), 3.
14. George Wilkins Kendall, *Narrative of the Texan Santa Fé Expedition* (New York: Harper and Brothers, 1844), 1:364-365.
15. Ibid., and Loomis, *Texan Santa Fé Pioneers*, are the foundation studies on the abortive Texan-Santa Fe fiasco.
16. Wilentz, *Andrew Jackson*, 161-163.
17. When he became president in 1845, Polk endorsed the earlier moves by his predecessor, John Tyler, which would assure that the vast land making up the Republic of Texas did, indeed, join the Union. Recent biographies of Polk include John Seigenthaler, *James K. Polk* (New York: Times Books, 2004); Walter R. Borneman, *Polk: The Man Who Transformed the Presidency and*

*America* (New York: Random House, 2009); and Robert W. Merry, *A Country of Vast Designs* (New York: Simon & Schuster, 2009). Also see Milo Milton Quaife, ed., *The Diary of James K. Polk During His Presidency, 1845-1848*, 4 vols. (Chicago: A. C. McClurg/Chicago Historical Society, 1910), its reprint (Columbia, TN: The James K. Polk Memorial Association, 2005), and the abridgment, Allan Nevins, ed., *Polk: The Diary of a President, 1845-1849* (New York: Longmans, Green, 1952) for essential information about the Mexican-American War and all of its manifestations, told in the words of the man who called the shots for the United States.

18. Nevins, *Polk*, xvii.
19. "Inaugural Address of James K. Polk," March 4, 1845, in James D. Richardson, *A Compilation of the Messages and Papers of the Presidents*, vol. 5 (New York: Bureau of National Literature, 1897), 2229-30.
20. Ibid., 2230.
21. Ibid., 2231.
22. Frank Blair to Andrew Jackson, February 28, 1845, quoted in Remini, *Andrew Jackson and the Course*, 3:511. Blair was the editor of the *Washington Globe*, and during Jackson's two terms as president, he and his newspaper had strongly supported the administration.
23. Andrew Jackson to Frank Blair, March 10, 1845, in ibid.
24. "First Annual Message from James K. Polk," December 2, 1845, in Richardson, *Compilation of the Messages*, 2238.
25. "Message to the Senate and House of Representatives," May 11, 1846, in ibid., 6:2290-91.
26. General Zachary Taylor to Adjutant General Roger Jones, April 26, 1846, quoted in Nevins, *Polk*, 83n3.
27. "Message to the Senate and House of Representatives," May 11, 1846, in Richardson, *Compilation of the Messages*, 6:2292.
28. Nevins, *Polk*, 86.
29. Ibid., 87-88.
30. "In Senate," May 12, 1846, in *The Congressional Globe*, 29th Cong., 1st sess. (Washington, DC: Blair & Rives, 1846), 804.
31. Nevins, *Polk*, 87n4.
32. Allan Nevins, ed., *The Diary of Philip Hone, 1829-1851* (New York: Dodd, Mead, 1927), 2:763.
33. Nevins, *Polk*, 93-94.
34. James A. Crutchfield, *Tennesseans at War: Volunteers and Patriots in Defense of Liberty* (Nashville: Rutledge Hill, 1987), 76; Tennessee Secretary of State, Tennessee State Library and Archives, www.tennessee.gov/tsla/exhibits/veterans/mexicanamerican.htm.
35. James K. Polk, *Occupation of Mexican Territory: Message from the President of the United States*, December 22, 1846, House Executive Document (HED) 19 (Washington, DC: 29th Cong., 2d sess., 1846), 5-7.

## Chapter Two: Looking West

1. Binkley, *Expansionist Movement*, 24-25, 178-79; *American Heritage Pictorial Atlas*, 161-63; Randall D. Sale and Edwin D. Karn, *American Expansion: A Book of Maps* (Lincoln: University of Nebraska Press, 1962), 12-15; Mark J. Stegmaier, *Texas, New Mexico*, 13, 28.
2. "The Compromise of 1850," in Henry Steele Commager, ed., *Documents of American History*, 6th ed. (New York: Appleton-Century-Crofts, 1958), 1:319-23.
3. Polk, *Occupation of Mexican Territory*, 5-7.
4. Zenon Trudeau to François Luis Hector Carondelet, October 7, 1792. Quoted in Noel M. Loomis and Abraham P. Nasatir, *Pedro Vial and the Roads to Santa Fe* (Norman: University of Oklahoma Press, 1967), 390.
5. A. P. Nasatir, ed., *Before Lewis and Clark: Documents Illustrating the History of the Missouri, 1785-1804*, 2 vols. (St. Louis: St. Louis Historical Documents Foundation, 1952), repr. (Lincoln: University of Nebraska Press, 1990), 1:28-31.
6. The Marqués de Casa Calvo to Don Pedro Cevallos, September 30, 1804. Quoted in ibid., 2:754-758, 1:113n106.
7. Ibid., 1:112-13.
8. "Pike's Observations on New Spain," in Donald Jackson, ed., *The Journals of Zebulon Montgomery Pike, with Letters and Related Documents* (Norman: University of Oklahoma Press, 1966), 2:59-62.
9. "Journal of the Western Expedition," in ibid., 1:391–97. Although Zebulon Pike was still a first lieutenant when he departed Saint Louis on his trip to the Southwest, he was promoted to captain less than one month later, on August 12, 1806. He eventually rose to the rank of brigadier general. Pike was killed April 27, 1813, at the Battle of York in Canada during the War of 1812. See Francis B. Heitman, *Historical Register and Dictionary of the United States Army*, 2 vols. (Washington, DC: Government Printing Office, 1903), repr. (Gaithersburg, MD: Olde Soldiers Books, 1988), 1:792.
10. Jackson, *Journals of Zebulon Montgomery Pike*, 1:350-52.
11. Ibid., 383-85.
12. Ibid., 391-92.
13. Ibid., 393-95.
14. "Pike's Dissertation on Louisiana," in ibid., 2:27-28. A new and comprehensive study of Zebulon Pike, his western explorations, and their ramifications is provided by Matthew L. Harris and Jay H. Buckley, eds., *Zebulon Pike, Thomas Jefferson, and the Opening of the American West* (Norman: University of Oklahoma Press, 2012).
15. John C. Luttig, *Journal of a Fur-Trading Expedition on the Upper Missouri, 1812-1813* (St. Louis: Missouri Historical Society, 1920), repr., Stella M. Drumm, ed. (New York: Argosy-Antiquarian, 1964), 142-43.
16. Rex W. Strickland, "James Baird," in LeRoy R. Hafen, ed., *The Mountain Men and the Fur Trade of the Far West* (Spokane: Arthur H.

Clark, 2001), 3:27-37; Rex W. Strickland, "Robert McKnight," in ibid., 9:259-268.

17. *American State Papers, Foreign Relations* (Washington, DC: Gales and Seaton, 1834), 4:211-13.

18. David Meriwether, *My Life in the Mountains and on the Plains: The Newly Discovered Autobiography* (Norman: University of Oklahoma Press, 1965), 89-102.

19. Ibid., 123–266.

20. *Franklin Missouri Intelligencer*, June 25, 1821, 3, quoted in Larry M. Beachum, *William Becknell: Father of the Santa Fe Trade* (El Paso: Texas Western Press, 1982), 17.

21. Ibid., 29.

22. Ibid.

23. Elliott Coues, ed., *The Journal of Jacob Fowler* (New York: Francis P. Harper, 1898), repr. (Minneapolis: Ross & Haines, 1965), 137–44.

24. Josiah Gregg, *Commerce of the Prairies, or the Journal of a Santa Fe Trader . . .* , 2 vols. (New York: Henry G. Langley, 1844), repr., Max L. Moorhead, ed. (Norman: University of Oklahoma Press, 1954), 14.

25. Ibid., 78.

26. Ibid., 332.

27. For a comprehensive and detailed history of Bent, St. Vrain & Company, as well as Bent's Fort, see Lavender, *Bent's Fort*. For a complete overview of the fur trade in the American Southwest, see David J. Weber, *The Taos Trappers* (Norman: University of Oklahoma Press, 1971).

## Chapter Three: Without Firing a Gun or Spilling a Drop of Blood

1. The standard work on Kearny is Dwight L. Clarke, *Stephen Watts Kearny: Soldier of the West* (Norman: University of Oklahoma Press, 1961). See also Dan L. Thrapp, *Encyclopedia of Frontier Biography* (Glendale CA: Arthur H. Clark, 1988), 3:762-63; Roger J. Spiller, ed., *Dictionary of American Military Biography* (Westport, CT: Greenwood Press, 1984), 2:549-52; Hans von Sachsen-Altenburg and Laura Gabiger, *Winning the West: General Stephen Watts Kearny's Letter Book, 1846-1847* (Boonville, MO: Pekitanou, 1998).

2. Heitman, *Historical Register and Dictionary*, 1:586.

3. Ibid., 376.

4. William L. Marcy to Stephen Watts Kearny, May 13, 1846, quoted in Ralph P. Bieber, ed., *Marching with the Army of the West, 1846-1848* (Glendale CA: Arthur H. Clark, 1936), repr. (Philadelphia: Porcupine Press, 1974), 23.

5. Adjutant General Roger Jones to Kearny, May 13, 1846, in ibid.

6. Marcy to John C. Edwards, May 13, 1846, quoted in ibid., 24.

7. Jones to Kearny, May 14, 1846, quoted in ibid.

8. President Polk's cabinet consisted of Secretary of State James Buchanan, Secretary of War William Marcy, Secretary of the Navy George Bancroft, Secretary of the Treasury Robert Walker, Attorney General John Mason, and Postmaster General Cave Johnson.

9. Nevins, *Polk*, 107.

10. Ibid.

11. Stephen Watts Kearny, "Report of a Summer Campaign to the Rocky Mountains," in David A. White, ed., *News of the Plains and Rockies* (Spokane: Arthur H. Clark, 1998), 4:115-33. The year before the war's outbreak, Colonel Kearny had led five companies of the 1st Regiment of Dragoons on a mission from Fort Leavenworth to the vicinity of South Pass in the Rocky Mountains. The purpose was to protect travelers on the Oregon Trail and to appeal to the region's Indian tribes to offer no resistance to the settlers' increasing numbers of wagon trains passing through their territory. During mid-June, near Fort Laramie, Kearny held a council with about one thousand two hundred Indians and asked them not to "disturb [the emigrants] in their persons or molest their property."

12. Nevins, *Polk*, 107.

13. Leo E. Oliva, *Soldiers on the Santa Fe Trail* (Norman: University of Oklahoma Press, 1967), 59.

14. Marcy to Kearny, June 3, 1846, in Polk, *Occupation of Mexican Territory*, 5.

15. Ibid., 5-7.

16. Daniel Tyler, *A Concise History of the Mormon Battalion in the Mexican War 1846-1847* (NP: privately printed, 1881), quoted in Philip St. George Cooke, *The Conquest of New Mexico and California in 1846-1848* (Chicago: Rio Grande Press, 1964), iv. The remainder of Kearny's detailed orders to Allen, which offer insight into the formation of the battalion and its similarity to a regular army unit, read: "the officers of each company will be a captain, first-lieutenant and second lieutenant, who will be elected by the privates and subject to your approval. The companies, upon being thus organized, will be mustered by you into the service of the United States, and from that day will commence to receive the pay, rations and other allowances given to the other infantry volunteers, each according to his rank."

17. Ibid., viii.

18. John T. Hughes, *Doniphan's Expedition; Containing an Account of the Conquest of New Mexico* (Cincinnati: J.A. & U.P. James, 1850), 25-26. John T. Hughes, a member of the 1st Regiment Missouri Mounted Volunteers, as the new unit was called, explained that: "For the space of twenty days, during which time portions of the volunteers remained at the fort, rigid drill twice per day, once before and after noon, was required to be performed by them, in order to render their services the more efficient. These martial exercises, upon a small prairie adjacent to the fort, appropriately styled by the

volunteers, 'Campus Martis,'[a corruption of Campus Martius in Roman military history] consisting of the march by sections of four, the sabre exercises, the charge, the rally, and other cavalry tactics, doubtless proved subsequently to be of the most essential service."

19. Ibid., 26-27; Oliva, *Soldiers*, 61-63.
20. Hughes, *Doniphan's Expedition*, 134-35.
21. Ibid.,135.
22. Ibid., 27, 29; Oliva, *Soldiers*, 61-63; Kearny to Jones, June 29, 1846, in *Stephen W. Kearny's Diary and Letter Book, 1846-1847*, in S. W. Kearny Papers, Box 2-2, Missouri Historical Society. Cited in von Sachsen-Altenburg and Gabiger, *Winning the West*, 154-56.
23. Captain H. S. Turner to Major Richard Cummings, June 20, 1846, in von Sachsen-Altenburg and Gabiger, *Winning the West*, 150-51.
24. Hughes, *Doniphan's Expedition*, 47.
25. LeRoy R. and Ann W. Hafen, "Thomas Fitzpatrick," in Hafen, *Mountain Men*, 7:87-105.
26. Hughes, *Doniphan's Expedition*, 56.
27. Thrapp, *Encyclopedia of Frontier Biography*, 1:34.
28. Thomas E. Chávez, *Manuel Alvarez, 1794-1856: A Southwestern Biography* (Niwot: University Press of Colorado, 1990), 114-15.
29. Samuel P. Arnold, "William W. Bent," in Hafen, *Mountain Men*, 6:61-84.
30. Harold H. Dunham, "Ceran St. Vrain," in ibid., 5:297-316; Ronald K. Wetherington, *Ceran St. Vrain: American Frontier Entrepreneur* (Santa Fe: Sunstone, 2012).
31. David Lavender points out in his book, *Bent's Fort*, that "Considerable discrepancy exists as to the fort's exact dimensions," 387n14. Even observers who visited the fort while it was operational—Lieutenant J. W. Abert, Ceran St. Vrain, John Hughes, and Lewis H. Garrard, among others—can't seem to agree on its shape, the number of rooms, or the walls' heights or thicknesses. For an interesting narrative—accompanied by measured drawings— of Bent's Fort's reconstruction during the mid-1970s, written by the general contractor in charge, see Emil Gimeno, *The Adobe Castle of the Santa Fe Trail: The History & Reconstruction of Bent's Old Fort* (Arvada, CO: privately printed, 2004).
32. George Frederick Ruxton, *Life in the Far West* (New York: Harper & Brothers, 1849), repr., Leroy R. Hafen, ed. (Norman: University of Oklahoma Press, 1951), 180.
33. George E. Hyde, *Life of George Bent Written from His Letters* (Norman: University of Oklahoma Press, 1968), 93.
34. "Proclamation of General Kearny," July 31, 1846, in Polk, *Occupation of Mexican Territory*, 19.
35. William H. Emory, *Notes of a Military Reconnoissance, from Fort Leavenworth, in Missouri, to San Diego, in California, Including Part of the*

*Arkansas, Del Norte, and Gila Rivers*, HED 41 (Washington, DC: 30th Cong., 1st sess., 1848), 18.

36. James W. Abert, *Report of Lieut. J. W. Abert, of His Examination of New Mexico, in the Years 1846-'47*, Senate Executive Document (SED) 23 (Washington, DC: 30th Cong., 1st sess., 1848), 25.

37. Susan Shelby Magoffin, *Down the Santa Fe Trail and into Mexico*, Stella M. Drumm, ed. (New Haven: Yale University Press, 1926, 1962), repr. (Lincoln: University of Nebraska Press, 1982), 80.

38. Ralph Emerson Twitchell, *The History of the Military Occupation of the Territory of New Mexico from 1846-1851* (Denver: Smith-Brooks, 1909), 60-63.

39. Emory, *Notes of a Military Reconnoissance*, 21.

40. Ibid., 21-22.

41. Ibid., 23.

42. Ibid., 25.

43. Ibid., 25-26. For the full texts of Kearny's and Armijo's letters, see "Notes and Documents," *New Mexico Historical Review* 26, no. 1 (Jan. 1951): 80-82.

44. Emory, *Notes of a Military Reconnoissance*, 27-28.

45. Ibid., 29.

46. Quaife, *Diary of James K. Polk*, 1:474.

47. Thomas Hart Benton, *Thirty Years' View; or, A History of the Working of the American Government for Thirty Years, from 1820 to 1850* (New York: D. Appleton, 1856), 2:683.

48. Kearny to Manuel Armijo, August 1, 1846, in "Notes and Documents," *New Mexico Historical Review* 26, no. 1 (Jan. 1951): 80.

49. Armijo to Kearny, August 12, 1846, in ibid., 81-82.

50. For details regarding the events surrounding the secret meetings between the American agent, Magoffin, and Armijo and Archuleta, see Bernard DeVoto, *The Year of Decision: 1846* (New York: Houghton Mifflin, 1942), repr. (New York: Book-of-the-Month Club, 1984); Paul Horgan, *Great River: The Rio Grande in North American History* (New York: Rinehart, 1954); and Lavender, *Bent's Fort*.

51. Emory, *Notes of a Military Reconnoissance*, 30-31. Also see Henry G. A. Caspers, "Journal," in Special Collections, Digital Collections, St. Louis Mercantile Library at the University of Missouri–St. Louis, no date, 3.

52. Rafael Chácon to Benjamin M. Read, May 4, 1910, in Benjamin M. Read, *Illustrated History of New Mexico* (Santa Fe: New Mexican Printing, 1912), repr. (New York: Arno, 1976), 431-33.

53. Max L. Moorhead, ed., "Report of the Citizens of New Mexico to the President of Mexico," September 26, 1846, in "Notes and Documents," *New Mexico Historical Review* 26, no. 1 (Jan. 1951): 69-76.

54. These are the same two letters referred to in notes 48 and 49 above.

55. "Report of the Citizens of New Mexico to the President of Mexico," September 26, 1846, in Moorhead, "Notes and Documents," 69-76.
56. "Report of Gov. Manuel Armijo to the Minister of Foreign Relations, Interior and Police," September 8, 1846, in ibid., 76-78.
57. Emory, *Notes of a Military Reconnoissance*, 31.
58. Ibid., 32.
59. *Niles' National Register* 70 (Aug. 29, 1846): 416.
60. *Richmond Enquirer*, November 6, 1846.

## Chapter Four: "Every Thing Here Is Quiet and Peaceable"

1. The latest research suggests that Santa Fe was founded between 1608 and 1610, depending on which source is consulted. See James C. Kelly and Barbara Clark Smith, "Introduction," in *Jamestown, Québec, Santa Fe: Three North American Beginnings* (Washington, DC: Smithsonian Books, 2007), 10; David J. Weber, "Santa Fe," in ibid., 136; Joseph P. Sánchez, "The Peralta-Ordóñez Affair and the Founding of Santa Fe," in David Grant Noble, ed., *Santa Fe: History of an Ancient City* (Santa Fe: School of American Research Press, 1989), 27ff.
2. Emory, *Notes of a Military Reconnoissance*, 34-35.
3. Abert, *Report of Lieut. J. W. Abert*, 32.
4. Hughes, *Doniphan's Expedition*, 91.
5. Frederick Adolphus Wislizenus, *Memoir of a Tour to Northern Mexico, Connected With Col. Doniphan's Expedition*. Senate Misc. Doc. 26 (Washington, DC: 30th Cong., 1st sess., 1848), 19-20, 28; Henry G. A. Caspers, "Journal," 3.
6. "Vigil y Alarid's Proclamation," August 17, 1846, in Read, *Illustrated History of New Mexico*, 430-31.
7. Hughes, *Doniphan's Expedition*, 79-80. See appendix B of the present book for Kearny's complete speech.
8. Twitchell, *History of the Military Occupation*, 74-75. See appendix C of the present book for Vigil y Alarid's complete speech.
9. Emory, *Notes of a Military Reconnoissance*, 33.
10. "Proclamation of General Kearny," August 22, 1846, in Polk, *Occupation of Mexican Territory*, 20-21. See appendix D of the present book for Kearny's complete proclamation.
11. Kearny to General Jonathan E. Wool, August 22, 1846, in Polk, *Occupation of Mexican Territory*, 21-22.
12. Emory, *Notes of a Military Reconnoissance*, 32.
13. Ibid.; L. Bradford Prince, *Old Fort Marcy* (Santa Fe: New Mexican Printing, 1912), 4-5. In the months following the army's occupation of Fort Marcy, the garrison was moved away from the fort and relocated in town some six hundred yards to the southwest. Soon to become known as the Post at Santa Fe, the installation was one of nearly one hundred army posts across the country that collected weather data for the US government in keeping

with an 1814 edict by the US surgeon general. See Gary K. Grice, "History of Weather Observing at Fort Marcy, New Mexico, 1849-1892" (Asheville, NC: Climate Database Modernization Program, NOAA National Climatic Data Center, 2005), 1-5.

14. Emory, *Notes of a Military Reconnoissance*, 36-43.

15. "Appointment, by General Kearny, of Civil Officers," in Polk, *Occupation of Mexican Territory*, 26; L. Bradford Prince, *Historical Sketches of New Mexico from the Earliest Records to the American Occupation* (New York: Leggat Brothers, 1883), 307-8; W. G. Ritch, *The Legislative Blue-Book of the Territory of New Mexico* (Santa Fe: Charles W. Greene, 1882), repr. (Albuquerque: University of New Mexico Press, 1968), 119.

16. Kearny to Adjutant General Roger Jones, September 22, 1846, in Polk, *Occupation of Mexican Territory*, 26; *Laws of the Territory of New Mexico* (Santa Fe: US Army of Occupation, 1846), repr., Nolie Mumey, ed. (Denver: Nolie Mumey, 1970), iii.

17. Emory, *Notes of a Military Reconnoissance*, 45.

18. Price's pre-Civil War career is explored in Robert E. Shalhope, *Sterling Price, Portrait of a Southerner* (Columbia: University of Missouri Press, 1971). Also, for a brief biography, see Twitchell, *History of the Military Occupation*, 357-360.

19. Although in some official documents, especially *Insurrection against the Military Government in New Mexico and California, 1847 and 1848*, Sen. Doc. 442 (Washington, DC: 56th Cong., 1st sess., 1900), Edmonson's name is clearly spelled "D. B. Edmonson," the Fort Leavenworth muster roles list him as "Benjamin B. Edmonson." The incorrect spelling is no doubt a typographical one, since *Insurrection* was a much later reprint of other, contemporary documents issued at the time of the war. Missouri Secretary of State website, http://www.sos.mo.gov/archives/soldiers/results, accessed June 22, 2013.

20. Hughes, *Doniphan's Expedition*, 132-34, 137-38; Oliva, *Soldiers on the Santa Fe Trail*, 61-66, 76-77; Missouri Secretary of State website, http://www.sos.mo.gov/archives/soldiers/results, accessed June 22, 2013.

21. William B. Drescher, *Traditional and Actual History and Genealogy of the Drescher Family*, 1906, Missouri History Museum Archives, St. Louis, 47.

## Chapter Five: Questions in the Nation's Capital

1. Emory, *Notes of a Military Reconnoissance*, 113-14.
2. Ibid., 109.
3. "Second Annual Message," December 8, 1846, in Richardson, *Compilation of the Messages*, 6:2344.
4. *The Congressional Globe*, December 17, 1846 (Washington DC, 29th Cong., 2nd sess., 1847), 33ff.

5. Polk, *Occupation of Mexican Territory*, 1.
6. *Laws of the Territory of New Mexico*, 3.
7. Quaife, *Diary of James K. Polk*, 2:281-82.
8. Ibid., 287.
9. Polk, *Occupation of Mexican Territory*, 2.
10. Ibid.
11. Marcy to Kearny, January 11, 1847, in *Message of the President of the United States*, HED 70 (Washington, DC: 30th Cong., 1st sess.), 13-14; James Madison Cutts, *The Conquest of California and New Mexico* (Philadelphia: Carey & Hart, 1847), repr. (Albuquerque: Horn & Wallace, 1965), 260-61.
12. Adjutant General Roger Jones to Marcy, December 17, 1846, in Polk, *Occupation of Mexican Territory*, 14.
13. Marcy to Polk, December 21, 1846, in ibid., 2-3.

## CHAPTER SIX: "WE WERE WITHOUT FOOD AND HAD NO COVERING"

1. Colonel Stephen W. Kearny to Adjutant General Roger Jones, September 16, 1846, in Polk, *Occupation of Mexican Territory*, 24-25.
2. Paul Wellman, *Glory, God, and Gold* (New York: Doubleday, 1966).
3. Carl Waldman, *Atlas of the North American Indian* (New York: Facts on File, 1985), 98; John L. Kessell, *Kiva, Cross, and Crown* (Washington, DC: National Park Service, 1979), 84-86.
4. Nan A. Rothschild, *Colonial Encounters in a Native American Landscape: The Spanish and Dutch in North America* (Washington, DC: Smithsonian Books, 2003), 61-62.
5. Joseph P. Sánchez, "Twelve Days in August: The Pueblo Revolt in Santa Fe," in Noble, *Santa Fe*, 39-52; David J. Weber, ed., *What Caused the Pueblo Revolt of 1680?* (Boston: Bedford/St. Martin's, 1999).
6. John L. Kessell, "By Force of Arms: Vargas and the Spanish Restoration of Santa Fe," in Noble, *Santa Fe*, 53-63.
7. Janet Lecompte, *Rebellion in Rio Arriba 1837* (Albuquerque: University of New Mexico Press, 1985), 7.
8. Ibid.
9. Ibid., 11-64.
10. "Proclamation of Provisional Governor Donaciano Vigil of the Territory to its Inhabitants," January 22, 1847, in *Insurrection against the Military Government*, 27-28.
11. "Vigil on Arms, Munitions, Trade, North Americans, and 'Barbaric' Indians," letter to the New Mexico Assembly, June 18, 1846, in David J. Weber, *Arms, Indians, and the Mismanagement of New Mexico: Donaciano Vigil, 1846* (El Paso: Texas Western Press, 1986), 1-8.
12. George F. Ruxton, *Adventures in Mexico and the Rocky Mountains* (New York: Harper & Brothers, 1848), 189.

13. Hughes, *Doniphan's Expedition*, 388.
14. *Insurrection against the Military Government* refers to Burgwin as "I. H. K." Burgwin. Heitman, in *Historical Register and Dictionary*, 263, lists him as "John Henry K." Burgwin. The incorrect spelling in *Insurrection* is no doubt a typographical error, since the report was a much later reprint of other, contemporary documents issued at the time of the war.
15. T. M. Pearce, ed., *New Mexico Place Names: A Geographical Dictionary* (Albuquerque: University of New Mexico Press, 1975), 152.
16. Hughes, *Doniphan's Expedition*, 388-89.
17. Ibid., 389-92; Cutts, *Conquest of California and New Mexico*, 217-18.
18. John Galvin, ed., *Western America in 1846-1847: The Original Travel Diary of Lieutenant J. W. Abert* (San Francisco: John Howell-Books, 1966), 74.
19. Ibid.
20. Ibid.
21. Cutts, *Conquest of California and New Mexico*, 221; Mark L. Gardner and Marc Simmons, eds., *The Mexican War Correspondence of Richard Smith Elliott* (Norman: University of Oklahoma Press, 1997), 117-18.
22. Galvin, *Western America*, 75.
23. Charles Bent to James Buchanan, December 26, 1846, in *Insurrection against the Military Government*, 6.
24. "Colonel Price's Report," February 15, 1847, in *Report of the Secretary of War*, HED 8 (Washington, DC: 30th Cong., 1st sess., 1848), 520-30.
25. Charles Bent to the Inhabitants [of New Mexico], January 5, 1847, in Cutts, *Conquest of California and New Mexico*, 218-20.
26. Lavender, *Bent's Fort*, 165.
27. Twitchell, *History of the Military Occupation*, 124-125.
28. William A. Keleher, *Maxwell Land Grant: A New Mexico Item* (Albuquerque: University of New Mexico Press, 1984), 39-40. Portions of the Miranda-Beaubien Land Grant, later called the Maxwell Land Grant after Beaubien's son-in-law Lucien B. Maxwell acquired it in 1864 upon Beaubien's death, have passed through several owners since the 1840s. In recent times, the Pennzoil Corporation purchased a large section of it in 1973 and several years later donated 150 square miles of the property to the US Forest Service for inclusion in the Carson National Forest. Today, a large portion of the original grant is owned by television mogul Ted Turner, who acquired it from Pennzoil in 1996. His property, called Vermejo Park Ranch, is operated as a guest ranch and corporate retreat. The Boy Scouts of America's Philmont Scout Ranch occupies around one hundred twenty-seven thousand acres of the original holdings, and the National Rifle Association's Whittington Center houses administrative offices, a museum, a research library, and firearms ranges on thirty-three thousand acres.
29. Ibid., 13-15; Weber, *Mexican Frontier*, 190-95.

30. Lawrence R. Murphy, "Charles H. Beaubien," in Hafen, *Mountain Men*, 6:30-31.
31. Charles Bent to Manuel Alvarez, February 24, 1846. "The Charles Bent Papers," *New Mexico Historical Review* 30, no 4 (Oct. 1955): 345-46.
32. Pearce, *New Mexico Place Names*, 162-63.
33. Howard Louis Conard, *"Uncle Dick" Wootton* (Chicago: W. E. Dibble, 1890), repr. (New York: Time-Life Books, 1980), 175.
34. Hughes, *Doniphan's Expedition*, 303.
35. Twitchell, *History of the Military Occupation*, 125-27; E. Bennett Burton, "The Taos Rebellion," *Old Santa Fe: A Magazine of History, Archaeology, Genealogy, and Biography* 1, no. 2 (1913): 182n6; Gardner and Simmons, *Mexican War Correspondence*, 139-45.
36. Ralph Emerson Twitchell, *The Leading Facts of New Mexican History*, vol. 2 (Cedar Rapids, IA: Torch Press, 1912), repr. (Santa Fe: Sunstone, 2007), 235n170.
37. Hughes, *Doniphan's Expedition*, 393. Several other accounts tell the story of the murders of Bent and his associates at Taos, some of them differing from others in detail. See Cutts, *Conquest of California and New Mexico*, 222-23; Gardner and Simmons, *Mexican War Correspondence*, 139-45; Hyde, *Life of George Bent*, 87-88; Ruxton, *Adventures in Mexico*, 226-30; Twitchell, *History of the Military Occupation*, 125-28; Prince, *Historical Sketches of New Mexico*, 317-18; Ralph Emerson Twitchell, *Old Santa Fe: The Story of New Mexico's Ancient Capital* (Santa Fe: New Mexican Publishing, 1925), 287-89; Edwin L. Sabin, *Kit Carson Days 1809-1868* (Chicago: A. C. McClurg, 1914), 303-6, 641-42; Stephen G. Hyslop, *Bound for Santa Fe: The Road to New Mexico and the American Conquest, 1806-1848* (Norman: University of Oklahoma Press, 2002), 386-88; Burton, "Taos Rebellion," 176-209; Horatio O. Ladd, *History of the War with Mexico* (New York: Dodd, Mead, 1883), 265-74.
38. Gardner and Simmons, *Mexican War Correspondence*, 139-45.
39. Murphy, "Charles H. Beaubien," in Hafen, *Mountain Men*, 6:31-32.
40. Albert D. Gonzalez, "Turley's Mill and the Archaeology of Westward Expansion" (n.p., n.d.), 3, from the Burgwin Research Center collection, Taos, NM.
41. Janet Lecompte, "Simeon Turley," in Hafen, *Mountain Men*, 7:301-14.
42. Ruxton, *Adventures in Mexico*, 227-28.
43. Ibid., 228.
44. Ibid.
45. Ibid., 229.
46. Hughes, *Doniphan's Expedition*, 393, lists the men killed at Turley's Mill as "S. Turley, A. Cooper, W. Harfield, L. Folque, P. Roberts, J. Marshall, and W. Austin." "Colonel Price's Report," February 15, 1847, in HED 8, *Report of the Secretary of War*, 520, lists the dead as "Simeon Turley, Albert Turbush, William Hatfield, Louis Tolque, Peter Robert, Joseph Marshall,

and William Austin." In *The Mexican War Correspondence of Richard Smith Elliott*, 146, the journalist gives the following list in his dispatch of February 15, 1847, to the Saint Louis *Weekly Reveille*: "Simeon Turley, Albert Cooper, Wm Hatfield (a volunteer), Louis Folque, Peter Robert, Jos. Marshall, Wm. Austin." In error, he also added "Mark Head and Wm. Harwood" to the names of those killed at Turley's Mill.

47. Conard, *"Uncle Dick" Wootton*, 180.
48. Ibid., 178-79.
49. Pearce, *New Mexico Place Names*, 128.
50. Ruxton, *Adventures in Mexico*, 226-27.
51. Captain W. S. Murphy to Colonel Sterling Price, January 25, 1847, in *Report of the Secretary of War*, HED 8, 533; Captain I. R. Hendley to Colonel Sterling Price, January 23, 1847, in *Report of the Secretary of War*, HED 8, 531-32; government proclamation published in Santa Fe dated February 15, 1847, in *Insurrection against the Military Government*, 24-26; James W. Goodrich, "Revolt at Mora, 1847," *New Mexico Historical Review* 47, no. 1 (Jan. 1972): 51.
52. Goodrich, "Revolt at Mora," 51-52.
53. "Colonel Price's Report," February 15, 1847, in *Report of the Secretary of War*, HED 8, 520.
54. Juan Romero, "Begetting the Mexican Adventure: Padre Martinez and the 1847 Rebellion," in Thomas J. Steele, Paul Rhetts, and Barbe Awalt, eds., *Seeds of Struggle/Harvest of Faith* (Albuquerque: LPD Press, 1998), 368n2.
55. Following his fur-trapping and army scouting careers, Carson served periods of time as the commandant at Fort Union, New Mexico, and Fort Garland, Colorado. He died in May 1868, less than a year after retiring from the army. He was buried in Colorado next to Josefa, who had died one month earlier after giving birth to the couple's seventh living child.
56. Paul A. F. Walter, "The First Civil Governor of New Mexico under the Stars and Stripes," *New Mexico Historical Review* 8, no. 2 (Apr. 1933): 122-23.
57. Fray Angelico Chávez, *But Time and Chance: The Story of Padre Martínez of Taos, 1793-1867* (Santa Fe: Sunstone, 1981), 158.
58. "Colonel Price's Report," February 15, 1846, in *Report of the Secretary of War*, HED 8, 520-30.
59. "The Provisional Governor of the Territory to its Inhabitants," January 22, 1847, in *Insurrection against the Military Government*, 27-28.
60. "Colonel Price's Report," February 15, 1846, in *Report of the Secretary of War*, HED 8, 521.
61. Pierce, *New Mexico Place Names*, 148-49.
62. "Road from Santa Fe to Don Fernandez, Memorial of the Legislative Council of New Mexico," HR Misc. Doc. No. 46 (Washington, DC: 33rd Cong.,1st sess., 1854), 1.
63. Eric Sloane, *Return to Taos* (New York: Wilfred Funk, 1960), 78.

64. Ruxton, *Adventures in Mexico*, 196.
65. "Colonel Price's Report," February 15, 1847, in *Report of the Secretary of War*, HED 8, 521-22.
66. Ibid., 522; Drescher, "Traditional and Actual History," 51; Alexander Byrdie Dyer, "Mexican War Diary of Lt. Alexander Byrdie Dyer," Fray Angélico Chávez History Library, Palace of the Governors, Santa Fe, entry dates, January 24, 25, and 26, 1847, in which he reveals, "The town [Cañada] is now being pillaged by the soldiery," action that was no doubt repugnant to the inhabitants.
67. "Colonel Price's Report," February 15, 1847, in *Report of the Secretary of War*, HED 8, 522-23; Dyer, "Mexican War Diary," entry date January 29, 1847.
68. Prince, *Historical Sketches of New Mexico*, 325.
69. Captain I. R. Hendley to Colonel Sterling Price, January 23, 1847, in *Report of the Secretary of War*, HED 8, 531-32.
70. Lieutenant T. C. McKarney to Colonel Sterling Price, January 25, 1847, in *Report of the Secretary of War*, HED 8, 532-33.
71. "Don Juan Jesus Vigil," HR Report No. 200 (Washington, DC: 33rd Cong., 1st sess., 1854), 1-2.
72. "Public Proclamation," February 15, 1847, in *Insurrection against the Military Government*, 24-26.
73. "Francisco Robaldo," HR Report 473 (Washington, DC: 35th Cong., 1st sess., 1858), 1-3; "Widow of Francisco Robaldo," HR Report 600 (Washington, DC: 36th Cong., 1st sess., 1860), 1-3.
74. "The Taos mountain" was not the summit that today looms over the region north of Taos Pueblo but was most likely in the neighborhood of Tetillas Peak, altitude 9,380 feet. *New Mexico Atlas & Gazetteer* (Yarmouth, ME: DeLorme, 1998), 16.
75. "Colonel Price's Report," February 15, 1847, in *Report of the Secretary of War*, HED 8, 523.
76. Ibid., 523-24.
77. Captain Woldemar Fischer to the Adjutant General, February 16, 1847, in *Insurrection against the Military Government*, 13-14.
78. "Colonel Price's Report," February 15, 1847, in *Report of the Secretary of War*, HED 8, 524-25; Dyer, "Mexican War Diary," entry date February 4, 1847, in which he writes, "When the white flag was raised on the pueblo fort, it was shot down and the firing continued until dark."
79. "Colonel Price's Report," February 15, 1847, in *Report of the Secretary of War*, HED 8, 525.
80. Dyer, "Mexican War Diary," entry dates February 6 and 7, 1847.
81. Conard, *"Uncle Dick" Wootton*, 184-86.
82. Cutts, *Conquest of California and New Mexico*, 232; Dyer, "Mexican War Diary," entry date February 13, 1847.

## Chapter Seven: "Dead! Dead! Dead!"

1. "Colonel Price's Report," in *Report of the Secretary of War*, HED 8, 520-30.
2. Nevins, *Diary of a President*, 218-19.
3. "Circular: Supreme Government of the Territory," February 12, 1847, in *Message of the President of the United States*, HED 70, 24.
4. "Trials for Treason in New Mexico," *Niles' National Register* 72 (May 15, 1847): 172-73; Hughes, *Doniphan's Expedition*, 398n.
5. Ibid. The proceedings of Montoya's court-martial are also found in the National Archives, Record Group 153, Records of the Office of the Judge Advocate General (Army), a typescript of which was kindly furnished to me by New Mexico historian Tim Kimball.
6. Donaciano Vigil to James Buchanan, March 23, 1847, in *Message of the President of the United States*, HED 70, 24-25.
7. Twitchell, *History of the Military Occupation*, 140-41.
8. Ibid., 139-40.
9. Ibid., 141.
10. "Trials for Treason in New Mexico," 172-73.
11. Twitchell, *History of the Military Occupation*, 141-42.
12. Robert J. Tórrez, "The New Mexican 'Revolt' and Treason Trials of 1847," *Tradición* 17, no. 1 (April 2012): 64.
13. Vigil to Buchanan, March 23, 1847, in *Message of the President of the United States*, HED 70, 24-25.
14. Ibid.
15. W. L. Marcy to Sterling Price, June 11, 1847, in *Message of the President of the United States*, HED 70, 31-33.
16. Benton, *Thirty Years' View*, 2:683; Tórrez, "New Mexican 'Revolt,'" 64.
17. Frank P. Blair to John Y. Mason, April 1, 1847, in *Message of the President of the United States*, HED 70, 26-27.
18. Marcy to James K. Polk, July 19, 1848, in *Message of the President of the United States*, HED 70, 10-13.
19. Marcy to Colonel Sterling Price, June 26, 1847, in *Message of the President of the United States*, HED 70, 33-34.
20. Marcy to Stephen W. Kearny, January 11, 1847, in *Message of the President of the United States*, HED 70, 13-14.
21. Francis T. Cheetham. "The First Term of the American Court in Taos, New Mexico," *New Mexico Historical Review* 1, no. 1 (Jan. 1926): 23-24.
22. Lewis H. Garrard, *Wah-To-Yah and the Taos Trail* (Cincinnati: H. W. Derby, 1850), repr. (Palo Alto: American West Publishing, 1968), 115.
23. Cheetham, "First Term of the American Court," 24-25.
24. Ibid., 28-29.
25. Ibid., 29-30.
26. Ibid., 30-31.

27. Ibid., 31-32.
28. Ibid., 33.
29. Ibid., 34-35.
30. Alberto Vidaurre, "1847 Revolt—Taos and Surrounding Area," in *Raíces y Ramas Journal* 3, no. 4 (Winter 2001): 2-7.
31. J. R. Logan, "The Other Side of the 1847 Insurrection," *Taos News*, September 29, 2013, http://www.taosnews.com/lifestyle/article_0ed1b5ec-2627-11e3-b94d-001a4bcf887a.html; author's telephone conversation with David Fernandez of Taos, Sept. 1, 2012; author's telephone conversation with Ouray Meyers of Taos, April 1, 2013.
32. Vidaurre, "1847 Revolt," 9; Drescher, *Traditional and Actual History*, 57. Of the execution of the five Taos Indians, Drescher wrote, "You should have seen the poor wifes of the Indians hung—heard their moans and observed their dispair—after the executions the misarable Indian wifes straped the dead bodies of their husbands not less than 200 to 275 # [pounds] each on their backs, and started for Pueblo their home 3 miles to give their husbands Indian burial."
33. Garrard, *Wah-To-Yah*, 162.
34. Ibid., 162-63.
35. Ibid., 163. Garrard mentioned no names, but since only Hipólito Salazar was found guilty of treason and hanged, it was likely his trial.
36. Antonio José Martínez to Manuel Alvarez, April 12, 1847, cited in E. A. Mares, "The Many Faces of Padre Antonio José Martínez: A Historiographic Essay," in *Padre Martinez: New Perspectives from Taos* (Taos: Millicent Rogers Museum, 1988), 27-28.
37. Antonio José Martínez to Sterling Price, April 12, 1847, in ibid., 28-30.
38. Garrard, *Wah-To-Yah*, 172. Vicente M. Martínez, the great-great-grandson of Padre Martínez, citing the 1877 Santiago Valdez biography of the padre, writes that this makeshift courtroom was located in the Martínez home. See "History of the Padre Martínez Home (1826-2009) From Generation to Generation," https://ghostsoftaos.files.wordpress.com/2013/10/abstract-hist-of-padre-ajm-home.pdf.
39. Garrard, *Wah-To-Yah*, 185.
40. Ibid., 187. William B. Drescher states that "Two Gallows were erected—a large one for the 5 Indians and a smaller for 4 Mexicans. Our battalion surrounded the place of execution. On Wagons—with ropes around their necks—the condemned were driven under the Gallows—The ropes adjusted to gallows—the teams started forward—the gallows creaked and the spirits of the unfortunate passed into that world where a merciful judge reigns ever." "Traditional and Actual History," 57.
41. Garrard, *Wah-To-Yah*, 188-89.
42. Ibid., 189.
43. Ibid.
44. Ibid., 190.

45. *Message of the President of the United States*, HED 70, 5. For the full text of the letter, see Marcy to Price, June 26, 1847, in *Message of the President of the United States*, HED 70, 33-34.
46. Ibid., Marcy to Kearny, January 11, 1847, 13-14.
47. Bernard C. Steiner, *Life of Roger Brooke Taney* (Baltimore: Williams & Wilkins, 1922), 287-89; Sister Mary Loyola, "The American Occupation of New Mexico, 1821–1852," *New Mexico Historical Review* 1, no. 3 (July 1939): 231n3.

Chapter Eight: "The New Mexicans Entertain Deadly Hatred against Americans"

1. *Niles' National Register* 72 (July 31, 1847): 343.
2. Bieber, *Marching with the Army*, 28-32.
3. Hughes, *Doniphan's Expedition*, 187.
4. Ibid., 188.
5. Governor Donaciano Vigil to Secretary of State James Buchanan, March 26, 1847, in *Message of the President of the United States*, HED 70, 25-26.
6. Ibid., 26.
7. Colonel Sterling Price to the Adjutant General of the Army, July 20, 1847, in *Insurrection against the Military Government*, 20-21.
8. Major B. B. Edmonson to Colonel Sterling Price, June 14, 1847, in *Report of the Secretary of War*, HED 8, 535-38.
9. Ibid.
10. Missouri Secretary of State website, http://www.sos.mo.gov/archives/soldiers/results, accessed June 22, 2013.
11. Edmonson to Price, June 14, 1847, in *Report of the Secretary of War*, HED 8, 535-38.
12. Hughes, *Doniphan's Expedition*, 401-3; Price to the Adjutant General, July 20, 1847, in *Insurrection against the Military Government*, 20-21.
13. Hughes, *Doniphan's Expedition*, 401-3; Price to the Adjutant General, July 20, 1847, in *Insurrection against the Military Government*, 20-21; *Niles' National Register* 73 (October 2, 1847): 76. The spellings of the names of the six insurgents hanged at Santa Fe on August 3, 1847, are reproduced as they were entered in the burial records of the parish registry by Padre José de Jesus Lujan. The deceased were interred in graves that are no longer identifiable in Rosario Cemetery in Santa Fe. "Court Martial Burials," by Tim Kimball, posted at www.kmitch.com/Taos/martial deaths.html; e-mail correspondence between author and Kimball, June 4, 6, 2013; January 10, 2014.
14. Hughes, *Doniphan's Expedition*, 403; Price to the Adjutant General, July 20, 1847, in *Insurrection against the Military Government*, 20-21; *History of Clay and Platte Counties, Missouri* (St. Louis: National Historical Company, 1885), 615, 623.
15. Price to the Adjutant General, July 20, 1847, in *Insurrection against the Military Government*, 20-21.

16. Hughes, *Doniphan's Expedition*, 403.
17. Ibid., 404.
18. Lt. John Love to Adjutant General Roger Jones, June 17, 1847, in *Niles National Register* 72 (July 31, 1847): 343-44.
19. Price to the Adjutant General, July 20, 1847, in *Insurrection against the Military Government*, 21-22.

## Chapter Nine: Causes and Consequences

1. Robert V. Remini, *Andrew Jackson and His Indian Wars* (New York: Penguin, 2002), 269-70.
2. Ibid.
3. Thomas Bryan Underwood, *Cherokee Legends and the Trail of Tears: From the Nineteenth Annual Report of the Bureau of American Ethnology* (Cherokee, NC: n.p., 2006), 27, quoted in A. J. Langguth, *Driven West: Andrew Jackson and the Trail of Tears to the Civil War* (New York: Simon & Schuster, 2010), 310-11.
4. George I. Sánchez, *Forgotten People* (San Francisco: R. and E. Research Associates, 1970), repr. (Albuquerque: University of New Mexico Press, 1996), 11-12.
5. Richard Bruce Winders, *Mr. Polk's Army: The American Military Experience in the Mexican War* (College Station: Texas A&M University Press, 1997), 84.
6. Charles Bent to Manuel Alvarez, May 3, 1846, in *New Mexico Historical Review* 31, no. 2 (Apr. 1956): 160; Bent to Alvarez, May 3, 1846, Benjamin Read Collection, No. 87, New Mexico State Records Center and Archives, Santa Fe; Alvarez to Vigil y Alarid, May 6, 1846, Benjamin Read Collection/Letter Book 54; Vigil y Alarid to Alvarez, May 5, 1846, Manuel Alvarez Papers, New Mexico State Records Center and Archives, cited in Chávez, *Manuel Alvarez*, 101. Bent wrote that "Blair & George were attacked by a mob in the squair of this place. Blair was in Liquor, and George was trying to take him home, when theas fellowes made an attack on them."
7. Winders, *Mr. Polk's Army*, 87.
8. Ruxton, *Adventures in Mexico*, 191-92.
9. Ibid., iv.
10. Ibid., 197.
11. Ibid.
12. Ibid., 189.
13. Ibid.
14. "Diary of Philip Gooch Ferguson, 1847–1848," in Bieber, *Marching with the Army*, 321.
15. W. L. Marcy to Colonel Sterling Price, June 26, 1847, in *Message of the President of the United States*, HED 70, 33-34.
16. *Niles' National Register* 73 (November 6, 1847): 155.
17. "Diary of Philip Gooch Ferguson, 1847-1848," in Bieber, *Marching with*

*the Army*, 321. The situation in Santa Fe prompted Ferguson to write, "The scenes of drunkenness daily and nightly enacted, filling the guardhouse with soldiers, demanded a reform in the dramshops;" Gary D. Lenderman, *The Santa Fe Republican: New Mexico Territory's First Newspaper, 1847–1849* (Seattle: CreateSpace Independent Publishing Platform, 2011), 11.

18. William Bowen Campbell, "Mexican War Letters of Col. William Bowen Campbell of Tennessee, Written to Governor David Campbell of Virginia, 1846–1847," *Tennessee Historical Magazine* (June 1915), repr. (n.p., Nabu Press, 2010), 135.
19. Ibid., 150-51.
20. Sánchez, *Forgotten People*, 47-48.
21. Lecompte, *Rebellion in Rio Arriba*, 7.
22. Ibid., 89.
23. Ibid., 91.
24. Ibid., 92.
25. "Vigil on Arms, Munitions, Trade, North Americans, and 'Barbaric' Indians," Letter to the New Mexico Assembly, June 18, 1846, in Weber, *Arms, Indians*, 1-8.
26. Twitchell, *History of the Military Occupation*, 74-75.
27. Luis Martinez, "The Taos Massacre—1847," Works Project Administration Files, Collection 1959-232, Folder 233a, New Mexico Records Center and Archives, Santa Fe, 1-2.
28. Ibid., 2-3.
29. Burton, "Taos Rebellion," 182.
30. Ibid.
31. Gardner and Simmons, *Mexican War Correspondence*, 139.
32. "Trials for Treason in New Mexico," 172-73; author's e-mail correspondence with Tim Kimball, June 4–6, 2013, and January 9–10, 2014.
33. Chávez, *Manuel Alvarez*, 114.
34. Ibid.
35. "The Provisional Governor of the Territory to Its Inhabitants," January 22, 1847, in *New Mexico and California, Message of the President of the United States*, HED 70, 21-22.
36. "The Provisional Governor of the Territory to Its Inhabitants," January 25, 1847, in ibid., 20-21.
37. "Circular—Supreme Government of the Territory," February 12, 1847, in ibid., 22-24.
38. "Army of the West—Massacre of Governor Bent and Other Americans at Taos—Battles of Cañada, Elemboda, Taos, and Moro—Americans Victorious" (Santa Fe: Government Printing Office, Feb. 15, 1847), in *Insurrection against the Military Government*, 24-26.
39. "Colonel Price's Report," Feb. 15, 1847, in *Report of the Secretary of War*, HED 8, 525.

40. Donaciano Vigil to James Buchanan, Feb. 16, 1847, in *Message of the President of the United States*, HED 70, 18-20.
41. Gardner and Simmons, *Mexican War Correspondence*.
42. Hughes, *Doniphan's Expedition*, 393.
43. Ruxton, *Adventures in Mexico*, 226–30.
44. Frank S. Edwards, *A Campaign in New Mexico* (Philadelphia: Carey & Hart, 1847), repr. (Naples, FL: Readex Microprint, 1966), 103–4.
45. Gardner and Simmons, *Mexican War Correspondence*, 139–146.
46. W. H. H. Davis, *El Gringo: New Mexico and Her People* (New York: Harper & Brothers, 1857), repr. (Lincoln: University of Nebraska Press, 1982), 97.
47. The three books are L. Bradford Prince's *Historical Sketches of New Mexico from the Earliest Records to the American Occupation*; Horatio O. Ladd's *History of the War with Mexico*; and Hubert Howe Bancroft's *History of Arizona and New Mexico 1530-1888*.
48. T. D. Bonner, *The Life and Adventures of James P. Beckwourth* (New York: Harper & Brothers, 1856), 483-84.
49. Rev. W. J. Howlett, *Life of the Right Reverend Joseph P. Machebeuf, DD*. (Pueblo, CO: Franklin Press, 1908), 228–29.
50. Thomas J. Steele, S.J., "The View from the Rectory," in *Padre Martínez*, 72.
51. Twitchell, *History of the Military Occupation*, 133–36.
52. Patricia Clark Smith, "Achaeans, Americanos, Prelates and Monsters: Willa Cather's *Death Comes for the Archbishop* as New World Odyssey," in *Padre Martínez*, 105-6.
53. James Kelly, "All-TIME 100 Novels: Critics Lev Grossman and Richard Lacayo Pick the 100 Best English-Language Novels Published Since 1923—the Beginning of TIME," *Time* magazine, Jan. 6, 2010, http//entertainment.time.com/2005/10/16/all-time-100-novels/slide/#times-list-of-the-100-best-novels.
54. Willa Cather, *Death Comes for the Archbishop* (New York: Alfred A. Knopf, 1927), repr. (New York: Vintage, 1971), 139-40. See Smith, "Achaeans, Americanos," in *Padre Martínez*, 122n4, for a rebuttal to the myth that Martínez double-crossed his parishioners.
55. Cather, *Death Comes*, 148-49.
56. Ibid., 140-41.
57. Smith, "Achaeans, Americanos," in *Padre Martínez*, 107.
58. Ibid., 106.
59. Diane H. Thomas, *The Southwestern Indian Detours* (Phoenix: Hunter, 1978, 2001), 41–50.
60. Henry Smith Turner, *The Original Journals of Henry Smith Turner with Stephen Watts Kearny to New Mexico and California, 1846–1847*, ed. Dwight L. Clarke (Norman: University of Oklahoma Press, 1966), 74.
61. Ibid., 73.

62. Hughes, *Doniphan's Expedition*, 120–21.
63. *Laws of the Territory of New Mexico* (Santa Fe: Press of the Palace of the Governors, 1979), i-ii; Gregg, *Commerce of the Prairies*, 142 and note 2.
64. Chávez, *But Time and Chance*, 48-49.
65. Ibid.
66. Ibid., 79-80; Juan Romero, *Reluctant Dawn: A History of Padre Antonio José Martínez, Cura de Taos* (Palm Springs, CA: Taos Connection, 2006), 33-34. Both of these references are based on Santiago Valdez, "Biografia del Rev. P. Antonio José Martínez, Cura-Párroco del Curato de Taos," an uncompleted, unpublished manuscript written in 1877 by Martínez's foster son, "amplified and translated" by Benjamin M. Read and located in the Ritch Collection, Huntington Library, San Marino, California; "Oliver P. Hovey, Report," HR (House Report) 60 (Washington, DC: 34th Cong., 3rd sess., 1857), 1.
67. "Oliver P. Hovey, Report," HR 60, 1; Mumey, *Laws of the Territory of New Mexico*, iii.
68. Commager, *Documents of American History*, 1:128-32.
69. Ibid., 144.
70. W. L. Marcy to Col. S. W. Kearny, June 3, 1846, in *Message from the President of the United States*, HED 19, 5-7.
71. "Proclamation of General Kearny," August 22, 1846, in ibid., 20-21.
72. Kearny to the Adjutant General, August 24, 1846, in ibid., 19-20.
73. James K. Polk to William H. Polk, October 2, 1846, in Wayne Cutler, ed., *Correspondence of James K. Polk* (Knoxville: University of Tennessee Press, 2009), 11:337.
74. Marcy to Kearny, January 11, 1847, in *Message of the President of the United States*, HED 70, 13-14.
75. Marcy to Sterling Price, June 26, 1847, in ibid., 33-34.
76. Prince, *Historical Sketches of New Mexico*, 313–14.

## Epilogue

1. Barry, *Beginning of the West*, 684-706.
2. William Hugh Robarts, *Mexican War Veterans: A Complete Roster of the Regular and Volunteer Troops in the War Between the United States and Mexico, from 1846 to 1848* (Washington, DC: Brentano's, 1887), 62.
3. Ibid., 45–46; Lee Myers, "Illinois Volunteers in New Mexico, 1847–1848," in *New Mexico Historical Review* 47, no. 1 (Jan. 1972): 5–31.
4. *Santa Fe Republican*, September 10, 1847, quoted in Lenderman, *Santa Fe Republican*, 4; "Diary of Philip Gooch Ferguson," in Bieber, *Marching with the Army*, 320.
5. *Santa Fe Republican*, September 10, 1847, in Lenderman, 5.
6. Ibid., September 17, 1847, in Lenderman, 9.
7. Ibid., September 24, 1847, in Lenderman, 11.
8. *Laws of the Territory of New Mexico*, 5-8.

9. Ritch, *Legislative Blue Book*, 98-99.
10. Ibid., 99.
11. Ibid., 99-100; "Petition of the People of New Mexico," October 14, 1848, Senate Misc. Doc. 5 (Washington, DC: 30th Cong., 2nd sess., 1848), 1-2.
12. *Journal of New Mexico Convention of Delegates to Recommend a Plan of Civil Government, September, 1849* (Santa Fe: Historical Society of New Mexico, 1907), repr. (n.p.: Nabu Press, 2010), 5-22.
13. "Memorial of Enrique Sanchez and Others, Citizens and Residents of the Territory and Valley of the Rio Grande, Praying The Establishment of a Territorial Government," February 27, 1850, Senate Misc. Doc. 61 (Washington, DC: 31st Cong., 1st sess., 1850), 1–3.
14. "Hugh N. Smith, Delegate from New Mexico," HR Report 220, April 4, 1850 (Washington, DC: 31st Cong., 1st sess., 1850), 4–6.
15. John Munroe, "Proclamation," May 28, 1850, in Annie Heloise Abel, ed., *The Official Correspondence of James S. Calhoun while Indian Agent at Santa Fé and Superintendent of Indian Affairs in New Mexico* (Washington, DC: Government Printing Office, 1915), 219–20.
16. Richard Melzer, Robert J. Tórrez, and Sandra Matthews-Benham, *A History of New Mexico Since Statehood* (Albuquerque: University of New Mexico Press, 2011), 8.
17. "Communication of R. H. Weightman," SED 76, September 12, 1850 (Washington, DC: 31st Cong., 1st sess., 1850), 1–11.
18. "Richard H. Weightman," HR Report 228, July 19, 1856 (Washington, DC: 34th Cong., 1st sess., 1856, 1.
19. Commager, *Documents of American History*, 1:319–23.
20. Abel, *Official Correspondence*, 296n2.
21. Daniel Webster to James S. Calhoun, January 9, 1851, in ibid., 296.
22. "Special Orders No. 12," March 2, 1851, in Abel, *Official Correspondence*, 296.
23. Francis Paul Prucha, *Guide to the Military Posts of the United States* (Milwaukee: State Historical Society of Wisconsin, 1964), 111, 85, 55, 100-101.
24. Abel, *Official Correspondence*, xii.
25. Calhoun to William Medill, September 25, 1849, in ibid., 21–25; Charles J. Kappler, *Indian Affairs: Laws and Treaties* (Washington, DC: Government Printing Office, 1904), 2:583–85, http://digital.library.okstate.edu/kappler/.
26. Calhoun to Orlando Brown, June 15, 1850, in Abel, *Official Correspondence*, 211–12.
27. Calhoun to Brown, July 15, 1850, in Abel, *Official Correspondence*, 216–18.
28. Calhoun to Medill, October 29, 1849, in Abel, *Official Correspondence*, 63–66; Paul Andrew Hutton, "Kit Carson's Ride," *Wild West* 19, no. 6 (Apr. 2007): 28–37; Hampton Sides, *Blood and Thunder: An Epic of the American*

*West* (New York: Doubleday, 2006), 247–59; William E. Hill, *The Santa Fe Trail, Yesterday and Today* (Caldwell, ID: Caxton Printers, 1992), 19–20; William E. Brown, *The Santa Fe Trail* (St. Louis: Patrice Press, 1988), 131–34.
29. Calhoun to Brown, November 30, 1849, in Abel, *Official Correspondence*, 88-89; Sides, *Blood and Thunder*, 257–58.
30. James H. Dunn to A. H. H. Stuart, October 9, 1850, in Abel, *Official Correspondence*, 272–273.
31. Sides, *Blood and Thunder*, 259.
32. Calhoun to Luke Lea, March 22, 1851, in Abel, *Official Correspondence*, 299–301.
33. Ibid., 300–301.
34. "Proposals to Raise Six Companies of Volunteers, for an Expedition to the Navajo Country," March 18, 1851, in Abel, *Official Correspondence*, 302–3.
35. Calhoun to the Cacique, Governors and Principals, March 19. 1851, in Abel, *Official Correspondence*, 301-2.
36. Calhoun to Millard Fillmore, March 29, 1851, in ibid., 305.
37. Calhoun to A. H. H. Stuart, March 31, 1851, in Abel, *Official Correspondence*, 306.
38. Calhoun to Lea, May 1, 1851, in Abel, *Official Correspondence*, 341–42.
39. Charles Beaubien to Calhoun, June 11, 1851, in Abel, *Official Correspondence*, 357–58.
40. John Munroe to Roger Jones, June 30, 1851, in Abel, *Official Correspondence*, 358–59.
41. "Pueblo Indians on the Warpath," *San Francisco Call*, May 14, 1910; "Liquor Cause of Indian Outbreak, *San Francisco Call*, May 15, 1910.

## Appendix H: The Taos Revolt in the Performing Arts and Literature

1. Jerry Tallmer, "Estelle Parsons Brings Back the Night," *Villager* 77 (October 10–16, 2007): 19, http://thevillager.com/232/estelleparsonsbrings.html.
2. Alberto Vidaurre, "1847 Revolt—Taos and Surrounding Areas," *Raíces y Ramas Journal* 3, no. 4 (Winter 2001): 3–4.
3. Maxwell Anderson, *Night over Taos: A Play in Three Acts* (New York: Samuel French, 1935), 29.
4. Vidaurre, "1847 Revolt," 3–4.
5. Ibid., 3.
6. Anderson, *Night over Taos*, 199. Actually, Montoya was tried in Taos by a military court-martial and hanged on the Plaza on February 7, 1847.
7. Victor Gluck, "Night Over Taos." http://www.theaterscene.net.
8. Caryn James, "Night of a Mexican Freedom Fighter," *New York Times*, October 2, 2007, http://theater.nytimes.com/2007/10/02/theater/ reviews/02taos.html?.

9. Everpoint (Joseph M. Field), *Taos: A Romance of the Massacre* (St. Louis: Reveille Office, 1847), repr. (Chimney Rock, CO: Rendezvous, 2006), 3.
10. E. A. Mares, *I Returned and Saw Under the Sun* (Albuquerque: University of New Mexico Press, 1989).

# BIBLIOGRAPHY

SOURCE MATERIAL

Abel, Annie Heloise, ed. *The Official Correspondence of James S. Calhoun while Indian Agent at Santa Fé and Superintendent of Indian Affairs in New Mexico*. Washington, DC: Government Printing Office, 1915.

Abert, J. W. *Journal of Lieutenant J. W. Abert, from Bent's Fort to St. Louis, in 1845*. Sen. Doc. 438. Washington, D C: 29th Cong., 1st sess., 1846.

———. *Report of Lieut. J. W. Abert, of His Examination of New Mexico in the Years 1846–'47*. SED 23. Washington, DC: 30th Cong., 1st sess., 1848. Reprint, Albuquerque: Horn & Wallace, 1962, as *Abert's New Mexico Report 1846–47*.

A Captain of Volunteers. *The Conquest of Santa Fe and the Subjugation of New Mexico by the Military Forces of the United States*. Philadelphia: H. Packer, 1847. Reprint, Farmington Hills, MI: Gale Sabin Americana, n.d.

*American State Papers, Foreign Relations*. Vol. 4. Washington, DC: Gales and Seaton, 1834.

Bancroft, Hubert Howe. *History of Arizona and New Mexico 1530–1888*. San Francisco: History Company, 1889.

Barry, Louise. *The Beginning of the West*. Topeka: Kansas State Historical Society, 1972.

Benton, Thomas Hart. *Thirty Years' View; or, A History of the Working of the American Government for Thirty Years, From 1820 to 1850*. 2 vols. New York: D. Appleton, 1854–56.

Bieber, Ralph P., ed. *Marching with the Army of the West, 1846–1848*. Glendale, CA: Arthur H. Clark, 1936. Reprint, Philadelphia: Porcupine Press, 1974. Contains the previously unpublished journals of Abraham Robinson Johnston, Marcellus Ball Edwards, and Philip Gooch Ferguson, all three of them soldiers with Stephen Watts Kearny's Army of the West.

Bonner, T. D. *The Life and Adventures of James P. Beckwourth*. New York: Harper & Brothers, 1856.

Campbell, William Bowen. "Mexican War Letters of Col. William Bowen Campbell of Tennessee, Written to Governor David Campbell of Virginia, 1846–1847," in *Tennessee Historical Magazine* (June 1915). Reprint, n.p.: Nabu Press, 2010.

Caspers, Henry G. A. "Journal." Special Collections, Digital Collections, St. Louis Mercantile Library at the University of Missouri–St. Louis. The Casper journal covers his army career with the Army of the West from June 13, 1846 to December 1848, and treats such events as the army's entry into Santa Fe, Governor Charles Bent's murder at Taos, Colonel Sterling Price's march to Taos, and the court-martial and execution of several New Mexicans involved in the killings of Captain R. T. Brown in August 1847.

Cheetham, Francis T. "The First Term of the American Court in Taos, New Mexico." *New Mexico Historical Review* 1, no. 1 (Jan. 1926): 23–41. Appended to Cheetham's background information about the court, its judges, and jury members are verbatim transcriptions of the grand jury and trial jury selection, verdicts, and sentencing of those arrested for murder and high treason during the uprising at Taos.

Commager, Henry Steele. *Documents of American History*. 6th ed. 2 vols. New York: Appleton-Century-Crofts, 1958.

Conard, Howard Louis. *"Uncle Dick" Wootton*. Chicago: W. E. Dibble, 1890. Reprint, New York: Time-Life Books, 1980.

*The Congressional Globe*. 29th Cong., 1st sess. Washington, DC: Blair & Rives, 1846.

———. 29th Cong., 2nd sess. Washington, DC: Blair & Rives, 1847.

Connelley, William Elsey. *Doniphan's Expedition and the Conquest of New Mexico and California*. Topeka: Privately Published, 1907.

Cooke, Philip St. George. *The Conquest of New Mexico and California in 1846–1848*. New York: G. P. Putnam's Sons, 1878. Reprint, Chicago: Rio Grande Press, 1964.

Coues, Elliott, ed. *The Journal of Jacob Fowler*. New York: Francis P. Harper, 1898. Reprint, Minneapolis: Ross & Haines, 1965.

Cutler, Wayne, ed. *Correspondence of James K. Polk*. 11 vols. Knoxville: University of Tennessee Press, 1969–2009.

Cutts, James Madison. *The Conquest of California and New Mexico*. Philadelphia: Carey & Hart, 1847. Reprint, Albuquerque: Horn & Wallace, 1965.

Davis, W. W. H. *El Gringo: New Mexico and Her People*. New York: Harper & Brothers, 1857. Reprint, Lincoln: University of Nebraska Press, 1982.

Drescher, William B. *Traditional and Actual History and Genealogy of the Drescher Family*. Missouri History Museum Archives, St. Louis,

1906. Drescher's memoir covers his army service from 1846–1848, including his duties in Santa Fe; his participation in the battles at La Cañada, Embudo, and Taos; and his observation of the Taos trials during April 1847.

Dyer, Alexander Byrdie. "Mexican War Diary of Lt. Alexander Byrdie Dyer." Undated. Fray Angélico Chávez History Library, Palace of the Governors, Santa Fe. The diary covers Colonel Sterling Price's move with his army to Taos during late January and early February 1847, to face those responsible for the murder of Governor Charles Bent. Included are references to the military actions at Cañada, Embudo, and Taos Pueblo, as well as Montoya's trial and hanging and Dyer's return to Santa Fe.

Edwards, Frank S. *A Campaign in New Mexico*. Philadelphia: Carey and Hart, 1847. Reprint, Naples, FL: Readex Microprint, 1966.

Emory, William H. *Notes of a Military Reconnoissance, from Fort Leavenworth, in Missouri, to San Diego, in California, Including Part of the Arkansas, Del Norte, and Gila Rivers*. HED 41. Washington, DC: 30th Cong., 1st sess., 1848. Reprint, Ross Calvin, ed. Albuquerque: University of New Mexico Press, 1951.

Galvin, John, ed. *Western America in 1846–1847: The Original Travel Diary of Lieutenant J. W. Abert*. San Francisco: John Howell-Books, 1966.

Gardner, Mark L., and Marc Simmons, eds. *The Mexican War Correspondence of Richard Smith Elliott*. Norman: University of Oklahoma Press, 1997.

Garrard, Lewis H. *Wah-To-Yah and the Taos Trail*. Cincinnati: H. W. Derby, 1850. Reprint, Palo Alto: American West, 1968.

Gregg, Josiah. *Commerce of the Prairies, or the Journal of a Santa Fe Trader, during Eight Expeditions across the Great Western Prairies, and a Residence of Nearly Nine Years in Northern Mexico*. New York: Henry G. Langley, 1844. Reprint, Max L. Moorhead, ed. Norman: University of Oklahoma Press, 1954.

Heitman, Francis B. *Historical Register and Dictionary of the United States Army*. 2 vols. Washington, DC: Government Printing Office, 1903. Reprint, Gaithersburg, MD: Olde Soldiers Books, 1988.

Historical Society of New Mexico. *Journal of New Mexico Convention of Delegates to Recommend a Plan of Civil Government, September, 1849*. Santa Fe: Historical Society of New Mexico, 1907. Reprint, n.p.: Nabu Press, 2010.

*History of Clay and Platte Counties, Missouri*. St. Louis: National Historical Company, 1885.

Hughes, John T. *Doniphan's Expedition; Containing an Account of the Conquest of New Mexico*. Cincinnati: J. A. & U. P. James, 1850.

Hyde, George E. *Life of George Bent Written from His Letters*. Norman: University of Oklahoma Press, 1968.

*Insurrection against the Military Government in New Mexico and California, 1847 and 1848*. Sen. Doc. 442. Washington, DC: 56th Cong., 1st sess., 1900.

Jackson, Donald, ed. *The Journals of Zebulon Montgomery Pike, with Letters and Related Documents*. 2 vols. Norman: University of Oklahoma Press, 1966.

Kappler, Charles J. *Indian Affairs: Laws and Treaties*. 2 vols. Washington, DC: Government Printing Office, 1904. Also see Oklahoma state website at http://digital.library.okstate.edu/kappler/.

Kendall, George Wilkins. *Narrative of the Texan Santa Fé Expedition*. 2 vols. New York: Harper and Brothers, 1844.

Ladd, Horatio O. *History of the War with Mexico*. New York: Dodd, Mead, 1883.

*Laws of the Territory of New Mexico*. Santa Fe: US Army of Occupation, 1846. Reprint, Nolie Mumey, ed. Denver: Nolie Mumey, 1970.

Lenderman, Gary D. *The Santa Fe Republican: New Mexico Territory's First Newspaper, 1847-1849*. Seattle: CreateSpace Independent Publishing Platform, 2011.

Luttig, John C. *Journal of a Fur-Trading Expedition on the Upper Missouri, 1812-1813*. St. Louis: Missouri Historical Society, 1920. Reprint, Stella M. Drumm, ed. New York: Argosy-Antiquarian, 1964.

Magoffin, Susan Shelby. *Down the Santa Fe Trail and into Mexico*, Stella M. Drumm, ed. New Haven: Yale University Press, 1926, 1962. Reprint, Lincoln: University of Nebraska Press, 1982.

McNierney, Michael, ed. *Taos 1847: The Revolt in Contemporary Accounts*. Boulder, CO: Johnson Publishing, 1980.

Meriwether, David. *My Life in the Mountains and on the Plains: The Newly Discovered Autobiography*. Norman: University of Oklahoma Press, 1965.

Moorhead, Max L., ed. "Notes and Documents." *New Mexico Historical Review* 26, no. 1 (Jan. 1951): 68–82.

Nasatir, A. P., ed. *Before Lewis and Clark: Documents Illustrating the History of the Missouri, 1785–1804*. 2 vols. St. Louis: St. Louis Historical Documents Foundation, 1952. Reprint, Lincoln: University of Nebraska Press, 1990.

Nevins, Allan, ed. *The Diary of Philip Hone, 1828–1851*. New York: Dodd, Mead, 1927.

———, ed. *Polk: The Diary of a President, 1845–1849*. New York: Longmans, Green, 1952.

*New York Herald*. October 3, 1846.

*Niles' National Register* 72 (May 15, 1847). "Trials for Treason in New Mexico."

Polk, James K. *New Mexico and California: Message from the President of the United States.* HED 70. Washington DC: 30th Cong., 1st sess., 1848.

———. *Occupation of Mexican Territory: Message from the President of the United States.* HED 19. Washington, DC: 29th Cong., 2d sess., 1846.

Prince, L. Bradford. *Historical Sketches of New Mexico from the Earliest Records to the American Occupation.* New York: Leggat Brothers, 1883.

———. *Old Fort Marcy.* Santa Fe: New Mexican Printing, 1912.

*Proceedings of the Drum-head Court Martial in the Case of Pablo Montoya, 1847.* Record Group 153, Records of the Office of the Judge Advocate General (Army), National Archives.

Quaife, Milo Milton. ed. *The Diary of James K. Polk During His Presidency, 1845 to 1849.* 4 vols. Chicago: A. C. McClurg, 1910.

———. *Kit Carson's Autobiography.* Lincoln: University of Nebraska Press, 1966.

Reeve, Frank D., ed. "The Charles Bent Papers." *New Mexico Historical Review* 29, no. 3 (July 1954): 234–39; 29, no. 4 (Oct. 1954): 311–17; 30, no. 2 (Apr. 1955): 153–67; 30, no. 3 (July 1955): 252–54; 30, no. 4 (Oct. 1955): 340–52; 31, no. 1 (Jan. 1956): 75–77; 31, no. 2 (Apr. 1956): 157–64; 31, no. 3 (July 1956): 251–53.

Remini, Robert V. *Andrew Jackson and the Course of American Democracy.* 3 vols. New York: Harper & Row, 1977–1984.

*Report of the Secretary of War.* HED 8. Washington, DC: 30th Cong., 1st sess., 1847.

Richardson, James D., ed. *A Compilation of the Messages and Papers of the Presidents.* 20 vols. New York: Bureau of National Literature, 1897.

"Road from Santa Fe to Don Fernandez, Memorial of the Legislative Council of New Mexico." HR Misc. Doc. 46. Washington, DC: 33rd Cong., 1st sess., 1854.

Robarts, William Hugh. *Mexican War Veterans: A Complete Roster of the Regular and Volunteer Troops in the War Between the United States and Mexico, from 1846 to 1848.* Washington, DC: Brentano's, 1887.

Robinson, Jacob S. *A Journal of the Santa Fé Expedition, under Col. Doniphan.* Portsmouth, NH: Portsmouth Journal Press, 1848. Reprint, Carl L. Cannon, ed. Princeton: Princeton University Press, 1932. Reprint, Santa Barbara, CA: Narrative Press, 2001.

Ruxton, George Frederick. *Adventures in Mexico and the Rocky Mountains.* New York: Harper & Brothers, 1848.

Ruxton, George Frederick. *Life in the Far West.* New York: Harper & Brothers, 1849. Reprint, Leroy R. Hafen, ed. Norman: University of Oklahoma Press, 1951.
Turner, Henry Smith. *The Original Journals of Henry Smith Turner with Stephen Watts Kearny to New Mexico and California, 1846–1847.* Edited by Dwight L. Clarke. Norman: University of Oklahoma Press, 1966.
Von Sachsen-Altenburg, Hans, and Laura Gabiger. *Winning the West: General Stephen Watts Kearny's Letter Book, 1846–1847.* Boonville, MO: Pekitanoui, 1998.
White, David A., ed., *News of the Plains and Rockies.* Spokane: Arthur H. Clark, 9 vols., 1996–2001.
Wislizenus, Frederick Adolphus. *Memoir of a Tour to Northern Mexico, Connected With Col. Doniphan's Expedition.* Senate Misc. Doc. 26. Washington, DC: 30th Cong., 1st sess., 1848.

## Secondary Material

*American Heritage Pictorial Atlas of United States History.* New York: American Heritage, 1966.
Anderson, Maxwell. *Night Over Taos, A Play in Three Acts.* New York: Samuel French, 1935.
Beachum, Larry M. *William Becknell: Father of the Santa Fe Trade.* El Paso: Texas Western Press, 1982.
Binkley, William C. *The Expansionist Movement in Texas, 1836–1850.* Berkeley: University of California Press, 1925.
Brown, William E. *The Santa Fe Trail.* St. Louis: Patrice Press, 1988.
Burton, E. Bennett. "The Taos Rebellion." *Old Santa Fe: A Magazine of History, Archaeology, Genealogy, and Biography* 1, no. 2 (Oct. 1913): 176–209.
Cather, Willa. *Death Comes for the Archbishop.* New York: Alfred A. Knopf, 1927. Reprint, New York: Vintage, 1971.
Chávez, Fray Angélico. *But Time and Chance: The Story of Padre Martínez of Taos: 1793–1867.* Santa Fe: Sunstone, 1981.
Chávez, Thomas E. *An Illustrated History of New Mexico.* Niwot: University Press of Colorado, 1992.
———. *Manuel Alvarez, 1794–1856: A Southwestern Biography.* Niwot: University Press of Colorado, 1990.
Christensen, Lena Maye. "Padre Martinez: New Mexican Champion of Defiance, 1793–1867." MA diss., Texas Technological College, Lubbock, 1961.
Crutchfield, James A. "Marching with the Army of the West," in *Black Powder Annual.* Union City, TN: Dixie Gun Works, 1991, 15–17, 89–91.

———. *Tennesseans at War: Volunteers and Patriots in Defense of Liberty.* Nashville: Rutledge Hill, 1987.

———. *Tragedy at Taos: The Revolt of 1847.* Plano: Republic of Texas Press, 1995.

Crutchfield, James A., Candy Moulton, and Terry A. Del Bene, eds. *The Settlement of America: Encyclopedia of Westward Expansion from Jamestown to the Closing of the Frontier.* Armonk, NY: Sharpe Reference, 2011.

Dawson, Joseph G., III *Doniphan's Epic March: The 1st Missouri Volunteers in the Mexican War.* Lawrence: University Press of Kansas, 1999.

DeVoto, Bernard. *The Year of Decision: 1846.* New York: Houghton Mifflin, 1942. Reprint, New York: Book of the Month Club, 1984.

Everpoint (Joseph M. Field). *Taos: A Romance of the Massacre.* St. Louis: Reveille Office, 1847. Reprint, Chimney Rock, CO: Rendezvous, 2006.

Fontana, Bernard L. *Entrada: The Legacy of Spain & Mexico in the United States.* Tucson: Southwest Parks and Monuments Association, 1994.

Gimeno, Emil. *The Adobe Castle of the Santa Fe Trail: The History & Reconstruction of Bent's Old Fort.* Arvada, CO: privately printed, 2004.

Gonzalez, Albert D. "Turley's Mill and the Archaeology of Westward Expansion." N.p., n.d. From the Burgwin Research Center collection, Taos, NM.

Goodrich, James W. "Revolt at Mora, 1847." *New Mexico Historical Review* 47, no. 1 (Jan. 1972): 49–60.

Grice, Gary K. "History of Weather Observing at Fort Marcy, New Mexico, 1849–1892," Asheville, NC: Climate Database Modernization Program, NOAA National Climatic Data Center, 2005.

Groneman, William III. *David Crockett: Hero of the Common Man.* New York: Forge Books, 2005.

Hafen, LeRoy R. *The Mountain Men and the Fur Trade of the Far West.* 10 vols. Glendale, CA: Arthur H. Clark, 1965–1972. Reprint, Spokane: Arthur H. Clark, 2000–2004.

Harris, Matthew L., and Jay H. Buckley, eds. *Zebulon Pike, Thomas Jefferson, and the Opening of the American West.* Norman: University of Oklahoma Press, 2012.

Herrera, Carlos R. "New Mexico Resistance to U. S. Occupation during the Mexican-American War of 1846–1848." In Erlinda Gonzales-Berry and David R. Maciel, eds. *The Contested Homeland: A Chicano History of New Mexico.* Albuquerque: University of New Mexico Press, 2000.

Hill, William E. *The Santa Fe Trail, Yesterday and Today.* Caldwell, ID: Caxton Printers, 1992.

Hollon, W. Eugene. *The Lost Pathfinder: Zebulon Montgomery Pike.* Norman: University of Oklahoma Press, 1949.

Horgan, Paul. *Great River: The Rio Grande in North American History.* 2 vols. New York: Rinehart, 1954.

Howlett, Rev. W. J. *Life of the Right Reverend Joseph P. Machebeuf, DD.* Pueblo, CO: Franklin Press, 1908.

Hutton, Paul Andrew. "Kit Carson's Ride." *Wild West* 19, no. 6 (Apr. 2007).

Hyslop, Stephen G. *Bound for Santa Fe: The Road to New Mexico and the American Conquest, 1806–1848.* Norman: University of Oklahoma Press, 2002.

Jenkins, Myra Ellen. "Rebellion Against American Occupation of New Mexico 1846–1847." Dissertation. Albuquerque: University of New Mexico, 1949. In Dorothy Woodward Papers, Collection 1959-231, Box 6, Folder 148, New Mexico Commission of Public Records, State Records Center and Archives, Santa Fe.

Johnson, David M., Chris Adams, Charles Hawk, and Skip Keith Miller. *Final Report on the Battle of Cieneguilla: A Jicarilla Apache Victory over the U.S. Dragoons March 30, 1854.* Washington DC: Government Printing Office, 2009.

Keleher, William A. *Maxwell Land Grant: A New Mexico Item.* Santa Fe: Rydal Press, 1942. Reprint, Albuquerque: University of New Mexico Press, 1984.

Kelly, James C., and Barbara Clark Smith, eds. *Jamestown, Québec, Santa Fe: Three North American Beginnings.* Washington, DC: Smithsonian Books, 2007.

Kessell, John L. *Kiva, Cross, and Crown.* Washington, DC: National Park Service, 1979.

Langguth, A. J. *Driven West: Andrew Jackson and the Trail of Tears to the Civil War.* New York: Simon & Schuster, 2010.

Lavender, David. *Bent's Fort.* Garden City, NY: Doubleday, 1954.

*Laws of the Territory of New Mexico.* Santa Fe: Press of the Palace of the Governors, 1979.

Lecompte, Janet. *Rebellion in Rio Arriba 1837.* Albuquerque: University of New Mexico Press, 1985.

Long, Jeff. *Duel of Eagles.* New York: William Morrow, 1990.

Loomis, Noel M. *The Texan-Santa Fe Pioneers.* Norman: University of Oklahoma Press, 1958.

Loomis, Noel M., and Abraham P. Nasatir. *Pedro Vial and the Roads to Santa Fe.* Norman: University of Oklahoma Press, 1967.

Love, Marian F. "The Demise of Turley's Mill," *Santa Fean* (March 1986), 24–26.
Loyola, Sister Mary. "The American Occupation of New Mexico, 1821–1852." *New Mexico Historical Review* 14, nos. 1, 2, and 3 (Jan., Apr., July 1939).
Mares, E. A. *I Returned and Saw Under the Sun*. Albuquerque: University of New Mexico Press, 1989.
Martínez, Luis. "The Taos Massacre—1847." Writers Project Administration (WPA) files, Collection 1959-232, Folder 233a. New Mexico Commission of Public Records, State Records Center and Archives, Santa Fe.
Martínez, Roger. "Our Lady of Guadalupe Has a Long History." *Taos News*, December 17, 2009.
Martínez, Vicente M. "History of the Padre Martínez Home (1826–2009) From Generation to Generation." https://ghostsoftaos.wordpress.com/taos-history/history-of-the-padre-martinez-home-1826-2009-from-generation-to-generation-%ef%a3%a9-2009-vicente-m-martinez/.
Melzer, Richard, Robert J. Tórrez, and Sandra Matthews-Benham. *A History of New Mexico Since Statehood*. Albuquerque: University of New Mexico Press, 2011.
Mumey, Nolie. *Old Forts and Trading Posts of the West*. Denver: Artcraft, 1956.
Murphy, Lawrence R. "The United States Army in Taos, 1847–1852." *New Mexico Historical Review* 47, no. 1 (Jan. 1972): 33–48.
Myers, Lee. "Illinois Volunteers in New Mexico, 1847–1848." *New Mexico Historical Review* 47, no. 1 (Jan. 1972): 5–31.
National Register of Historic Places. Nomination form, "Governor Bent House," prepared March 1, 1978, by John O. Baxter, archivist, New Mexico State Records Center and Archives, Santa Fe.
———. Nomination form, "Taos Downtown Historic District," prepared March 1, 1978, by John O. Baxter, archivist, New Mexico State Records Center and Archives, Santa Fe.
Noble, David Grant. "Pecos Pueblo, December 31, 1590," in *Exploration*. Santa Fe: School of American Research Press, 1981.
———, ed. *Santa Fe: History of an Ancient City*. Santa Fe: School of American Research Press, 1989.
Oliva, Leo E. *Soldiers on the Santa Fe Trail*. Norman: University of Oklahoma Press, 1967.
*Padre Martinez: New Perspectives from Taos*. Taos: Millicent Rogers Museum, 1988.
Pearce, T. M., ed. *New Mexico Place Names: A Geographical Dictionary*. Albuquerque: University of New Mexico Press, 1965.

Powell, Donald M. *New Mexico and Arizona in the Serial Set, 1846–1861*. Los Angeles: Dawson's Book Shop, 1970.

Prucha, Francis Paul. *Guide to the Military Posts of the United States*. Milwaukee: State Historical Society of Wisconsin, 1964.

Read, Benjamin M. *Illustrated History of New Mexico*. Santa Fe: New Mexican Printing, 1912. Reprint, New York: Arno, 1976.

Remini, Robert V. *Andrew Jackson and His Indian Wars*. New York: Penguin, 2002.

Ritch, W. G. *The Legislative Blue-Book of the Territory of New Mexico*. Santa Fe: Charles W. Greene, 1882. Reprint, Albuquerque: University of New Mexico Press, 1968.

Romero, Juan. *Reluctant Dawn: A History of Padre Antonio José Martínez, Cura de Taos*. Palm Springs, CA: Taos Connection, 2006.

Rothschild, Nan A. *Colonial Encounters in a Native American Landscape: The Spanish and Dutch in North America*. Washington, DC: Smithsonian Books, 2003.

Sabin, Edwin L. *Kit Carson Days (1809–1868)*. Chicago: A. C. McClurg, 1914.

Sale, Randall D., and Edwin D. Karn. *American Expansion: A Book of Maps*. Lincoln: University of Nebraska Press, 1962.

Sánchez, George I. *Forgotten People*. San Francisco: R. and E. Research Associates, 1970. Reprint, Albuquerque: University of New Mexico Press, 1996.

Sánchez, Pedro. *Memories of Antonio José Martínez*. Edited by Guadalupe Baca-Vaughn. Santa Fe: Rydal Press, 1978.

Shalhope, Robert E. *Sterling Price, Portrait of a Southerner*. Columbia: University of Missouri Press, 1971.

Sherman, John. *Taos: A Pictorial History*. Santa Fe: William Gannon, 1990.

Sides, Hampton. *Blood and Thunder: An Epic of the American West*. New York: Doubleday, 2006.

Sloane, Eric. *Return to Taos*. New York: Wilfred Funk, 1960.

Spiller, Roger, ed. *Dictionary of American Military Biography*. Westport, CT: Greenwood Press, 1984.

Steele, Thomas J., Paul Rhetts, and Barbe Awalt, eds. *Seeds of Struggle/Harvest of Faith: The Papers of the Archdiocese of Santa Fe Catholic Cuarto Centennial Conference on the History of the Catholic Church in New Mexico*. Albuquerque: LPD Press, 1998.

Stegmaier, Mark J. *Texas, New Mexico, and the Compromise of 1850*. Kent, OH: Kent State University Press, 1996.

Steiner, Bernard C. *Life of Roger Brooke Taney*. Baltimore: Williams & Wilkins, 1922.

Thomas, David Yancey. *A History of Military Government in Newly Acquired Territory of the United States*. Studies in History, Economics, and Public Law, vol. 20, no. 2. New York: Columbia University, 1904. Reprint, New York: AMS Press, 1967.

Thomas, Diane H. *The Southwestern Indian Detours*. Phoenix: Hunter, 1978, 2001.

Thrapp, Dan L. *Encyclopedia of Frontier Biography*. 4 vols. Glendale, CA: Arthur H. Clark, 1988–94.

Tórrez, Robert J. "The New Mexican 'Revolt' and Treason Trials of 1847." *Tradición* 17, no. 1 (April 2012), 60–70.

Twitchell, Ralph Emerson. *The Conquest of Santa Fe 1846*. Truchas, NM: Tate Gallery, 1967.

———. *The History of the Military Occupation of the Territory of New Mexico from 1846 to 1851*. Denver: Smith-Brooks, 1909.

———. *The Leading Facts of New Mexican History*. 5 vols. Cedar Rapids, IA: Torch Press, 1911–17. Vols. 1 and 2 reprinted Santa Fe: Sunstone, 2007.

———. *Old Santa Fe: The Story of New Mexico's Ancient Capital*. Santa Fe: New Mexican Publishing, 1925.

———. *The Story of the Conquest of Santa Fe, New Mexico, and the Building of Old Fort Marcy, A.D. 1846*. Santa Fe: Historical Society of New Mexico, n.d.

Urwin, Gregory J. W. *The United States Cavalry: An Illustrated History*. Poole, UK: Blandford Press, 1983.

Vásquez, Dora Ortiz. *Enchanted Temples of Taos*. Santa Fe: Rydal Press, 1975.

Vidaurre, Alberto. "1847 Revolt—Taos and Surrounding Areas." *Raíces y Ramas Journal* 3, no. 4 (Winter 2001): 2–16.

Waldman, Carl. *Atlas of the North American Indian*. New York: Facts on File, 1985.

Walker, Dale L. *Pacific Destiny: The Three-Century Journey to the Oregon Country*. New York: Forge, 2000.

Walter, Paul A. F. "The First Civil Governor of New Mexico under the Stars and Stripes." *New Mexico Historical Review* 8, no. 2 (Apr. 1933), 98–129.

Weber, David J., ed. *Arms, Indians, and the Mismanagement of New Mexico: Donaciano Vigil, 1846*. El Paso: Texas Western Press, 1986.

———, ed. *Foreigners in Their Native Land: Historical Roots of the Mexican Americans*. Albuquerque: University of New Mexico Press, 2003.

———. *The Mexican Frontier, 1821–1846: The American Southwest under Mexico*. Albuquerque: University of New Mexico Press, 1993.

———. *On the Edge of Empire: The Taos Hacienda of los Martínez*. Santa Fe: Museum of New Mexico Press, 1996.

———. *The Taos Trappers*. Norman: University of Oklahoma Press, 1971.

———, ed. *What Caused the Pueblo Revolt of 1680?* Boston: Bedford/St. Martin's, 1999.

Website of the Missouri Secretary of State.

Wetherington, Ronald K. "Cantonment Burgwin: The Archaeological and Documentary Record." *New Mexico Historical Review* 81, no. 4 (Fall 2006), 391–411.

———. *Ceran St. Vrain: American Frontier Entrepreneur*. Santa Fe: Sunstone, 2012.

Wilentz, Sean. *Andrew Jackson*. New York: Times Books, 2005.

Winders, Richard Bruce. *Mr. Polk's Army: The American Military Experience in the Mexican War*. College Station: Texas A&M University Press, 1997.

# ACKNOWLEDGMENTS

One cannot recount events that occurred nearly 170 years ago without owing a tremendous debt to many people from the past—historians, writers, and artists—not to mention those contemporary professionals—librarians, publishers, editors, illustrators, and photographers—who contribute so much to present-day historical research and documentation.

For assistance with the present volume, the writer would like to thank the following individuals and institutions, listed in no particular order:

The late Alberto Vidaurre, Taos; Frankie King, librarian, Tennessee State Library and Archives, Nashville; Carol Fletcher and Miriam Barrett, Nashville Metropolitan Public Library, Nashville; Patrick McMurray, librarian, University of New Mexico, Taos Library, Taos; Carol Baker, librarian, Fort Burgwin–Southern Methodist University at Taos; Skip Miller, archaeologist, US Forest Service, Taos; David Fernandez, Taos; Joan Livingston, *Taos News,* Taos; Professor Meg Frisbee, Colorado State University, Pueblo; John Carson, Bent's Old Fort National Historic Site, La Junta, Colorado; Thomas Chávez, Albuquerque; Tom Leech and James Bourland, Press of the Palace of the Governors, Santa Fe; Tomas Jaehn, Angelico Chávez History Library, Santa Fe; Greta Lindquist, University of California Press, Berkeley; Emily Brock, senior archivist, New Mexico State Archives, Santa Fe; Ellen Goldberg, editorial assistant, School for Advanced Research, Santa Fe; Rachel Preston Prinz, chief visionary officer, Archinia LLC, Taos; Cindy Tyson, administrative assistant, New Mexico Historical Review, Albuquerque; Nita Murphy, director, Southwest Research Center, University of New Mexico–Taos; Mike Adler, director, Fort Burgwin–Southern Methodist University at Taos; Tim Kimball, Corrales, New Mexico, who alerted me to the existence of the journals of Henry George Anton Caspers and A. B. Dyer; Crown Publishers, New York; Camille Cazedessus, Pagosa Springs, Colorado; Ouray Meyers, Taos; André Dumont and Nicholas Potter, whose antiquarian bookstores in Santa Fe have provided a gold mine for anyone interested in New Mexico history; Rick Hendricks, New Mexico state historian, Santa Fe; *New Mexico Historical Review* former editor Paul Andrew Hutton and former office manager Nancy Brown, Albuquerque; Molly Kodner, associate archivist, Missouri History Museum, St. Louis; J. R. Logan, *Taos News*, Taos, from whom I learned about the William B. Drescher journal; my brother, Sam S. Crutchfield, Alexandria, Virginia; Dolores Benavides, Alexandria, Virginia; Alfredo Benavides, Washington, DC; Candy Moulton, Encampment, Wyoming, and Dale Walker, El Paso, Texas, for their many years of friendship and their encouragement and support of my writing career over the past three decades; and Mary Bray Wheeler, Nashville, for her longtime friendship and editorial services.

To my publisher, Bruce H. Franklin of Westholme Publishing, and his fine colleagues—manuscript editor Ron Silverman, jacket designer Trudi Gershenov, cartographer Tracy Dungan, indexer Kendra Millis, and proofreader, Mike Kopf—I extend my sincerest thanks and admiration.

Finally, I thank my wife, Regena, who has consistently supported me in all of my writing endeavors.

The conclusions in this book are my own, and I take responsibility for any errors.

# INDEX

Abert, J. W., 36, 48, 67, 68, 69
Abréu, Ramón, 144
Acoma, 62–63
Adams, John Quincy, 3
*Adventures in Mexico and the Rocky Mountains* (Ruxton), 138
Alamo, 4–5
Albert, John D., 80, 80*ph*
Alcalde, Señor, 99
Alencaster, Joachin del Real, 17
Allen, James, 29, 30–31
Alvarez, Manuel, 72, 110, 153
Angney, William A., 30, 84, 93, 99, 152
Apache Canyon, 38, 39, 41–44, 44*ph*
Archuleta, Diego, 41, 50, 67, 67*ph*, 68, 133, 137, 138
Archuleta, Pantaleón, 103
Armijo, Manuel, 8, 32, 32*ph*, 37–38, 39–44, 50, 52–53, 65, 71, 135
arms and ammunition, import of, 65–66
Army of the West
 Bent and, 70
 at Bent's Fort, 34
 en route to New Mexico, 31, 36–37
 formation of, 13, 26, 29–31
 occupation by, 14, 43–46, 44*ph*
Asencio, 108
Atkinson, Henry, 19
Austin, Mary, 141, 142–143
Austin, Moses, 1–2
Austin, Stephen, 2, 4
Austin, William, 82
Autobees, Charles, 106

Avila, Juan Antonio, 108

Baird, James, 18–19
Barbee, Thomas, 54, 99
Barcelo, Trinidad, 103
Barry, James S., 106
Beaubien, Charles (Carlos), 53, 71, 78, 105, 105*ph*, 107, 108, 109, 151, 157–158
Beaubien, Narciso, 71, 75, 78, 82, 105
Becknell, William, 21–22
Beckwourth, James P., 139
Bent, Charles
 background of, 24
 Bent's Fort and, 32–33
 Buchanan and, 69
 burial of, 82, 97
 as governor, 53
 murder of, xvii, 73, 75, 78, 100, 133–134
 on planned rebellion, 70
 portrait of, 55*ph*
 in Taos, 69–72
Bent, George, 106, 127
Bent, Teresina, 73–74
Bent, William, 24, 32–33, 34, 105
Benton, Thomas Hart, 11–12, 27–28, 40, 90, 103
Bent's Fort, 24, 32–34, 35*ph*
Bingo, Antonio Jose, 106
Blair, Francis P., Jr., 53, 102, 103–104, 103*ph*, 106, 127
Blumner, Charles, 53
Boggs, Rumalda Luna, 73, 110
Bowie, James "Jim," 5
Brooke, George M., 28
Brown, James, 30

Brown, Orlando, 155
Brown, Robert T., 117, 118
Buchanan, James, 57, 69, 103, 116, 137
Burgwin, John Henry K., 67, 83, 87–88, 93, 97
Burnett, John G., 122–123
Burr, Aaron, 16
Burton, E. Bennett, 133–134

Cabanne, Lewis, 81
Calhoun, James S., 154, 155, 156, 157, 158
Calhoun, John C., 8, 9, 10, 12
*Campaign in New Mexico, A* (Edwards), 138
Campbell, William Bowen, 130–131
Cañada, battle at, 85–87, 86*m*
*Carbine Manual* (Kearny), 27
Carson, Josefa Jaramillo, 73, 82, 110
Carson, Kit, 73, 82, 156
Cather, Willa, 140, 141–143
causes of revolt, 122–136
Cementerio Militar, El, 82
Chácon, Rafael, 42
Chalifoux, Jean-Baptiste, 106
Chambers, Samuel, 18–19
Chaves, Manuel, 156–157
Chávez, Manuel, 67
Chávez, Thomas E., 135
Chavis, Pablo (Chávez), 69, 96, 137, 138
Chimayó Rebellion, 64–65, 132
Chouteau, Auguste P., 19
citizenship issue, 50, 58–60, 104, 145–149
Clamorgan, Jacques, 18
Clark, Meriwether Lewis, 30
Clark, William, 15, 19
Clarkson, R. Hunter, 143
Clay, Henry, 8–9, 20, 154
*Commerce of the Prairies* (Gregg), 22–23
Compromise of 1850, 13, 154
Connelly, Henry, 153
*Conquest of California and New Mexico, The* (Cutts), 137

Cooke, Philip St. George, 28, 32, 40–41, 54
Cordoval, Jose, 106
Cordoval, Ramonde, 106
Cortez, Hernanado, 62
Cortez, Manuel, 69, 81, 117, 136–137, 138
Crockett, David "Davy," 5
Cuervo, El, 107–108
Culver, Romulus E., 81
Cutts, James M., 137

Dallam, Richard, 53
Davis, Daniel, 30
Davis, Edward T., 150
Davis, Garett, 57
Davis, W. H. H., 138–139
de Mun, Jules, 19
*Death Comes for the Archbishop* (Cather), 140, 141–143
d'Eglise, Jacques, 15–16
Dent, John C., 54
Dios Maes, Juan de, 89
Dodge, Henry, 26
Doniphan, Alexander W., 29–30, 30*ph*, 54, 115–116, 117*ph*
*Doniphan's Expedition* (Hughes), 137–138
Douglas, Stephen A., 57
Drescher, William B., 55
drunkenness, 129–130, 151
Duran, Jose Tomas, 118–119
Durocher, Lorenzo, 15–16
Dyer, A. B., 84, 93

Easton, L. J., 99
Edmonson, Benjamin B., 55, 67, 83, 117–118
Edwards, Benjamin, 2–3
Edwards, Frank S., 138
Edwards, Haden, 2–3
Edwards, John C., 27, 29
*El Gringo* (Davis), 138–139
Elliott, Richard Smith, 75, 78, 117, 134, 138
Embudo, battle at, 87–88, 88*m*
Emory, William H., 36, 37–38, 37*ph*, 41–42, 44–45, 47–48, 49, 50, 52, 56

# Index

Fannin, James W., 5
Federal Writers Project, 133
Ferguson, Philip Gooch, 129
Fillmore, Millard, 154, 157
Fischer, Woldemar, 30, 92
Fitzpatrick, Thomas "Broken Hand," 31–32
*Forgotten People* (Sánchez), 131
Fort Brown, 11
Fort Marcy, 52, 82
Fowler, Jacob, 22
Fredonia, Republic of, 3
Frémont, John Charles, 28
Funk, Joseph, 81

Garcia, José Manuel, 106–107, 108
Garrard, Lewis H., 105, 109–112
Giddings, N. B., 54
Gilmer, Jeremy F., 50, 52
Gilpin, William, 30, 115
Glenn, Hugh, 22
Gonzales, José, 64–65
Graham, Joseph M., 106
Great American Desert myth, 18
Great Depression, 125
Green, Charlotte, 34
Gregg, Josiah, 22–23, 23*ph*, 144
Grier, William N., 156
Guadalupe Hidalgo, Treaty of, 152
Guerrera, Pablo, 108

Hall, Willard P., 54
hangings, 111–112
Haralson, Hugh A., 57
Harvey, Fred, 143
Harwood, William, 81, 82, 138
Hatfield, William, 82
Head, Mark, 81, 82, 138
Hendley, Israel R., 55, 67, 89–90, 91
Higgins, Nelson, 30
Hollaway, John (Holloway), 54, 117
Holley, William C. (Halley), 54
Hone, Philip, 12
Horine, Thomas, 54
Houghton, Joab, 53, 101, 102–103, 104, 105–106, 109
Houston, Sam, 5

Hovey, Oliver Perry, 144–145, 150
Howlett, W. J., 139–140
Hudson, Thomas B., 30
Hughes, John T., 48, 119, 137–138, 144
Hunt, Jefferson, 30
Hunter, Jesse, 30

Indian Detours, 143
Indian raids, 115–120, 154–158
Indian Removal Act (1830), 122–123
Ingalls, Rufus, 99

Jackson, Andrew, 3, 8, 10, 12, 122
Jackson, H., 54
Jackson, Hancock, 30
Jaramillo, Maria Ignacia (Bent), 33, 70, 70*ph*, 75, 110–111
Jaramillo, Pablo, 75, 78, 82
Jones, Roger, 27, 59, 120, 158

Kearny, Stephen Watts
  address from, 166
  appointments by, 53
  Armijo and, 42–44, 52–53
  background of, 26–27
  citizenship issue and, 58–59, 104, 146–148
  directive of, 34–36
  en route to New Mexico, 31–32
  guarantees of, 115
  Martínez and, 144
  on New Mexicans, 61–62
  occupation of New Mexico by, 38–39, 39*ph*, 41–42, 45*ph*, 49–50
  orders to, 28–29
  portrait of, 27*ph*
  proclamation of, 169–170
  recruitment by, 29
  at San Pasqual, 56
  at Santa Fe, 44–45, 49, 132
  *See also Laws of the Territory of New Mexico*
Kendall, George Wilkins, 8
Kit Carson Cemetery, 82

La Lande, Baptiste, 15–16
Lamar, Mirabeau B., 6, 8
Lamy, Juan Bautista, 141
Largo, Sarcilla (Zarcillos Largos), 115–116, 117*ph*
Larkin, John, 119
Latour, Jean Marie, 141
*Laws of the Territory of New Mexico*, 53–54, 57–59, 59*ph*, 144–145, 151
Lea, Luke, 156, 157
Leal, James W., 69–70, 75, 78, 82
Lecompte, Janet, 64, 132
Ledoux, Antoine, 106
Lee, Elliott, 75, 100–101, 106, 134, 138
Lee, Stephen Louis, 69, 71, 71*ph*, 75, 78, 82, 106
Lewis, Meriwether, 15
Lisa, Manuel, 18
Lobato, Buenaventura, 133–134
Love, John, 120
Lucero, Juan Antonio, 107–108
Lucero, Pedro, 107
Luhan, Mable Dodge, 141

Machebeuf, Joseph Projectus, 139
Maclean, L. A., 52
Magoffin, James Wiley, 40–41, 41*ph*, 50
Magoffin, Samuel, 40
Magoffin, Susan Shelby, 36–37, 40
Mallet, Paul and Pierre, 15
Manifest Destiny, 122, 123
Marcy, William L., 27, 28–29, 52, 58–59, 103–104, 113, 130, 146, 147, 148
Marshall, Joseph, 82
Martin, Juan Domingo, 107–108
Martin, Mariano, 106
Martin, Pedro, Carpio, and Deonicio, 119
Martínez, Antonio José, 65, 65*ph*, 71, 75, 82, 100, 108, 110, 136–145, 152
Martínez, Jose Gregory, 106
Martínez, Luis, 133
Martínez, Mariana, 155

Martínez, Pascual, 140
Martínez, Santiago, 106
Martínez, Ventura, 106
Mason, John Y., 103–104
Mason, W. S., 119
Masservy, W. S., 153–154
Maxwell, Lucien, 106
Maxwell Land Grant, 71
McClanahan, James M., 118
McKissack, William M. D., 91
McKnight, John, 22
McKnight, Robert, 18–19
McMillan, S. H. (McMillin), 54
Medina, Antonio, 106
Melgares, Don Facundo, 21
Meriwether, David, 19–20
Meteyer, Jeanot, 15–16
Mexican independence, 21
Mexican-American War
 end of, 152
 lead-up to, 1–11
 reactions to, 12
 start of, 11–12
Meyers, Ralph, 76–77*m*
Miera, Manuel, 107–108
Miranda, Guadalupe, 71
Miranda-Beaubien Land Grant, 71
Mitchell, D. D., 55
Monroe, John, 157–158
Montoya, Pablo, 65, 69, 96, 98–101, 134–135, 136–137, 138
Mora, battle at, 81, 89–90, 89*ph*, 91
Morin, Jesse B., 55, 91, 119
Mormon Battalion, 28, 29, 30, 54
Morrison, William, 15–16
Moss, Oliver Perry, 30
Mountain Route of Santa Fe Trail, 21
*Mr. Polk's Army* (Winders), 127
Muñoz, Don Pedro, 42
Murphy, William S., 30

Nacogdoches, 2–3
Naranjo, Francisco, 107–108
*Narrative of the Texan Santa Fe Expedition* (Kendall), 8

New Mexico
  description of, 171
  invasion of, 26–46
  occupation of, 13, 14
  trade with, 14–19, 21–24
Newby, Edward W. B., 150, 151
Northwest Ordinance (1787), 146
Noyes, Mr., 81
Nuestra Señora de Guadalupe, 72, 73*ph*, 82, 108

O'Falon, John, 19
Onate, Don Juan de, 62
*One of Ours* (Cather), 141
Ortiz, Antonio, 106
Ortiz, Juan Felipe, 68, 144
Ortiz, Tomás, 67, 68, 138, 144
Otero, Antonio José, 53
Overton, John, 3
Owens, W. (Owen), 119
Owl Woman, 33
Oxley, Clare, 90–91

Pacheco, Juan, 107–108
Palo Alto, 11
Parsons, Monroe M., 30
Pérez, Albino, 64
Pierce, Franklin, 20, 91
Pike, Zebulon, 16–18
Pillsbury, Timothy, 57
Pino, Nicholas and Miguel, 67
Poinsett, Joel, 3
Point of Rocks, 155–156
Polk, James K.
  Congress and, 57–58, 60
  criticism of, xviii
  election of, 8–10
  expansion and, 124
  Magoffin and, 40
  Mexican-American War and, 11–12
  New Mexico occupation and, 27–29
  portrait of, 11*ph*
  Price and, 54, 98
  territorial status and, 145–149
  Texas annexation and, 1, 10, 11, 13
  treason issue and, 112–113
  Trujillo and, 103
Ponett, Ola, 81
Popé, 63
Price, Sterling
  at Cañada, 85–87
  citizenship issue and, 104
  command of, xvii, 54–55, 114
  at Embudo, 87
  Indian raids and, 116–117, 119
  Marcy's dispatch to, 130
  Martínez and, 110
  Montoya and, 98–99, 101
  Mora and, 89
  portrait of, 83*ph*
  report from, 98, 137
  response from, 81–82, 83–84
  at Taos, 91–92
  Taos Pueblo and, 93, 96
  troops of, 66–67, 127–128
  Trujillo and, 103
Prince, L. Bradford, 148
Pruett, Benjamin, 81
Pueblo people, 63, 131
Purcell, James (a.k.a. Pursley), 16

Quisenbury, Charles (Quesenberry), 118

racial issues, 124–125
Ralls, John, 150
Raton Pass, 36–37
Read, Benjamin M., 42
rebellion
  history of, 62–65, 131–132
  thwarted, 67–68, 70
  *See also* Taos Revolt
Reid, John W., 30, 115
*Report on the Exploring Expedition to the Rocky Mountains* (Frémont), 28
Resaca de la Palma, 11
Rhett, Robert, 57
Rio Colorado, 81
Rivole, Francisco (Revali), 107, 108
roads, condition of, 84–85, 84*ph*
Robaldo, Francisco, 91
Robert, Peter, 82

Robinson, Benjamin, 55, 117
Rodgers, Charles E., 30
Rodriges, George (Rodriguez), 119
Romero, Felipe, 106
Romero, Isidor (Ysidro) Antonio, 107, 108
Romero, José Gabriel, 107–108
Romero, Manuel Antonio, 107, 108
Romero, Tomás (Tomacito), 69, 96, 137, 138
Roosevelt, Franklin, 133
Rowland, Thomas, 99
Ruff, C. R., 30
Ruxton, George F., 66, 79, 81, 85, 128–129, 138

Saens, Manuel, 119
Salazar, Hipólito (Polo), 107, 108, 113
San Géronimo de Taos, 89*ph*, 92–94, 97*ph*, 108
San Pasqual, battle at, 56
Sanchez, Enrique, 152–153
Sánchez, George I., 125, 131
Sanchez, Miguel, 106
Sandoval, Antonio, 152
Sandoval, Jose Maria, 99
Sandoval, Manuel, 107–108
Santa Anna, Antonio Lopez de, 4, 5, 5*ph*
Santa Fe
  description of, 47–48, 66
  map of, 51*m*
  trade with, 14–19, 21–24
*Santa Fe Republican*, 150–151
Scott, Winfield, 12, 122, 124, 152
Seitzendorfer, Eugene, 53
sheep, seizure of, 90–91
Shepherd, Samuel, 119
Slack, William Y., 54, 93, 99
Sloane, Eric, 84–85
Smith, Andrew Jackson, 31, 54, 55
Smith, Hugh N., 152–153
Smith, Patricia Clark, 142
Snively, Jacob, 32
soldiers, behavior of, 129–130, 151. *See also* volunteer troops
Spry, 38

St. Vrain, Ceran, 24, 32, 33, 84, 85–86, 87, 93, 105*ph*, 106
Steele, Thomas J., 139–140
Stephenson, John D., 30
Stuart, A. H. H., 156, 157
Sumner, Edwin V., 28

Tafoya, Felipe, 108
Tafoya, Jesus Maria, 69, 87, 101, 102, 134, 137, 138
Tafoya, Rafael, 107–108
Tafoya, Varua, 108
Taney, Roger B., 113
Taos
  description of, 172–173
  map of, 74*m*, 76–77*m*
  people of, 131
Taos Pueblo, battle at, 92–93, 92*ph*, 94–95*m*, 96–97
Taos Revolt
  casualties of, 174–179
  causes of, 122–136
  chronology of, 159–165
  description of, 73–75, 78
  in performing arts and literature, 180–182
Taylor, Zachary, 11, 12, 124, 155
territorial status, 145–149, 151–154
Texan-Santa Fe Expedition, 6, 8
Texas
  annexation of, 1, 8–11
  boundary of, 5–6
  independence movement in, 4–5
  map of, 7*m*
Texas and New Mexico Act, 154
Texas Declaration of Independence, 1, 4
Thruston, Lucian, 99
Tobin, Thomas, 80
Tolque, Louis, 82
Town, Charles, 106
Trail of Tears, 122–123
Travis, William B., 4–5
treason issue, 60, 102, 103–104, 107, 108, 109–110, 112–113, 145, 147–148
trials
  citizenship issue and, 103–104

Garrard on, 109–111
of Montoya, 98–101
Polk and, 112–113
proceedings of, 105–108
of Trujillo, 102–103
Trujillo, Antonio Maria, 102–103
Trujillo, Juan Ramón, 107, 108
Turbush, Albert, 82
Turley, Simeon, 78–80, 82, 138
Turner, Henry Smith, 143–144
Twitchell, Ralph Emerson, 102, 140
Tyler, John, 8, 9

Urrea, José, 5
Ussel, Gabriel, 139–140

Valdez, Jean Bennette, 106
Valdez-Lobato, Juana Catalina, 134
Valentine, Mr., 81
Van Buren, Martin, 8
Vargas, Don Diego de, 63
Vial, Pedro (Pierre), 15
Vigil, Cornelio, 70, 71, 75, 78, 82
Vigil, Don Juan Jesus, 90
Vigil, Donaciano, 53, 65–66, 83–84, 83*ph*, 103, 116, 132, 136–137, 152
Vigil, Gabriel, 106
Vigil, Jose Angel, 106
Vigil, Matias, 106
Vigil, Pedro, 103
Vigil y Alarid, Juan Bautista, 44, 48–49, 132, 167–168
volunteer troops, 126–127, 128, 130–131, 150–151, 156–157

*Wah-To-Yah and the Taos Trail* (Garrard), 105
Waldo, David, 30, 54
Waldo, Lawrence L., 81
Walton, William P., 30
Washington, J. M., 155
Webster, Daniel, 154
Weightman, Richard H., 30, 153–154
Wellan, Paul, 62
White, James M., 155–156
White, Lieutenant, 99

Whitworth, Edward G., 118
Wilkinson, A. S., 119
Wilkinson, James, 16, 17
Williams, R. E., 54
Willock, David, 55, 119
Winders, Richard Bruce, 127, 128
Wislizenus, Frederick Adolphus, 48
Wool, Jonathan E., 50, 54
Wootton, Dick, 72, 80–81, 80*ph*, 96
Wright, J. A., 119

Young, Brigham, 29